Explorations in Cognitive Neuropsychology

For my mother and in memory of my father

Explorations in Cognitive Neuropsychology

ALAN J. PARKIN

Laboratory of Experimental Psychology
University of Sussex

BLACKWELL
Publishers

First published 1996
Reprinted 1997

Blackwell Publishers Ltd
108 Cowley Road
Oxford OX4 1JF, UK

Blackwell Publishers Inc.
238 Main Street
Cambridge, Massachusetts 02142, USA

British Library Cataloguing in Publication Data
A CIP catalogue record for this book is available from the British Library

Library of Congress Cataloging in Publication Data
Parkin, Alan J.
Explorations in cognitive neuropsychology / Alan J. Parkin
p.   cm.
Includes bibliographical references and index.
ISBN 0–631–19472–X (hbk : alk. paper)
ISBN 0–631–19473–8 (pbk : alk. paper)
1. Cognitive disorders. 2. Clinical neuropsychology.
3. Cognitive neuroscience. I. Title.
RC553.C65P37   1996   95–34845
616.8—dc20   CIP

Typeset in 10 on 12pt Sabon
by CentraCet Ltd, Cambridge
Printed and bound in Great Britain by Hartnolls Ltd, Bodmin, Cornwall

This book is printed on acid-free paper

Contents

Preface

When I first studied experimental psychology the investigation of human brain damage played only a small role in our attempts to understand human cognition. Now, in the mid-1990s, the situation has changed beyond recognition and the discipline of cognitive neuropsychology occupies a major position in psychological science. This growth has been acknowledged in the major expansion of publications in this area and the birth of many new journals. Most notably the journal *Cognitive Neuropsychology* has set the standard for in-depth investigation of individual case histories. Another notable step was the APA's decision to adopt and relaunch *Neuropsychology* – a sign that this subject has finally gained recognition within the psychological establishment.

Faced with the explosion of literature in cognitive neuropsychology I have had to be extremely selective in deciding which areas to cover. My principal aim was to address those areas of the subject where research is extremely active and where elements of controversy exist. In this way I hope I can convey to the reader the vibrant nature of research in this area.

I have a number of people to thank in the preparation of this book. Argye Hillis went well beyond the call of duty in providing a very thorough set of comments on the whole book and Elaine Funnell gave me detailed criticisms of the language chapters. John Marshall and Peter Halligan gave very helpful comments on the Neglect chapter and Mike

Corballis's thoughts on the split-brain sharpened up chapter 6. In addition the Amnesia chapter benefits greatly from my continuing collaboration with Nicola Hunkin. However, as always, the final responsibility for content rests entirely with me. I would also like to thank the numerous students who have taken the course from which this book evolved – their comments on the material have been extremely valuable in shaping the book. I am deeply grateful to Ella Squires for all her editorial work and to Frances for staying up half the night figuring out how Endnote prints out 670 references. Finally I hope that readers of this book will spare a thought for the subjects of cognitive neuropsychology. I have always been impressed by how readily brain-injured people offer themselves as subjects in full knowledge that the experiments they take part in will not help them personally in any way. I think this type of contribution, often within the context of adverse or even tragic circumstances, is something both to be acknowledged and admired.

Alan Parkin
Brighton June 1995

1

Cognitive Neuropsychology as a Science

We have our sandwiches on a hill outside Weston with a vast view over Somerset. She wants to say, 'What a grand view' but her words are going too. 'Oh,' she exclaims. 'What a bit lot of About.' There are sheep in the field. 'I know what they are,' she says, 'but I don't know what they are called.' Thus Wittgenstein is routed by my mother.

Alan Bennett (*Writing Home*, 1994)

Cognitive neuropsychology is founded on the principle that one of the easiest ways to understand how a system works is to observe what happens when it goes wrong. By carefully recording and analysing the various errors that can occur in a system you can build up a picture of how its components are organized and how they operate. Before considering how this approach can be applied to the complex functions of the human brain consider how it might be applied to the relatively simple task of understanding how a television works. In an intact television you are not aware of the various components that contribute to the output. However, if you observed enough faulty televisions you might begin to develop ideas about how they work. You would, for example, notice that televisions can lose sound but not vision and *vice versa*. This is an important observation because it tells us that these two components are **independent** because they can each function when the other is not working. Another observation you might make is that the picture can lose its colour. However, the opposite observation, colour without picture, never occurs. This means that the systems governing picture generation and colour are not independent because one, the production of colour, seems critically dependent on the presence of picture. Nonetheless the continual observation of colour loss with a normal black and white picture suggests that the production of colour involves a separate component of the television.

The above example is based on the assumption that the observer has no prior knowledge of televisions or any other concepts that might help understanding of how the television works. In practice many observers would have both prior knowledge and intuitions about what to look for. Thus their observations would not be naïve but guided by various assumptions such as an existing knowledge about the separation of audio and visual channels and the fact that televisions have colour controls that enable the colours to be manipulated independent of picture quality. In short your observations of faulty televisions would be **theory-driven** in that you use pre-existing knowledge to both guide and interpret your observations.

The aim of cognitive neuropsychology is to provide a greater under-standing of how the brain carries out mental operations based on the observation of people who have developed specific deficits as the result of brain damage. Cognitive neuropsychology is heavily dependent on careful observation of the behaviour exhibited by brain damaged people but it is also guided by the theoretical framework provided by **cognitive psychology**.

Cognitive Psychology and Modularity – A Very Brief Overview

Before 1960 the dominant approach to understanding human mental processes was provided by behaviourists such as Skinner. Behaviourism takes the view that behaviour cannot be explained by making any appeal to internal structures or processes within the brain. Instead behaviourists sought to account for all human behaviour in terms of the relations between inputs (stimuli) and outputs (responses). In 1959 the linguist Chomsky wrote a powerful critique of the behaviourist approach and, in essence, came to the conclusion that the nature of mental life could not be investigated effectively without some theory about how the structures and processes of the brain were organized and the principles by which they operated (Chomsky, 1959).

Experimental psychologists face a challenge encountered in no other science except perhaps sub-atomic physics. There is little disagreement that mental processes take place in the brain and, from microscopic examination, we can see that the brain comprises nerve cells and fibres which interact with one another within a complex network. However, knowing that the mental processes that we seek to understand are a product of the interaction between nerve cells does not help us comprehend how mental processes take place. In short the explanation of psychological processes cannot, at present, be reduced to an understanding of how the brain works at a physiological level. Because of this psychologists are forced to use **analogy** or **metaphor** in explanation; that is they attempt to explain the workings of the mind in terms of something else that we do understand.

Cognitive psychology can be defined as the branch of psychology which attempts to provide a scientific explanation of how the brain carries out complex mental functions such as vision, memory, language and thinking. Cognitive psychology arose at a time when computers were beginning to make a major impact on science and it was perhaps natural that cognitive psychologists should draw an analogy between computers and the human brain. The computer analogy was used frequently to draw up a model of the brain in which mental activity was characterized in terms of the flow of **information** between different stores.

Perhaps the most well known of these models was the model of memory put forward by Atkinson and Shiffrin (1968). In this model (see figure 1.1) the human memory system comprises three stores: New information (external stimulation) first enters sensory store where, after initial processing it passes to short-term store. While in the short-term store information can be actively processed guided by the intentions of the individual. Thus new information can be stored in the permanent repository of memory known as long-term store or be discarded. The system also needs to be able to retrieve stored information at a later date and for this reason the model embodies a two-way flow of information between short- and long-term store. The interaction envisaged between short- and long-term store very much resembles the interactions that occur between the central processing unit of a computer and its permanent database. It is important to stress that the computer analogy attempted to emphasise the similarity between the organization of the human mind and that of a computer. It was evident from the outset that the precise manner in which computers operated, that is the binary coding system employed, was not an appropriate basis for understanding cognitive processes themselves.

The computer analogy, in modified form, continued to dominate cognitive psychology for the next 20 years. A vast range of models were

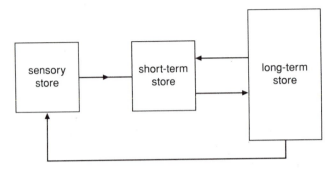

Figure 1.1   The multistore model of memory.

produced each attempting to explain some form of mental activity in terms of a series of processing stages intervening between an input and an output. Despite their widespread use, information processing accounts of mental abilities have not been without criticism. Indeed this approach has been characterized by some commentators as nothing more than 'boxology' – defined by Stuart Sutherland as 'The construction and ostentatious display of meaningless flow charts by psychologists as a substitute for thought' (Sutherland, 1989, p. 58). These criticisms arose because cognitive psychologists became increasingly happy to specify mental processes in terms of information processing systems without offering any explanation of how any of the supposed stages worked.

Modularity

More recently the cognitive approach has been strongly influenced by the concept of **modularity**. This has gone some way to addressing the accusation of boxology because properties are assigned to the processing elements, or **modules**, that comprise any system. The term modularity derives from computer programming and refers to the principle that it is important to make the different components of the program as independent from one another as possible. Modularity will then make any debugging operations much easier to carry out because the nature of the fault will tend to be an accurate indicator of which program module is at fault. An important feature of a modular system, therefore, is that the components are **autonomous** in that they remain functionally intact when other components of the same system become corrupted.

Marr (1976) proposed that the brain might also have a modular organization because modularity imparts considerable advantage to any complex system that is attempting to evolve. The reason for this is that a modular system is easier to correct or improve because changes can be made to specific parts of a system without the need for parallel changes elsewhere. In vision, for example, improvements might occur in modules concerned with extracting information about depth without the need to improve the modules integrating the resulting depth information into the final percept.

The idea of modularity has been extensively developed by Fodor (1983) in his book *The Modularity of Mind*. Fodor's major contribution was to specify a number of properties that he assumed modules had.

1 Informational encapsulation: Modules carry out their operations in isolation from what is going on elsewhere. These operations are not amenable to 'cognitive penetration'. Fodor illustrates this by pointing out that we are unable to overcome visual illusions even though we know full well that they are illusions.

2 Domain specificity: Each module can only process one type of input. Modules therefore deal in only one source of information.

3 Mandatory: Each module operates in an all-or-none fashion. Once activated it will carry out the entire processing operation for which it is responsible.

4 Innate: The modules of the cognitive system are innate and not acquired through development. This is a highly controversial claim which we can highlight by considering this statement from the neurologist Geschwind:

> the overwhelming majority of humans who have ever lived have been illiterate, and even today I believe it is the case that a very large percentage ... of the world's population have never had the opportunity to learn to read. Most of us come from families that four generations ago did not possess the ability to read

We can interpret the above fact in two basic ways. First we could argue that the short history of reading in humans means that reading is carried out by modules that pre-existed to carry out other functions. Support for this view can be found in the study of developmental dyslexia where it can be found that dyslexia often occurs in association with deficits in more basic abilities such as sequencing and left-right discrimination. Alternatively we could argue that the innate assumption is wrong and that new modules can evolve within a developing brain. Arguments supporting this view would be the existence of highly specific acquired dyslexias in which the process of reading seems selectively disrupted (see below and chapter 7).

For our present purpose it is fortunate that the two aspects of modularity most important to cognitive neuropsychology, information encapsulation and domain specificity, are the least controversial. It is important to note, however, that Fodor's definition of modules is not strictly adhered to within cognitive neuropsychology in that modules are often defined as accepting different types of input whereas Fodor considers modules to be input-specific.

Identifying modules cannot, however, be the only goal of cognitive psychology. For a proper explanation we also need to understand how the processes operating within hypothesized modules are carried out. Fodor's view in this area is highly controversial. He accepts that some scientific explanation of how modules operate can be achieved. However, only more basic cognitive processes are held to be modularized and more complex processes such as thinking and deciding are thought to be highly interactive with one another. For Fodor this level of interactivity precludes effective scientific investigation because it is not possible to offer any precise theory about how more complex activities might be carried out.

In general cognitive psychology has not gone along with Fodor's viewpoint and theories abound to explain all manner of human cognitive processes. A good example of a cognitive model embodying both modular and non-modular components is the working memory model of Baddeley and Hitch (Baddeley and Hitch, 1977; Baddeley, 1990). This model is a development of Atkinson and Shiffrin's concept of short-term store (see figure 1.2). It comprises a central executive and two auxiliary components, an articulatory loop and a visuo-spatial scratch pad. The central executive represents the locus of control of the cognitive system. It is responsible for determining how inputs should be dealt with and for retrieving information from long-term storage. It is also multi-modal and not domain-specific, able to combine information from both different sensory modalities and different types of stimulus input.

In contrast the two auxiliary components have very much the character of modules. The articulatory loop is considered a limited capacity system specifically dedicated to the processing of phonological information. Similarly the visuo-spatial scratch pad is solely dedicated to the representation of a limited amount of information in terms of its visuo-spatial characteristics. Working memory is just one example of a large number of models that currently exist to explain human cognition at various levels of complexity. The scale of this enterprise is too vast to even attempt a summary here. Instead the reader will have to be content in knowing that relevant theories will be explained at appropriate points in the text.

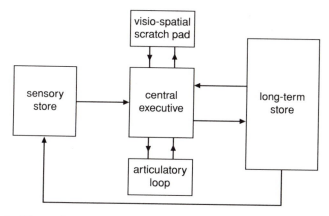

Figure 1.2   The multistore model of memory revised to incorporate the concept of working memory.

Parallel Distributed Processing

Most recently the study of cognitive processes has undergone an almost revolutionary change with the advent of **parallel distributed processing** (**PDP**) or, as it is more often known, **connectionism** (McClelland and Rumelhart, 1986). PDP models are implemented as computer programs known as **networks**. Unlike the models we have considered so far, in which each component of the model is explicitly stated (e.g. central executive, articulatory loop), connectionist models learn by themselves and set up their own representation of any given set of information.

A network comprises a series of **nodes** or **units** linked to each other by connections which can be either inhibitory or excitatory in nature. In addition the strength of any connection can be modified by assigning a particular weight. It is an important feature of these models that information about any concept is distributed across many nodes and not the property of a single node. Different pieces of information thus correspond to different patterns of activity within the same network (see figure 1.3).

PDP networks are able to learn by using rules or **algorithms** to change interconnections between the nodes of the network. One method of learning is the **back-propagation algorithm** which is a means of making an output conform to a desired state. For any input, the system is informed about what the resulting output should be. This information is compared with the actual state of the network when the stimulus is present and an adjustment is made. This process is incremental and

Output patterns

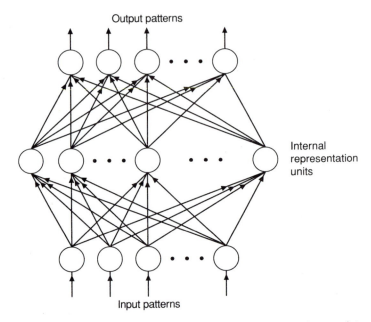

Internal
representation
units

Input patterns

Figure 1.3 A prototype connectionist network comprising a layer of input units, a layer of internal 'hidden units', and a layer of output units. The network learns to associate a particular input pattern with an output pattern. This is achieved via the hidden units which recode input patterns so that they can be more easily differentiated from each other. Thus in a network learning to read the inputs CAT and CAR would be distinguished by different patterns of hidden unit activity. From McClelland and Rumelhart (1986), *Parallel Distributed Processing*. Reproduced by permission of MIT Press.

networks need many exposures to a stimulus before they learn the correct output. Methods like back propagation allow a network to represent information. But because human learning is not characterized by having pre-existing knowledge of the desired outcome, algorithms like back-propagation have obvious limitations. However, proponents of PDP models argue that it is the properties of the established network that are of interest to psychologists rather than the manner in which they become established.

Because PDP models are active learning networks cognitive neuropsychologists have explored the effects of damaging them in a way that might be considered analogous to the effects of a brain lesion on a real neural network. Thus a network that has learnt to read a set of words might be deprived of 30 per cent of its nodes and the resultant effects on reading the target word set re-observed. Later in the book we will examine several instances where the results of degraded PDP networks produce impaired response patterns similar to a particular pattern of deficit caused by brain damage and consider the implications they have for developing theories about real brain function.

Neurological Specificity and Double Dissociation

Within modern cognitive neuropsychology the assumption that different mental functions occupy different brain regions is known as neurological specificity. For some the assumption of neurological specificity is purely abstract in that no attempt is made to describe the brain regions underlying mental functions that appear dissociated. However, the majority of cognitive neuropsychologists do provide neurological data on the brain injuries suffered by their patients and in a number of cases these data may be important for the arguments being made.

The assumption of neurological specificity, combined with acceptance of the modularity principle (see above) underlies a good deal of the work taking place in cognitive neuropsychology. Central to this is the method of **double dissociation**. In a neuropsychological investigation a psychologist wishes to specify the independent existence of the various modules comprising a system. To do this it is necessary to have demonstrations of each module working in the absence of the other. Thus, if we believe that a process has two modules, A and B, we need evidence of A operating in the absence of B and vice versa.

With the television example we considered earlier we are left in no doubt about dissociability because we can easily observe no picture with sound or vice versa. This constitutes what is known as a classic double dissociation (Shallice, 1988) in that performance on one function is deficient while the other is normal. In cognitive neuropsychology double dissociations are usually claimed on the basis of differing degrees of relative impairment. Thus Patient 1 might be better on a task tapping module A and Patient 2 better on a task reflecting module B. However, in neither case do the patients perform normally on any of the tasks. This is a difficult issue for neuropsychologists because dissociations are commonly claimed on this sort of evidence but they could be artefactual. It may be that uncontrolled differences between the two patients underlies their differential impairment rather than real qualitative differences in the nature of their cognitive deficit. Classic double dissociation is much harder to explain in this way but, unfortunately, instances of this are hard to come by.

By observing patterns of dissociation the cognitive neuropsychologist can develop an account of the modular organization of a particular cognitive ability. However, it must be stressed that using the logic of double dissociation to make increasingly fine distinctions between processing elements in the brain is not a sufficient goal in cognitive neuropsychology. This point was addressed by Roediger (1990) when he noticed a report by Gazzaniga (1989):

> One patient, for example, was unable to name the colour of fruits that were red. Thus, in response to the question, 'What is the colour of an apple?' there was a chance performance. Yet, the same patient was easily able to name the colour of a banana. Additionally, the same patient was easily able to name the colour of fire engines and school houses. It is conceivable that her incapacity to identify the colour of red fruits was due to crucial fibres being interrupted within her left hemisphere that connected together the appropriate information sources. (p. 949)

Roediger expresses concern at the rapidity with which modular dissociations can grow and the possibility that modular theorists might discover hundreds of similar fine-grained distinctions in the absence of any organizing principles. He draws a comparison with Gestalt psychology in which, at one time, there were 114 laws of perception. However, as greater understanding developed many of these laws became subsumed under more general headings. It is not enough, therefore, to argue for increasingly complex patterns of modular organization. There must, in addition, be a theoretical framework within which modular accounts of the cognitive system can be evaluated.

Phonological and Surface Dyslexia – An Example of Investigation in Cognitive Neuropsychology

Figure 1.4 presents a rather simplified idea of how the modules responsible for reading a word aloud might be organized in the brain. The word is first identified at module A but from here it can go along a pathway to module B or module C, before a pronunciation of the output is achieved at module D. This model has not been determined by cognitive neuropsychology but by pre-existing theory and observation based on normal readers. Fluent readers of English have the ability to pronounce both real words, for example, MINT, ROAD, and **nonwords**, for example, SINT, FOAD. Another ability is to deal with the large amount of irregularity in English pronunciation. Estimates vary but around 20 per cent of English words contain some irregularity in that if you tried to pronounce them by rule you would make a mistake, examples of these **irregular words** are PINT and BROAD.

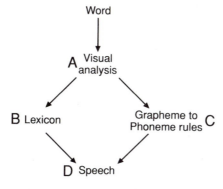

Figure 1.4   A much simplified modular system for pronouncing words.

The demands of being able to read both nonwords and irregular words mean that there must be at least two systems available for converting the printed word into sound. First we must have a set of rules, usually called letter-to-sound or **grapheme-to-phoneme correspondence rules**, which enable us to produce a pronunciation for nonwords such as SINT and FOAD. However, because they are based on the commonest correspondences between letters and sounds, these rules would also deal effectively with regularly pronounced words such as MINT and ROAD. Where these rules would come unstuck is with irregular words because here the incorrect 'regularized' pronunciation would be produced (e.g. PINT →; BROAD → BRODE). Because of this difficulty it is necessary to propose that we have an additional word-specific or **lexical basis for** specifying the pronunciation of individual words and it is only this system that allows the correct pronunciation of irregular words.

It is generally thought that these two paths to pronunciation operate in parallel. For regular words the correct response can be achieved via either path and nonwords can only be pronounced using grapheme to phoneme rules. In contrast irregular words will only be correctly pronounced if the lexical path is used. This model is based on both intuition and experimental evidence. We know, for example, that it takes longer to start pronouncing irregular words compared with regular words under speeded conditions and that when doing this subjects will tend to 'regularize' irregular words (Parkin, 1982a). However, perhaps our strongest motive for believing in two routes to pronunciation comes from our observations of **acquired dyslexia** – the sudden loss of reading ability due to a brain lesion. This evidence also provides us with a good introduction to the logic underlying much current neuropsychological investigation.

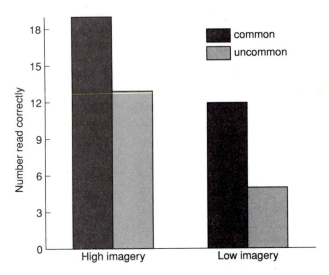

Figure 1.5   Norman's ability to read common and uncommon words differing in imageability (data courtesy of Elaine Funnell).

There are many forms of acquired dyslexia and we will examine some of them in detail at a later point. For now we will consider only two types of reading problem exemplified in these case histories:

> *Norman* suffered a stroke which, due to damage in his left cerebral hemisphere, has resulted in considerable language difficulties even though his ability to communicate verbally is generally good. Norman's problem is that he can no longer write, or read books. On tests of reading simple familiar words (e.g. *dog, man, tree*) he has no difficulty and, although he finds it more difficult, he can also read less meaningful words such as *it, when* and *how*. However, not all words can be read. We can divide words very roughly into those that enable us to form an image easily (e.g. door, bird) and those for which an image does not spring easily to mind (gist, desire). We can also divide words into common and uncommon on the basis of how frequently we see or hear them. Norman was given a simple experiment in which he had to read words that differed along these two dimensions and the results are shown in figure 1.5. He does reasonably well in three of the categories but has obvious difficulty with uncommon words low in imagery. It is also notable that when he fails to read a word he either says nothing or offers another more common word instead (syllable → label).
>
> In a second experiment Norman was asked to <u>read nonwords</u>. This he could not do at all and when he did respond he produced a real word that resembled the nonword (e.g. vith → with; fage → age).

Norman's deficit does not, on its own, allow us to conclude the separable existence of lexical and grapheme-to-phoneme correspondence rules. One could, for example, argue that there is a single process that converts all types of print into sound and that, for some reason, it works less efficiently for unfamiliar patterns of letters – hence Norman's greater difficulty with nonwords. In order to argue for two routes, therefore, we need evidence for a double dissociation – a pattern of disturbed reading that can be explained in terms of a defective lexical route.

> TOB developed language problems very slowly due to an evolving dementing illness centred on his left temporal lobe. He gradually lost vocabulary to the point where he could only name very common objects. Thus although he was able to drive his car perfectly well he could not name any of the parts. Along with the problem of naming things TOB also developed a reading problem. He found it hard to define what words meant even when his word-finding problems were by-passed by asking him to match words to pictures. In an experiment TOB was asked to read different types of words and nonwords aloud. TOB had little difficulty reading aloud regular words and nonwords, but had great difficulty reading aloud irregular words. This problem was emphasized by TOB's inability to read even the simplest irregular words (e.g. *chord, ache*) despite fluent pronunciation of very uncommon regular words such as *indiscoverable, chitterling*, and *huckaback*.

The reading problems shown by Norman and TOB are very different. Norman reads most words well but cannot read anything that is not a word. TOB can read words without difficulty as long as the words obey English grapheme-to-phoneme correspondence rules; he also has no problem reading nonwords. These two patterns of reading impairment have been observed many times and are described as **phonological dyslexia** and **surface dyslexia** respectively.

In phonological dyslexia there is a primary problem in reading nonwords. In terms of our simple modular account of reading this suggests that Norman no longer possesses any ability to convert graphemes to phonemes. However, Norman can read most words thus indicating that he does have a lexical basis for reading words. This evidence suggests that the simple modular account put forward in figure 1.4 may well be correct because this would predict the pattern we have observed. However, Norman's data alone do not clinch the argument because we need evidence for a double dissociation. This is, of course, provided by TOB because he reads regular words and nonwords equally effectively but has gross difficulty reading any irregular word accurately. TOB's reading errors thus suggest that he is reliant on grapheme-to-phoneme correspondence rules because he has no access to lexically-based pronunciation.

The above evidence thus provides us with a good example of double dissociation and supports the modular theory outlined in figure 1.4. However, it should be noted that the model does not fully account for the available facts. Why, for example, does Norman read high-imagery words better than low-imagery words? To explain this we must refine our ideas of how the lexical pathway operates. In addition our investigation has not told us anything about how the various modules work. How does the grapheme-to-phoneme module work? What rules does it use? This can only be achieved by more detailed exploration.

Another important point to notice is that the modular theory examined in this example pre-existed on the basis of evidence from normal subjects. In this instance, therefore, cognitive neuropsychology's role is confirmatory in that it serves to reinforce theories we have about the cognitive system. This is a common role for cognitive neuropsychology and we will see many instances of this throughout this book. However, it must be emphasized that cognitive neuropsychology can do more than this by providing insights into brain organization that are not apparent from studying normal people. Blindsight, the topic of the next chapter, is one example, and the work conducted on language (chapters 7 and 8) also provides instances of cognitive neuropsychology leading the development of theory.

Methods in Cognitive Neuropsychology – Single Cases or Groups?

In the preceding example we compared data from two people and came to a particular theoretical conclusion about the organisation of the reading system. However, we noted that both phonological and surface dyslexia had been observed in other people. To some scientists this latter fact would come as some relief because they would be uneasy about accepting a particular theoretical position on the basis of observing just two individuals with different deficits. However, within cognitive neuropsychology, this is not a universal position and many believe that only single cases should be studied.

To understand the arguments in this section let us first imagine an experiment in which there are two conditions A and B. Our hypothesis is that A will produce better performance than B. If we were to then test only one randomly selected subject in condition A and one in condition B would we be in a position to argue about the relative effectiveness of the two conditions? No. Because experimental subjects naturally vary in their ability to do any experimental task and, with only one subject in each condition, there is an obvious danger that any apparent difference arises from sampling error. To control for this problem we test a substantial number of subjects in each condition and use inferential statistics to check whether any group difference we observe is significant given the overall variability in task performance.

At first sight it does not seem a difficult step to apply the same logic to experiments in cognitive neuropsychology. However, a number of authors have argued that extension of the group study logic to brain damaged populations is invalid (e.g. Badecker and Caramazza, 1985; Caramazza, 1984; Caramazza, 1986; Caramazza and Badecker, 1989; Caramazza and Badecker, 1991; McCloskey, 1993; McCloskey and Caramazza, 1988; Sokol, McCloskey, Cohen and Alimnosa, 1991). The basis of the argument is that group studies on normal subjects rest on the reasonable assumption that the cognitive processes under investigation are homogeneous – it being unlikely that a basic ability such as perception or memory would be carried out in a qualitatively different manner across individuals. In a normal group study, therefore, all one has to do is control for variability in a function whose neural representation can be considered similar across individuals.

Turning to brain damaged subjects one can still assume homogeneity of pre-morbid cognitive function but what can be assumed about the patients' current cognitive abilities? Opponents of group studies argue that very little can be gained from group studies because lesions cause such variation in damage that it is impossible to be sure that any two patients have the same form of cognitive deficit. This criticism can certainly be applied to a good number of neuropsychological studies where groups of subjects have been loosely defined. Many studies, for example, have simply compared the effects of left and right hemisphere damage – a crude classification which, without doubt, results in the grouping together of patients with very different patterns of impairment.

Supporters of group studies (e.g. Robertson, Knight, Rafal and Shimamura, 1993; Zurif, Swinney and Fodor, 1991; Zurif, Gardner and Brownell, 1989) have countered these arguments by proposing various ways in which the heterogeneity problem can be overcome. One approach is to group patients together on the basis of syndromes. A syndrome can be defined as a set of symptoms which co-occur with sufficient regularity to suggest that they reflect a single underlying deficit. A large number of syndromes have been described in neuropsychology and many experimental studies have been carried out using syndromes as a basis for specifying groups of subjects.

The success of the syndrome-based approach to group classification depends critically on how the syndrome is defined. If the criteria are too loose and patients with qualitatively different deficits are grouped together, conclusions based on averaging their performance will be misleading. Opponents of the group-based approach have argued that syndrome-based groups often show dramatic individual variation which undermines treating them as a single group. Supporters of the group approach argue that syndromes have proved very useful in medicine even though not all patients show all the defining features of a given syndrome.

An alternative argument favouring group studies can be termed the significance implies homogeneity rule. Put simply this rule states that if a group of subjects exhibits significant heterogeneity then they will not be capable of generating statistically significant group differences. However, this rule has also been attacked because of mistaken assumptions it makes about the nature of statistical significance. Intuitively one considers that demonstration of a significant effect in a group of subjects means that the majority of subjects show the effect. However, analysis of statistical procedures shows that a significant effect can sometimes be obtained when less than 50 per cent of subjects show the effect (providing, of course, that the remaining subjects show no effect rather than an effect in the opposite direction).

A further attempt at strengthening the rationale of group studies is to use neurological data. As we have seen cognitive neuropsychology assumes a degree of neurological specificity. So, on the assumption that patients all had similar neurological specificity prior to their brain injury, it is valid to assume that all those with damage to the same part of the brain also have similar functional problems. An optimal arrangement, therefore, would be to construct experimental groups each defined as having a discrete lesion in a different part of the brain and then examine their patterns of cognitive impairment. Although in theory possible, this type of experiment is extremely uncommon for a number of reasons. First many of the dissociations that have been observed arise from damage to the same general brain area and neuroradiology does not enable us to map structure to function in fine enough detail. Moreover, our assumption that neurological specificity is consistent across subjects may not hold in all circumstances. For example, people show great individual variation in how the blood supply to their brain is organized. Thus, two patients might be considered similar in terms of suffering damage to the same brain artery but the consequent damage might be very different.

The alternative approach, sometimes called 'ultra' or 'radical' cognitive neuropsychology, is to consider only data from single-case studies. This approach overcomes problems concerning heterogeneity because any study only involves one subject but it opens up a different range of problems. The most obvious of these is the problem of generalization. How can we be sure that the conclusions derived from the study of one individual reflect the population as a whole? Supporters of the radical approach employ the following logic:

> The radical single-patient approach avoids the population heterogeneity problem in a simple way: The concept of a patient population is not invoked in linking data to theory . . . In a radical single-patient study, the results are first used to draw conclusions about the patient's previously normal cognitive mechanisms and functional damage to these mechanisms. Then, on the assumption that the cognitive mechanisms are shared by some normal population, the conclusions about the patients premorbid cognitive mechanisms are generalised directly to that normal population. (McCloskey, 1993, p. 728)

There are a number of points to notice about this methodology. Most importantly there is the assumption that the patient's pre-morbid cognitive functions were similar to those of the normal population. A problem here is that the patient may have been atypical from the start (something Caramazza has dubbed 'The Martian among us problem'). While this might not be a frequent problem there is, in my opinion, at least one clear instance where data from an atypical patient has been central to a neuropsychological theory.

Speaking and spelling disorders tend to go together and this supported a traditional view in which spelling evolved on a pre-existing speech production system. A key piece of evidence against a theory of this kind would be someone who could write but not speak. In considering the issue of a separate spelling system (Ellis and Young, 1988) laid considerable emphasis on data from a patient known as EB (Levine, Calvanio and Popovics, 1982). EB continued to be able to read and write despite total mutism and an inability to appreciate even inner speech (the natural tendency to hear words in your head as you are reading). This seems compelling support for a modular separation of speaking and spelling systems but it is notable that Levine et al. considered their patient to be somewhat special:

> Another possible factor, perhaps related to his talent for mental imagery, was his unusual premorbid reading strategy. While a young man (age 20) . . . he took a 16 week course in speed reading, which he practised hard and used ever since . . . always read fast. In this course he was taught to avoid saying the printed words to himself and to focus instead on their meanings. He wrote 'Learning to and practising speed reading required super concentration on sense of words within idea contexts. Individual words and the phonetics of words was suppressed in order to be proficient

at high speed reading. Now I am slow and ponderous but still only 'see' words as ideas not sounds' (p. 406).

EB was 54 when he suffered his stroke so he had been reading in his abnormal fashion for over 30 years. It is not unreasonable to suppose, therefore, that his reading and related skills may have been organized abnormally. More specifically, his background suggests that he may have developed a reading and writing strategy that did not rely on phonology at all thus making preserved writing in the absence of speech a distinct possibility. This makes it difficult to assume that EB is a patient whose cognitive system was organized normally prior to brain damage. One could, of course, argue that EB's achievements are an indication that speaking and spelling are separable but the counter-argument here is that cognitive neuropsychology must explain what is typical not what may be possible.[1]

Fortunately, other less controversial data now supports the separate existence of a spelling system (see chapter 8). Nonetheless one can see that if EB had been the only case of preserved spelling in the absence of speech, we might well have been misled. This emphasizes another difficulty for single case approaches – replication. In science a theory will not be accepted if the findings that generated it are not capable of replication. However, the radical approach seemingly fails to meet this basic tenet of scientific investigation. Imagine a situation in which one person suffers a brain lesion that results in a selective inability to read poetry as opposed to other written material and a second shows the reverse deficit. Within radical cognitive neuropsychology this would necessitate a distinction being made between the processing of poetry and other written material. More importantly the conclusions derived from these single cases would hold even if that pattern of impairment were never observed again. How could the single-case methodology ensure that the above dissociation was a genuine reflection of normal cognitive processes?

Supporters of the radical approach argue that testing flaws can be avoided by using extensive testing regimes in which converging evidence for a conclusion is derived from performance across a number of tasks. A more difficult problem is to combat inclusion of a patient whose data are atypical from the outset (see above). Care can be taken to avoid any patient who may have evidence of abnormal brain development, and the appearance of findings that are inconsistent with the developing theoret-

---

[1] An interesting case in point is the mnemonist S (Luria, 1968). This man had an incredible memory based largely on the use of imagery. No one doubts the power of the data but it does not figure in any current theory of normal memory function.

ical framework could also indicate that the data are mistaken in some way. A danger here, however, is that the inclusion or exclusion of cases becomes increasingly guided by theory rather than objective fact – a tactic, incidentally, that can be as easily employed in studies based on group data. These conditions may reduce the risk of misleading information being incorporated into theorizing but one must still feel uneasy about dissociations based on the observation of just one or two patients. The answer here is to strengthen an idea by the collation of patients with similar deficits – something that appears to be done even by those most strongly associated with the single-case position.

At the time of writing both viewpoints seem firmly entrenched (see McCloskey, 1993 and Robertson et al., 1993) but, emerging from the criticisms of both sides, we can see how both approaches might be modified so as to become more acceptable. Group studies could benefit from stricter criteria for subject inclusion and the use of more stringent statistical procedures could reduce the inclusion of atypical group members. Proponents of the single-case approach would achieve greater support if they were to take some steps towards dealing with the issue of replication. In particular the development of some means of aggregating patients with similar deficits would dispel much of the current criticism.

In writing this book I was posed with a dilemma as to which viewpoint to adopt. Unlike Ellis and Young (1988), who chose the single-case viewpoint and thus mainly excluded group-based data, I have opted for a less radical approach and decided to use both single case and group-based data. This has inevitably exposed me to a much wider database and has the benefit of introducing some additional topics – particularly in the area of memory impairment.

Animal Studies

One of the more contentious areas of cognitive neuropsychology concerns its links with research on animals. Human neuropsychology is disadvantaged because the lesions suffered by patients lack precision in that they do not selectively target specific brain regions. Animal studies do not suffer from this drawback but a serious problem is whether the data from animal studies are relevant to understanding human cognition. This is a difficult issue, all the more so because of the ethical debate that continues.

Within neuropsychology it appears that animal studies seem most relevant in relation to 'lower' levels of cognition. In chapter 2, for example, we will see some overlap between human and animal data concerning the visual system. Similarly object recognition and attention may also be areas in which animal work is informative about the organisation of human abilities. Memory is an area in which animal studies have been of varying influence. The work of Montreal group (see chapter 10) has shown some definite links between the role of the frontal lobes in the memory performance of non-human primates and humans. However, the classic work of O'Keefe and Nadel (1978), in which the rat hippocampus was specifically proposed as a cognitive map does not appear to generalize to human hippocampal function.

At the highest levels of human cognition: language, thought, executive function and consciousness; animal studies are likely to be of least relevance because here it is most likely that we are dealing with developments within the brain that are unique to humans.

The vastness of the animal literature along with my own doubts about how far one can generalize from animals to humans means that animal studies are not prominently featured. However, where animal research has provided some necessary clarification or enlightenment I have included it in my account.

Neuroimaging Techniques

Within the last 15 years there have been dramatic developments in neuroimaging techniques and these are having an increasing impact on neuropsychological research. A large number of patients now routinely receive **computerized axial tomography (CAT)** scanning. This is a technique based on X-rays which allows a three-dimensional picture of the brain to be created. CAT scans do serve many useful purposes but they are limited in terms of the detail they show – it is not unusual for patients with quite severe neurological difficulties to have a clear CAT scan.

A more recent and refined means of obtaining a structural picture of the brain is **magnetic resonance imaging (MRI)** sometimes known as **nuclear magnetic imaging (NMR)**. This technique involves momentarily aligning atoms in a particular direction within a magnetic field using radio waves. When these waves are turned off the atoms produce a voltage (magnetic resonance) and this is used to construct an image. Plate 1.1 shows a CAT scan and an MRI scan and shows the greater degree of detail available in the latter. MRI scans are primarily used to identify which regions of the brain have been damaged. However, more recently, MRI techniques have been adapted in order to measure physiological changes in the brain, a technique known as **functional magnetic resonance imaging (fMRI)** (see Moonen, 1995, for a recent review of this technique and its applications).

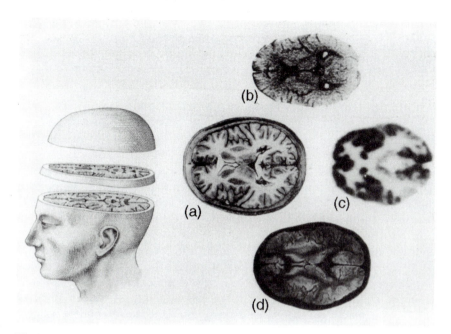

Plate 1.1   Four different ways of imaging the brain: (a) a photograph, (b) CAT scan, (c) PET scan (normally different areas of activation would be shown in different colours), (d) MRI scan. From Posner & Raichle, *Images of Mind*. Copyright © 1994 Scientific American Library. Used with permission of W. H. Freeman.

Although use of functional MRI is increasing **Positron Emission Tomography (PET)** scanning is the most widely used means of detecting physiological abnormalities in the brain. PET involves injecting a patient with a water solution containing a positron emitting radioactive isotope. After a minute or so the radioactive isotope accumulates in the brain in direct proportion to the local blood flow – thus the greater the brain activity the greater the radioactive emission. In this way the extent of regional blood flow can be measured and those areas with greater or lesser activity identified. The results of PET scans are shown on images where brighter colours indicate higher levels of activity (see Plate 1.1).

Recently there has been increasing use of PET scanning as a means of investigating functional localisation in normal brains. The basic technique involves placing an individual into a PET scanning machine and then asking them to perform a particular cognitive task. By examining the different patterns of activation with different tasks it is possible to specify which brain structures are active during which tasks. Even greater accuracy can be obtained by combining PET with MRI which enables the mapping of metabolic activity on to a detailed structural image of the same brain (for a very clear account of PET scanning see Posner and Raichle, 1994).

About the Rest of this Book

Hopefully this opening chapter has given you an introduction into the nature and the various methods of cognitive neuropsychology. The rest of this book covers the various research areas currently being investigated. In choosing and describing the topics I have tried to emphasize those areas where debate and controversy is occurring. It is for this reason I begin with blindsight. This is a relatively small topic in neuropsychology but it is one that reveals the fascination of neuropsychology along with the methodological and interpretive problems that so often cause difficulty. Next I deal with visual agnosia, an area which has undergone marked expansion as the complexity of the disorder is realised. Deficits in facial processing follow this and here a primary emphasis is placed on the use of a single model to accommodate a range of experimental findings. Chapter 5 deals with neglect: an intriguing area but one where the reader may feel that the demonstration of phenomena is rather ahead of a unifying theory. In chapter 6 I describe the split-brain research. Typically this area has stayed outside mainstream cognitive neuropsychology, perhaps due to the atypicality problem concerning these patients, but these issues raised by these extraordinary cases are so fascinating that I could not leave this topic out. Chapters 7 and 8 cover spoken and written language impairments. This area has been dominated by more radical cognitive neuropsychologists and what I hope to have provided is a fair account of their ideas. In producing these chapters I am greatly indebted to Andrew Ellis and Andy Young for the theoretical framework so clearly stated in their highly influential 1988 book *Human Cognitive Neuropsychology*. Chapter 9 covers my own field, memory impairment, an area somewhat eschewed by the radical group because of its much higher use of group data. The final chapter tackles the frontal lobes and examines the case for a central executive.

A Note about Brain Anatomy and Clinical Neuropsychology

It has not been my intention to require an understanding of brain anatomy as a prerequisite for understanding the material in this book.

For the most part deficits are discussed in the abstract without reference to underlying lesions (issues of this nature are thoroughly dealt with by McCarthy and Warrington, 1990). However, if you know very little about the neuroanatomy of the brain you may find it useful to look at a text such as Kolb and Whishaw (1996). Also it was not feasible to cover all neuropsychological deficits encountered in the clinic so my emphasis has been on those deficits which have been most prominent within cognitive neuropsychology. For more clinically-oriented approaches the reader is referred to Heilman and Valenstein (1993).

Summary

Cognitive neuropsychology is founded on the idea that psychological processes can be investigated by examining how different aspects of mental ability break down following brain damage. An influential idea is that the cognitive system is to some extent modular and this, coupled with the assumption of neurological specificity, provides a primary rationale for cognitive neuropsychology. A fundamental method in cognitive neuropsychology has been the demonstration of double dissociations and this is exemplified in the comparison of surface and phonological dyslexia. More recently neuropsychologists have also employed connectionist networks as a means of simulating normal and impaired brain function. Currently there is a major controversy surrounding the use of both group studies and single-case designs in neuropsychological research. Neuroimaging techniques are becoming increasingly important in neuropsychology as they become able to shed light on functional relationships within the brain.

2

Blindsight

One of the important benefits of neuropsychological investigation is that it can reveal components of a system that cannot be observed separately under normal conditions. The phenomenon of blindsight provides a particularly good example of this in that it enables us to observe components of the visual system that would not be apparent in people with normal vision.

Our account of blindsight begins with a few facts about the organisation of the human visual system. Information leaves the retina via the optic nerve and most of the fibres (around 90 per cent) project more or less directly to the striate cortex – a region of the visual cortex so called because of its distinctive striped appearance. The striate cortex connection is not direct because the fibres from the retina terminate in a region of the diencephalon known as the dorsal lateral geniculate nucleus (DLGN) from where new fibres project into the striate cortex itself. Involvement of the DLGN as a relay has led to this pathway becoming known as the **geniculo-striate pathway**.

There are, however, a number of other branches of the optic nerve which terminate in non-cortical areas. Most notable of these is the branch terminating in the **superior colliculus.** This pathway comprises approximately 100,000 fibres which makes it larger than the auditory nerve (see figure 2.1). In addition it is also known that a few thousand

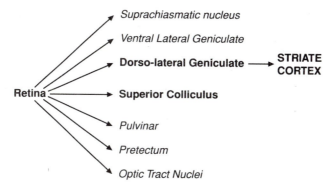

Figure 2.1 A simplified diagram showing some of the neural pathways from the eye to the brain (based on Cowey and Stoerig, 1991). Little is known about the function of structures shown in italics.

fibres from the DLGN project to other **extrastriate** regions of the visual cortex (Cowey and Stoerig, 1991).

In order to follow the material in this chapter it is important to properly understand how lesions to different parts of the brain affect the visual fields. First, remember that the left visual fields of both eyes project to the right hemisphere and that the right visual fields of each eye project to the left hemisphere. Figure 2.2 shows that a lesion occurring in the optic nerve will disrupt both visual fields but only for one eye. A lesion at the optic chiasm will result in the loss of the left field for one eye and the right field of the other. Lesions of the geniculo-striate pathway will disrupt the same visual field of both eyes. In the cases we are about to consider there has been damage to the geniculo-striate system. Thus, in all cases, the patients will have visual field defects associated with both eyes.

Experiments on Non-Striate Vision

Anatomical considerations thus indicate that there is a considerable flow of information away from the retina which does not terminate in the striate cortex. On the assumption that pathways other than the geniculo-striate are functional one could plausibly expect some visual functions to remain if the geniculo-striate pathway became inoperative due to, for example, damage to the striate cortex. Under these conditions, therefore, it might be possible to establish the nature of visual processes not dependent on the geniculo-striate system – processes we will term **non-striate vision**.

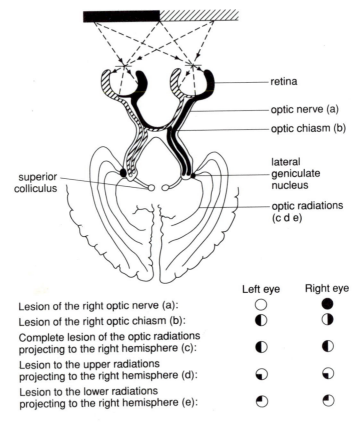

	Left eye	Right eye
Lesion of the right optic nerve (a):	○	●
Lesion of the right optic chiasm (b):	◐	◑
Complete lesion of the optic radiations projecting to the right hemisphere (c):	◐	◐
Lesion to the upper radiations projecting to the right hemisphere (d):	◵	◵
Lesion to the lower radiations projecting to the right hemisphere (e):	◔	◔

Figure 2.2 The geniculo-striate pathway from eye to brain. Damage at different points results in different forms of field defect. In all cases lesions of the same sites on the left side of the brain will produce equivalent field defects in the right visual field. Adapted from Humphreys and Riddoch (1987a), *To see but not to see*. Reprinted by permission of Lawrence Erlbaum Associates Ltd., Hove, UK.

Animal research, particularly involving monkeys, has played an important role in characterizing the nature of non-striate vision. Humphrey, (1970) performed a number of experiments on a chimpanzee, named Helen, who had undergone complete removal of the striate cortex (an animal in this unfortunate condition is described as 'destriate'). Helen was studied over a number of years and Humphrey was able to demonstrate her visual sensitivity in a variety of settings. She could, for example, pick up small pieces of paper and peanuts although she could not distinguish them without touching them. Summarizing this research

Humphrey notes that 'After six years she still does not know a carrot when she sees one, nor apparently can she recognize my face, despite an excellent ability to locate visual events in her environment and to avoid obstacles by vision alone' (Humphrey, 1972, p. 684).

Following on from this other researchers showed that destriate monkeys could learn to discriminate between different patterns and different levels of brightness. Destriate monkeys can also detect **gratings** – these are stimuli used a great deal in vision research and they are, in effect, a series of stripes alternating in either brightness or colour. Gratings can vary in their **spatial frequency** which can be defined as the rate at which the stripes alternate. High spatial frequency gratings thus comprise thin stripes and low-frequency gratings have broader stripes. The higher the spatial frequency that can be discriminated either from another grating or a blank field of equal visual flux constitutes a measure of **visual acuity**. Destriate monkeys were able to detect gratings of relatively low frequency but were not able to detect those with higher frequencies thus indicating some visual acuity. Monkeys without striate cortex can also discriminate lines differing in orientation as little as eight degrees (Weiskrantz, 1986).

Studies in Humans

Research in non-human primates had indicated that a considerable amount of visual processing can take place in the absence of striate cortex thus suggesting that the non-striate pathways were functional. The next step was to establish whether this was also true for man.

The first positive indication came from a study by Poppel, Held, and Frost (1973). They studied four patients who suffered brain lesions in parts of the striate cortex. The effect of these lesions is to create various regions of total blindness known as scotoma which can be mapped accurately using the method of perimetry (see Figure 2.3). Because patients were fixating centrally Poppel et al. were then able to flash a target stimulus in the part of the visual field that was now a scotoma. Following target presentation, which lasted 100 msec, the subjects were then asked to 'guess' where the light had been presented. Because the subjects could not 'see' anything, target presentation had to be accompanied by a click so that they knew the target had occurred. Subjects indicated target location by moving their eyes to where they 'guessed' the stimulus had been presented. The subjects found this task very difficult. One commented 'How can I look at something I have never seen?' yet all four patients produced patterns of eye movements that accurately reflected the location of the targets.

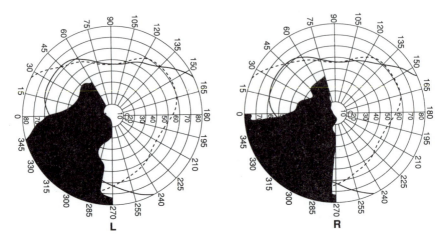

Figure 2.3 DB's visual field defect as measured by perimetry. Perimetry is measured by asking the patients to fixate centrally and then requiring responses to lights that appear randomly at different locations within the visual fields. By noting those lights not responded to the area of defective vision can be established. Note also that the field defect occupies mainly the lower left quadrant for each eye. This indicates damage to upper radiations of right visual cortex. From L. Weiskrantz, *Blindsight: A case study and implications*. Reproduced by permission of Oxford University Press.

The Case of DB

Around the same time as this report a young man known as DB entered hospital to be treated for chronic and severe migraine. The cause was traced to an ateriovenous malformation in the right occipital lobe and the only effective treatment was surgical removal of the malformation. The operation involved removal of most of the calcarine cortex, an area which includes the striate cortex. The operation was a success in that his migraine largely disappeared but, as expected, he was left with a left visual field defect. For the first three years this defect encompassed virtually all of the left visual field but some recovery occurred resulting in a scotoma centred on the lower left quadrant of the visual field (see figure 2.3).

DB came to the attention of neuropsychologists Larry Weiskrantz and Elizabeth Warrington. They were intrigued by reports that DB could 'see' things presented in his defective visual field. Initially they explored this by asking him to point to the position of markers on a wall or to decide whether a stick presented in his blind field was horizontal or vertical. He was able to perform these tasks without error but, as this brief conversation shows, he had no idea how he was performing the task:

'Did you know how well you had done?'

'No I didn't because I couldn't see anything; I couldn't see a darn thing.'

'Can you say how you guessed – what it was that allowed you to say whether it was vertical or horizontal?'

'No, I could not because I did not see anything; I just don't know.'

'So you really did not know you were getting them right?'

'No.'

DB thus appeared to have some form of vision that was independent of awareness and for this reason the investigators described the phenomenon as **blindsight**. What followed was a highly detailed investigation of DB's blindsight which is fully described in Weiskrantz's book *Blindsight: A Case Study and its Implications* (Weiskrantz, 1986 see also Weiskrantz, 1989). In the short account that follows I describe some of the key findings that emerged from this investigation.

In all the experiments the same basic procedure was used. DB was seated with his head resting on a chin rest. He was asked to maintain a central fixation so that the position of his scotoma within his visual field could be accurately established. On any given trial a 'ready' signal would be given and a stimulus projected into the scotoma or into the sighted field if required. Using this procedure it was established that, within his scotoma, DB could:

Detect the location of stimuli by pointing or, less reliably, by directing his gaze.

Perform well above chance on deciding whether a stimulus was present or absent.

Show reasonable visual acuity, as measured by sensitivity to the spatial frequency of gratings.

Detect the presence of moving versus stationary stimuli.

Discriminate both lines and gratings presented horizontally versus vertically, and horizontally versus diagonally.

Make some types of discrimination based on form. Thus he could reliably distinguish X from O and also performed quite well when attempting to discriminate between five letters, **A, C, D, R,** and S. He could also discriminate between a square and a diamond matched for flux and performed well on a figure-ground clustering task (see figure 2.4a). However, DB could not distinguish between a triangle and **X**, curved versus normal triangles, or squares and rectangles matched for flux (see figure 2.4b and c).

Discriminate direction of contrast in that he could tell the difference between a grey disc presented on a white background or the same grey disc on a black background.

The above findings indicate that DB possessed a range of perceptual abilities in his scotoma. However, he did not seem to have the ability to identify form. His ability to detect the difference between **X** and **O** was almost certainly based on his ability to detect orientation differences because he could not detect the difference between **X** and a triangle, in which lines of the same orientations as the **X** appear, nor could he distinguish squares from rectangles. Similarly, his apparent ability to discriminate triangles from squares could be based on the detection of different orientations.

An important feature of Weiskrantz's account of DB is the attention paid to DB's verbal commentaries on his own performance. On many of the tasks where his performance was close to perfect he would deny being able to see anything at all. In one detection experiment he commented 'It's a dead area. No sensation. Just guessing' even though he was 93 per cent accurate. On other tasks DB did report sensations although these rarely related to the actual visual qualities of the stimulus being presented and on no occasion did he regard himself as seeing the stimuli. On one task he described the stimuli as coming out from the surface rather like a 'billiard cue' and on another task stimuli were described as 'little curved waves coming out from the wall about a quarter of an inch'. On detecting movement in a vertical line he commented 'I did not see the line. There was a kind of pulsation. I did not see the light or anything, but I could *feel* the movement, and I was absolutely sure of it'. In some instances the occurrence of these reports correlated with higher accuracy but this was not always the case.

Figure 2.4   (a) Figure-ground clustering stimuli used by Weiskrantz. DB could reliably distinguish 1,2,3, and 4 from 6 – a performance only midly inferior to controls. However, he could not distinguish between rectangles of different sizes (b) (note that both sets of stimuli are matched internally for intensity), nor could he tell the difference between a straight triangle and a series of curved triangles (c). L. Weiskrantz, *Blindsight: A case study and implications*. Reproduced by permission of Oxford University Press.

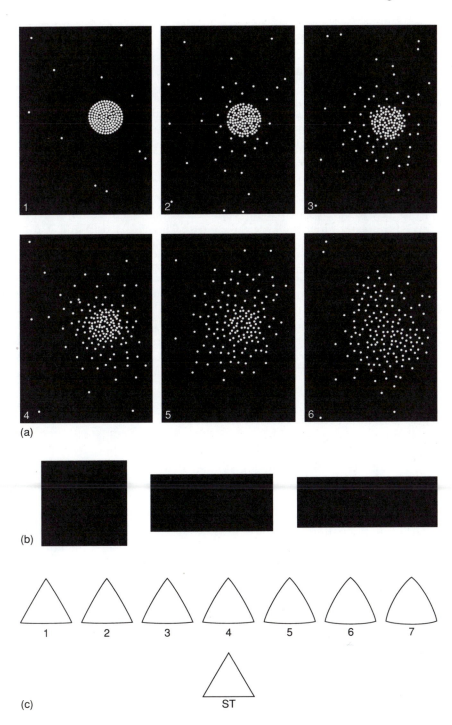

The Stray Light Hypothesis

One potential problem for the interpretation of blindsight is that DB, like other patients who have shown the phenomenon (see below), are only partially blind and thus have a good deal of intact visual field. Campion, Latto and Smith (1983) put forward the view that blindsight could be an artefact of **stray light**. The basis of their idea was that light emitted from presentation of the target in the scotoma could stray into the sighted field and then provide a clue to the target's location or identity. To illustrate this point they investigated a patient who, like DB, appeared able to discriminate horizontal from vertical lines in his scotoma. However, this patient volunteered that a horizontal bar produced a greater glow towards the centre of his visual field and it may, therefore, have been this cue that was the basis of his responding.

Following this up Campion et al. devised an experiment with normal subjects in which the left eye and the right field of the right eye were covered over. Stimuli were presented to the right visual field but, because of the covering over, they could not be seen directly. Any information about those stimuli could only be obtained by information picked up in the left visual field of the right eye. A detection task was used in which subjects were asked to point to the location of lights presented at six different locations. Even though the stimuli could not have been seen in any way by the right visual field, their position was accurately detected. The authors thus concluded that stray light picked up in the left visual field must have been the basis for responding.

Campion et al.'s data show that phenomena resembling some features of blindsight can be simulated in experiments which allow stray light to be a valid cue for discriminating stimuli. However, can the phenomena of blindsight really be explained by stray light? The answer is almost certainly no.

One of the features of Campion et al.'s simulation was that the background lighting was very low, as it had been in some of the experiments testing detection in DB. Stray light emitted by the targets is most likely to be an effective cue if there is little other ambient light. However, in one study, it was shown that DB's ability to reach accurately for targets in his scotoma remained even when the ambient light levels were extremely high.

A more rigorous test of the stray light hypothesis involves the **blind spot control**. Figure 2.5 shows the position of the blind spot in relation to DB's scotoma and it can be seen that the blind spot lies closer to the intact field than most of the scotoma. If detection of a target depends on stray light entering the intact field it follows that detection of targets

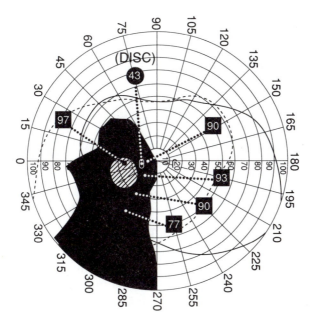

Figure 2.5 Results of blind spots control experiment on DB. Figures indicate DB's accuracy as a percentage for detecting whether or not a flash of light appeared at each location. Note that his performance is at chance when the light is flashed on to the blind spot. However, in all other places performance is well above chance, including areas further away from the intact visual field than the blind spot. Hatching estimates area in which DB had a 'feeling' that he might be able to see something. From L. Weiskrantz, *Blindsight: A case study and implications*. Reproduced by permission of Oxford University Press.

presented to the blind spot should be as good as adjacent areas of the scotoma. However, as the figure shows, detection of stimuli in the blind spot was at chance even though detection within the scotoma was extremely reliable.

Another major problem for the stray light hypothesis is that DB showed a degree of visual acuity being able to distinguish gratings of different spatial frequency. It is not easy to see how degraded diffuse light could provide information about spatial frequency. Similarly, it is also hard to explain how diffuse light could provide information about orientation and stimulus form. Finally Zihl and Werth (1984) demonstrated that localization performance in the scotoma of two patients was actually worse when stray light was manipulated as a cue to target position.

Our conclusion must be that although stray light may be manipulated to mimic some of the phenomena associated with blindsight it seems highly unlikely that it is the cause of the phenomenon itself.

Blindsight as Degraded Normal Vision

A second objection raised by Campion et al. was that the visual abilities demonstrated in blindsight studies were not the product of non-striate visual mechanisms but, instead, represented degraded normal vision – the argument being that the operative procedures may have left some striate cortex in place and it is this which mediates responding. On this basis blindsight would be interpreted as simply weak striate vision rather than as the output of a qualitatively different visual system.

One argument against the degraded normal vision argument was the striking similarity between the phenomena found in monkeys known to be completely destriate and the phenomena associated with blindsight. Furthermore it is notable that DB's verbal reports, where given, rarely bore any resemblance to the stimuli he was being shown. If a degraded striate system were at work one might well expect the reports to have some overlap with the visual qualities of the stimuli being used.

Additional evidence against the degraded normal vision theory came from an ingenious experiment where the first step was to find a region of the intact field in which DB's ability to distinguish a grating from a blank stimulus of similar flux was at chance. At the same location DB was tested on his ability to distinguish an **X** from a triangle and on this task he performed with 90 per cent accuracy.

Next a location was found in the scotoma where his ability to distinguish a grating from a blank stimulus was near perfect at 93 per cent correct. The final step was to examine how well he performed on the **X** versus triangle distinction and here he performed at chance. Together these data provide an important double dissociation. At a place in the intact field where grating detection is at chance, discrimination of form is extremely good. In contrast a location in the scotoma allows excellent grating detection but no discrimination of form. On the basis of this finding it is impossible to argue that blindsight is simply degraded normal vision because, if this were the case, the task performed most accurately in the intact field should also be performed best in the scotoma. This was not so and thus suggests that the visual processing undertaken in the scotoma and the intact field are qualitatively different.

Other Instances of Blindsight

Other cases of blindsight have been reported. Most notable is case GY who has been shown to demonstrate a wide variety of blindsight phenomena. Barbur, Ruddock and Waterfield (1980) demonstrated that

GY reliably judged the speed of moving stimuli in his scotoma even though he was unable to discriminate either the shape or size of the stimuli. This study also ruled out the possibility of stray light providing a cue (see also Blythe, Bromley, Kennard and Ruddock, 1986). Barbur, Forsyth and Findlay (1988) showed that GY could reliably direct eye movements to stimuli projected in the blind field. Most recently Weiskrantz, Harlow and Barbur (1991) showed that GY could reliably detect gratings in his scotoma providing appropriate conditions are met.

There have also been larger-scale studies. Blythe, Kennard and Ruddock (1987) studied 25 subjects with scotoma and found that 5 had residual vision characteristic of blindsight. Marzi, Tassinaari, Aglioti and Lutzemberger (1986) examined 20 patients with striate cortex damage and found 4 with evidence of blindsight as measured by a spatial summation task. In this task subjects are asked to respond as quickly as possible to a flash of light and performance is faster when two flashes are presented simultaneously. Why blindsight should occur variably is not clear. Marzi et al. suggest that their methods may have been relatively insensitive. Another possibility is that practice in making saccadic eye movements into the scotoma may influence the demonstration of some blindsight phenomena (Zihl and Werth, 1984).

Recently Gazzaniga (1994) has raised a number of concerns about blindsight. He notes the lack of eye movement monitoring in many of the early studies and the possibility that GY's residual vision may reflect unusual cortical reorganisation because his brain injury was sustained early in life. He also highlights the fact that, in group studies, the majority of patients do not appear to show blindsight (see above). Another issue is whether some blindsight phenomena might reflect isolated pockets of residual cortical vision. Fendrich, Wessinger and Gazzaniga (1992) report a patient known as CLT who had a left hemianopia in which there was a small area of residual vision for which he was unaware. Since blindsight did not occur in the blind field surrounding this small region the authors conclude that this residual vision must be cortically mediated.

What is the Function of Blindsight?

While Gazzaniga's comments urge caution in accepting all instances of blindsight as reflections of non-striate vision, the available evidence suggests that the phenomenon is sound. This raises a further question, what is blindsight for?

One extreme hypothesis concerns the concept of encephalization which asserts that, with evolutionary development, the cerebral cortex increasingly dominates brain function and that the activity of sub-cortical structures becomes far less important. Thus with vision it might be that the non-striate pathways still function and indeed have some residual abilities. However, in a brain with an intact striate cortex these functions are completely redundant and the visual world of the individual is based entirely on striate vision. One argument against the extreme encephalization position is that it would simply be uneconomical for the brain to maintain all these non-striate pathways when they are of no functional significance.

Alternatively, it has been proposed that two visual systems, one striate and one non-striate, have evolved to perform different functions. Schneider (1967) showed that lesions in the visual cortex of hamsters resulted in an inability to discriminate patterns from one another, but no difficulty in localizing the spatial position of stimuli. In contrast lesions to the superior collicus, a major component of the non-striate pathways, produced the reverse result. This gave rise to a view that one system, the striate system, was concerned with 'what things are' whereas the other, non-striate system, was concerned with 'where things are'.

Evidence in favour of a non-striate visual mechanism operating in normal humans is provided by Meeres and Graves (1990). They briefly exposed students to stimuli which, on 50 per cent of occasions, comprised an open circle presented at one of six locations (indicated by positions on the clock face) whilst on the other trials the stimulus was a blank field. Presentation of the stimuli was made increasingly brief and was also 'masked' by a subsequent patterned stimulus. The subjects' task was to detect whether a circle had been presented or not and, if so, whereabouts it was presented. As presentation duration decreased subjects' detection accuracy decreased to a point where they could no longer reliably decide whether a circle had been presented or not. However, when pressed to guess location at this point they were still detecting location well above chance.

The above study suggests that information about the location of a stimulus can be detected even when the subject fails to see the stimulus (see also Graves and Jones, 1992). This is a similar phenomenon to what we encountered in blindsight and thus suggests that non-striate vision may have a functional role in normal visual activity. Further evidence that non-striate vision has a functional role comes from a phenomenon known as 'inhibition of return'. If a subject is asked to make an eye movement to a stimulus in a particular location a further movement to that location will be inhibited if attempted within the next couple of seconds – a mechanism which is thought to promote novelty in visual scanning. Studies of patients who have suffered supra-nuclear palsy, a disease which causes degeneration of the superior colliculus, indicate that these patients do not show **inhibition of return** (Posner, Rafal, Choate and Vaughan, 1985). This shows that an aspect of normal vision is disrupted by damage to a non-striate pathway thus indicating that this pathway at least has a role in normal vision. This is supported by Hood's (1994) developmental study showing that very young children, in whom full striate vision has not yet developed, nonetheless show inhibition of return.

Spatial processing is certainly one of the prime abilities shown by blindsight patients but they can also perform other tasks such as movement detection, discriminate orientations, distinguish certain types of form, and most recently, discriminate colours (Weiskrantz, 1990; Stoerig and Cowey, 1992; Stoerig, 1993). In addition Rafal, Smith, Krantz, Cohen and Brennan (1990) have shown that stimuli presented in the scotoma can inhibit eye movements in the sighted field. This suggests that the mere detection of spatial location is not the only property of the non-striate system. One speculation is that it represents a more primitive visual system that is able to detect and locate moving shapes and some basic perceptual forms. The collection of abilities manifest in blindsight might, therefore, comprise some early visual system able to perform certain vital functions but, with the course of evolution, the complexities of cortical vision have become superimposed.

Summary

Blindsight is a form of residual visual ability in which people appear able to make certain forms of visual discrimination in the absence of any conscious visual perception. It is found in patients who have suffered damage to the geniculo-striate pathway and is thought to reflect the properties of other visual pathways such as that involving the superior colliculus. Among the visual abilities shown in blindsight are detection of location, movement, stimulus intensity along with some crude detection of form and colour. Doubts have been expressed about the nature of blindsight and attempts made to attribute it to poor control over eye movements, artefactual stimulation of the sighted field by stray light and residual cortical vision. While caution must be observed with this phenomenon the evidence points clearly to a form of residual vision that can be detected in the scotoma of patients with cortical blindness. It is possible that blindsight represents a more primitive visual system that has been superceded by that mediated by the cortex. Evidence does, however, suggest a functional role for this earlier system.

3

Visual Agnosia

I tried one final test. . . . I had thrown my coat and gloves on the sofa.
'What is this?' I asked, holding up a glove.
'May I examine it?' he asked, and, taking it from me, he proceeded. . . .
'A continuous surface,' he announced at last, 'infolded on itself. It
appears to have' – he hesitated – 'five outpouchings, if this is the word.'
'Yes,' I said cautiously. 'You have given me a description. Now tell me
what it is.'
'A container of some sort?'
'Yes,. . . . what would it contain?'
'It would contain its contents!'. . . . 'There are many possibilities. It could
be a change purse. . . . for coins of five sizes. It could. . . .'
I interrupted. . . . 'Does it look familiar? Do you think it might contain,
might fit, a part of your body?'
No light of recognition dawned on his face. (Sacks, 1985)

Recognizing things seems so easy that it is often difficult to understand
recognition problems such as those shown by Sack's patient Dr. P.
However, it has long been appreciated that brain damage can impair the
ability to recognize objects in a number of ways – a condition known as
visual agnosia. This can be defined as the inability to identify objects by
sight in the absence of any significant visual or intellectual impairment.
Lissauer, (1890) was one of the first to explore visual agnosia and he

suggested that visual agnosia could be divided into two basic forms, **apperceptive and associative**. In the apperceptive case the patient fails to identify an object because they are unable to form a stable representation or **percept**. In the associative case there is a normal percept but no ability to attribute identity, 'a percept stripped of its meaning' (Teuber, 1965).

In clinical neuropsychology apperceptive and associative agnosia are usually distinguished in terms of the patient's ability to copy pictures. Figure 3.1 shows the copying performance of two patients. In one case the patient is unable to copy even simple shapes and he also fails a very simple matching task. In contrast the second patient has remarkably good copying ability but is unable to name any of the pictures he has drawn. However, as we shall see later, accurate copying is not necessarily indicative of normal apperceptive processes.

In Lissauer's theory agnosia arose because of some disruption of the processes intervening between visual analysis and the attribution of meaning. It was thus a theory about how a specific object recognition system could become disordered. However, it is interesting to note that there was considerable early resistance to the idea of visual agnosia. In particular, Bay (1953) argued that all supposed instances of visual agnosia were either attributable to visual impairments that had not been properly assessed or due to intellectual impairment. As Farah (1990) points out, these objections seem a little curious from our current perspective in which we have models of visual recognition which propose intervening stages between visual analysis and identification of objects. But, presented with a theory that distinguished simply between perceptual processes and knowledge, it was relatively easy for these critics to re-interpret visual agnosia in terms of impaired vision or intellect.

Modern Studies of Visual Agnosia

Warrington and her colleagues (e.g. Warrington, 1985) have provided much of the recent experimental work on visual agnosia and initially used it to propose a two-stage account similar to Lissauer's original apperceptive/associative distinction. An important aspect of this work has been to provide sound evidence that any observed impairments in object recognition could not be attributed to lower-level sensory deficits.

Ruling out impairments due to sensory problems is not a straightforward matter because it requires an objective distinction between sensory and non-sensory aspects of visual processing. In her account Warrington identifies three patterns of visual impairment which she considers to be of a sensory nature. Any deficits of object recognition arising in association with one or more of these deficits cannot be

a)

 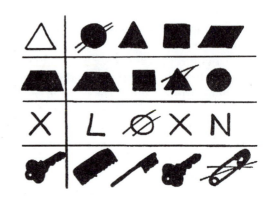

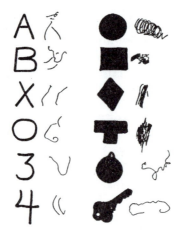

b)

I still don't know

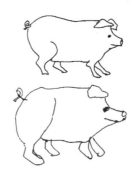

Could be a dog or any other animal.

considered as true agnosia but are instead considered as instances of pseudo-agnosia.

Warrington proposed that impaired colour discrimination and problems with visual orientation indicated defective sensory processes. In addition she also included impaired **shape discrimination** as an indicator of sensory impairment. This view owed much to the case of Mr S. reported by Efron (1968) who was recovering from cortical blindness following carbon monoxide poisoning. Mr S was experiencing major problems indentifying pictures, objects and people by sight. This could have indicated agnosia but Efron argued that the patient's problems arose from a more fundamental problem with shape discrimination. This was demonstrated by Mr S.'s inability to distinguish between a square and a rectangle matched for total flux.

The idea that fundamental problems in shape discrimination do not constitute a proper agnosia is a controversial one which we shall return to later. For the moment we will consider a number of highly influential studies of visual agnosia carried out by Warrington and her colleagues. One of the most important perceptual abilities we possess is the ability to identify an object despite it being presented in many different orientations, at various distances, and in differing lighting conditions. This is known as **object constancy**. Warrington and Taylor (1973) examined the capacity for object constancy in the two patient groups with lesions to either the right or the left hemisphere who were further subdivided as to whether their lesion was anterior, medial or posterior. Their investigation involved an **unusual views test** which was devised by photographing 20 objects both from a **prototypical** or **canonical** viewpoint and an unusual, unconventional viewpoint (see figure 3.2). Subjects were first shown the unusual views and asked to name or describe the picture (some of the left hemisphere patients had language difficulties). The procedure was then repeated for the canonical view pictures.

Five of the patient groups performed similarly to controls on the unusual views but one group, the right posterior group, performed much worse. The poor performance of the right posterior group did not arise because the subjects did not know what the objects were because, on canonical views, performance was extremely good in all groups. This, in conjunction with the absence of any sensory impairment, indicates that

---

Figure 3.1   (a) Shape matching and copying ability of two apperceptive agnosic patients. In matching task patient must match target shape on left with one of four choices. The patient's choices are marked; (b) copies of drawings by an associative agnosic along with his attempts to name them. From Farah, *Visual Agnosia*, (1990), reprinted by permission of MIT Press and Bauer (1993) reprinted by permission of Oxford University Press.

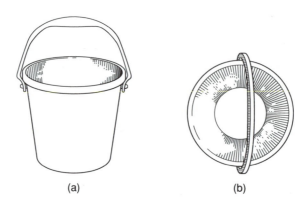

(a)   (b)

Figure 3.2   Example of items from an unusual views test. Item is presented in (a) conventional view and (b) unconventional view and subject must decide whether items are same or different. From Beaumont and Davidoff (1992). Reproduced with permission from Blackwell Scientific Publications.

impairment on the unusual views test is due to some problem within the perceptual system itself – the system which derives the representation of an object from the sensory input and attempts to match that input with our knowledge about objects.

Warrington and Taylor (1978) conducted a second experiment on object constancy using a modified version of the unusual views test. Instead of naming, which had caused difficulty for some left hemisphere patients, they used a task in which subjects saw pairs of photographs in which one was photographed from its canonical view and one from an unusual view. On half the trials both pictures were of the same object and on the other of a different object. Subjects merely had to decide whether the objects were the same or not and, in line with previous studies, it was only the right posterior group who found this task more difficult than controls.

This study also involved a matching to function test which is illustrated in Figure 3.3. Here subjects must decide which of two objects is most similar, functionally, to a test item. On this task it was found that both left and right posterior lesion groups performed at comparably worse levels than controls. However, a further analysis revealed an important difference between the two posterior lesion groups. For patients with right hemisphere lesions their deficit was neatly predicted by their recognition errors in that function matching errors occurred for objects that they failed to match in the unusual views test. However, when these errors were corrected for in the left hemisphere group it was still necessary to postulate an additional deficit to account for their bad performance.

Figure 3.3 Examples of the matching to function test. Subject must decide which of the two objects at the top has the same function as the lower object. From Warrington (1982), reproduced with permission.

Warrington and Taylor used their data as the basis for developing a model of object recognition that had much in common with Lissauer's earlier distinction between apperceptive and associative agnosia. In this model the first stage involves **visual analysis** and this occurs equally in both hemispheres. The next stage is termed **perceptual categorization** and represents those processes that enable object constancy to occur by establishing that two different views of an object are in fact representations of the same thing. This system is located in the right hemisphere because it was right posterior patients who had particular difficulty in performing a task of object constancy. After this comes **semantic categorization** which involves the attribution of meaning to the percept. This system is placed in the left hemisphere because it was left posterior patients who showed an independence between the ability to achieve object constancy and knowledge about the function of objects.

Agnosia and Marr's Theory of Vision

One of the most influential theories of vision is that of Marr (1976). Marr's theory is complex but can be summarized as dividing vision into four basic stages:

Primal Sketch: A scene is represented in terms of its fundamental perceptual elements such as edges and bars whose attributes such as length, contrast and orientation are also represented. These elements may also be grouped into features such as a conjunction between two lines of differing orientation.

$2\frac{1}{2}$D Sketch;   Information such as depth cues, figure ground discrimination, and surface texture are added. At this point the representation of the stimulus is still **viewer-centred** in that the nature of the internal representation is still determined by the observer's viewpoint.

3D Sketch: An **object-centred** representation of the object is established. This can be defined as a representation of the object that is independent of the specific viewpoint. At this stage a full structural description of the object becomes available. Thus, even though many important features of an object might be obscured in the current viewpoint, achievement of the 3D sketch means that our full knowledge of the object's structure becomes available.

Semantic Interpretation: Meaning is attributed to the stimulus.

There is an obvious correspondence between Marr's theory and the model developed by Warrington and Taylor. The proposed perceptual categorization process can be seen as analogous to the transition from a $2\frac{1}{2}$ to 3D sketch. Additionally, failure of semantic categorization could be attributed to a deficit in semantic interpretation. However, these similarities are rather general and it is possible that many other theories of vision might also accommodate the variations in object identification deficits observed by Warrington and her colleagues.

Experiments on agnosic patients were, however, thought to have some more precise bearing on Marr's theory. In particular, it was thought that agnosic patients might provide evidence about the exact mechanism underlying object constancy. In Marr's theory object constancy occurs when a given $2\frac{1}{2}$D sketch activates a stored structural description (3D Sketch). In work leading to this idea Marr and Nishihara (1978) had argued that a key component in establishing a 3D sketch was the assignment of a **principal axis** to the $2\frac{1}{2}$D sketch. The principal axis

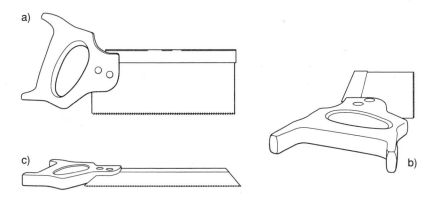

Figure 3.4 Examples of a saw shown with (a) its principal axis apparent (b) foreshortened so as to de-emphasize the principal axis, (c) rotated so as to obscure its defining physical feature. From Riddoch and Humphreys (1995), *Birmingham Object Recognition Battery*. Reproduced by permission of Lawrence Erlbaum Associates Ltd., Hove, UK.

reflects the fact that an object in its canonical view is bisected by an axis in a particular plane (see Figure 3.4). It was argued that if this axis could not be achieved then object recognition would be impeded.

Marr considered the results of Warrington and Taylor's studies to be highly relevant to the development of his theory. Discussing this Shallice (1988) notes that Marr considered the majority of Warrington and Taylor's unusual view stimuli to be ones in which the principal axis had been largely obscured. He thus suggested that the locus of the right posterior patients' difficulty with the unusual views test arose from an inability to derive the principal axis of the stimuli.

Warrington and Taylor did not consider the absence of a principal axis as the basis for recognition failure in the unusual views test. They adhered to the view of Sutherland (1973) in which object recognition depended on matching features of the percept with those of stored structural descriptions. Because objects share many common features, recognition depends critically on matching any distinctive or unique features of the stimulus with those of its stored description. Failure on unusual views thus arose because these pictures would tend to obscure distinctive features of the objects.

Humphreys and Riddoch (1984) set out to contrast these two opposing accounts of object recognition. They created a series of 26 stimuli each of which was photographed in three ways: a canonical view; a foreshortened view in which the principal axis was de-emphasized; and a view in from which the primary distinctive feature of the object was difficult to see (see Figure 3.4). The study involved five patients, four of whom had right hemisphere lesions. The fifth patient, HJA, who we will learn more about later, had bilateral posterior lesions. Subjects were presented with three stimuli, a target, the target rotated into either a foreshortened or minimal distinctive feature position, and an unrelated target. The task was to decide which of the three stimuli was different.

The results of the experiment showed that the four right hemisphere patients made substantial errors on the foreshortened stimuli averaging 43 per cent correct compared with 86 per cent correct for the other stimuli. However, HJA performed much better overall but produced a lower score for the stimuli in which the distinctive feature had been obscured (77 per cent versus 92 per cent). Humphreys and Riddoch took these data to be evidence for two routes to object constancy, one involving derivation of the principal axis and one requiring identification of distinctive features. However, this conclusion has come under considerable attack, most notably from Shallice (1988).

First, there was a statistical error in the analysis which when corrected indicated that one could no longer conclude that HJA's error pattern was the reverse of the right hemisphere group. Second, Shallice points out that, aside from statistical problems, HJA's higher level of performance makes an interpretation in terms of different forms of deficit difficult to pursue (see Shallice, 1988 for a more detailed discussion).

Putting aside problems with the interpretation of HJA's result, Humphreys and Riddoch's data from the four right hemisphere patients appeared to provide additional evidence that failure to derive an object's principal axis was the underlying cause of recognition failure. In support of this a further experiment used the same procedure but with additional depth cues present so as to emphasize the principal axis. This had a marked effect on patients' performance with performance improving to an average of 71 per cent.

These data thus seem to support a theory in which object constancy depends on establishing an object's principal axis. However, as Shallice notes, this does not square with other available data. Warrington (1982) presented stimuli in different lighting conditions. When the lighting was changed by, for example, lighting from the other side rather than above, a right posterior group performed more poorly even though changed lighting did not have any obvious influence on the availability of the principal axis.

Equally problematic for the Humphreys and Riddoch view is the study carried out by Warrington and James (1988). Subjects viewed three-dimensional silhouettes of objects which were slowly rotated around either the vertical or horizontal axis so that they became easier to

Figure 3.5 Examples of stimuli used by Warrington and James (1988). Reproduced with permission.

identify. The effect of this manipulation was that for some rotations the principal axis was immediately available whereas for others it did not appear until the object had been considerably rotated (see figure 3.5). If the principal axis is essential to object identification then it follows that those stimuli in which the principal axis becomes available earlier should be more quickly identified, but this was not the case.

The above studies show very clearly that agnosic patients have problems with object constancy, which can be shown easily with various forms of the unusual views test. However, the data do not support the view that derivation of an object's principal axis is a necessary component in establishing object constancy. The nature of the mechanism underlying object constancy must await further research.

Further Fractionation of Apperceptive Agnosia

Warrington's account of agnosia essentially involves two levels of categorization: perceptual and semantic. However, as work on agnosia continues it is becoming clear that a simple division between perceptual and semantic categorization impairments does not capture the variation in deficits shown by visual agnosics. Kartsounis and Warrington (1991) describe Mrs FRG who had developed object recognition problems following cortical degeneration. She succeeded on all the standard tests of visual acuity including shape discrimination but was unable to perform even the simplest figure-ground discrimination. In the example shown in figure 3.6 she described it as 'a triangle in the middle and a line across the top'. The right posterior patients who did poorly on the unusual views test were all able to perform these figure-ground discriminations so, minimally, it would appear that there is a separable stage mediating figure-ground discrimination that intervenes between sensory processing and perceptual categorization.

As we noted earlier Warrington's account restricts the use of the term agnosia to those patients whose visual identification impairments cannot be explained in terms of sensory loss. Where the latter is observed the

Figure 3.6   Stimulus used by Kartsounis and Warrington (1991). Reproduced with permission.

patient is described as pseudo-agnosic instead. While there is no problem in accepting impaired visual orientation, brightness discrimination or colour vision as evidence of sensory loss there has been considerable discussion as to whether patients with impaired shape discrimination should also be defined as pseudo-agnosic. At a clinical level, for example, a patient with normal brightness discrimination and colour vision who is unable to perceive shapes would be termed an apperceptive agnosic (a good example being illustrated in figure 3.1). However, within Warrington's scheme this patient would be pseudo-agnosic with the term apperceptive agnosia being restricted to patients with normal shape discrimination whose deficit lies in an inability to match two different views of the same object.

If the proposed distinction between pseudo-agnosia and agnosia were only of clinical relevance then we could probably drop the matter here. However, the issue does have important theoretcial implications as well when one attempts to relate visual identification impairments to models of visual recognition. Humphreys and Riddoch (1987a) have argued that an impaired ability to copy shapes should be considered a type of agnosia. Their argument is primarily based on theoretical claims that the process of object constancy allowing successful matching of different viewer-centred descriptions of an object does not necessarily occur independently of lower level processes involved in the perception of form (Humphreys and Quinlan, 1987). As a result it is not possible to divorce mechanisms of shape perception from higher level processes such as the achievement of object constancy.

Humphreys and Riddoch therefore propose that the terms agnosia should be applied to any impairment in the ability to perceive form. Their classification would, for example, still define impaired brightness discrimination as sensory loss but an ability to discriminate shapes in the presence of normal sensory abilities is termed shape agnosia. In addition to shape agnosia Humphreys and Riddoch have proposed the term transformation agnosia to describe patients who are able to identify objects from their canonical view but fail when the objects are foreshortened or their defining physical features are de-emphasized. In addition the Humphreys and Riddoch approach is perhaps best known for the identification of a third form of apperceptive agnosia which we consider in the next section.

Integrative Agnosia

The third form of apperceptive agnosia identified by Humphreys and Riddoch has emerged largely from the detailed study of one agnosic patient (Humphreys and Riddoch, 1987b, Riddoch and Humphreys, 1987a). HJA was a businessman who suffered a bilateral stroke which left him with marked visual difficulties. These could not be due to basic sensory difficulties because he showed normal discrimination of line length, orientation and position and also responded normally to various visual illusions.

Figure 3.7 shows HJA's copy of an etching and, on the basis of its accuracy, one would assume that he is an associative agnosic. However, this would be misleading because this drawing has been produced by a slavish line-by-line procedure which took six hours to carry out. This indicates caution in the interpretation of accurate copying performance but more importantly suggests that HJA may well have some form of apperceptive problem. Figure 3.7 also illustrates three simple drawings that he failed to identify. His commentary on trying to name these and other objects is enlightening:

Carrot: 'I have not the glimmerings of an idea. The bottom point seems solid and the other bits are feathery. It does not seem logical unless it is some sort of brush.'

Nose: 'a soup ladle.'

Onion: 'I'm completely lost at the moment. You don't put it on. It has sharp bits at the bottom like a fork. It could be a necklace of sorts.'

(Humphreys and Riddoch, 1987b, pp. 59–60)

The most noticeable feature of HJA's errors is that he seems unable to grasp the overall relation between the parts of the objects. Inability to perceive the whole object leads him to try and extrapolate the item's identity from just one or two features. Observations like these are well known in the agnosia literature. Luria, for example, argued that 'One fact stands out clearly in every case [of apperceptive agnosia] so far described: The structure of the visual act is incomplete. The patient identifies a particular sign from a complex object or picture or sometimes

Figure 3.7 HJA's copy of an etching and three simple line drawings which he failed to name. From Humphreys and Riddoch (1987b), *To see but not to see*. Reprinted by permission of Lawrence Erlbaum Associates Ltd., Hove, UK.

he may manage to pick out a second sign, but he cannot synthesize these signs visually and he cannot convert them into the components of an integral whole' (Luria, 1980, pp. 161–2).

The type of object recognition deficit shown by HJA has sometimes been described as **simultanagnosia**, meaning 'impaired simultaneous perception'. However, this term is slightly problematic because it can be used to describe a more precise and different form of impairment in which the patient is unable to identify more than one object in an array at any point in time (Wolpert, 1924). For this, and other reasons which will soon become apparent, Humphreys and Riddoch (1987a,b) chose the term **integrative agnosia** to describe the object recognition deficit shown by HJA.

Humphreys and Riddoch have carried out an extensive number of experiments in an attempt to characterize the basis of HJA's object naming impairment. The first, and most obvious explanation, is that he has somehow lost his stored knowledge about objects. This can be ruled out easily because, as we have seen, HJA has excellent knowledge about

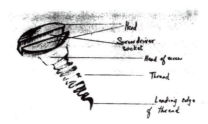

Figure 3.8 HJA's drawing of a screw from memory including his labelling of the various parts. From Humphreys and Riddoch (1987a), *To see but not to see*. Reprinted by permission of Lawrence Erlbaum Associates Ltd., Hove, UK.

the objects he cannot name and can also produce reasonable drawings of them (see figure 3.8).

In one experiment HJA was shown fragmented pictures in which the fragments were either aligned along the contours of the object or misaligned by a significant degree (see figure 3.9). HJA was asked to judge whether each pair of pictures depicting the same object were the

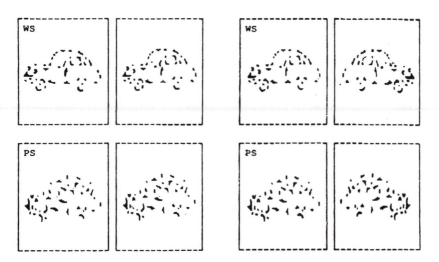

Figure 3.9 Matching task used by Boucart and Humphreys (1992). WS = well structured. PS = poorly structured. The computation of perceptural structure from collinearity and closure: Normality and pathology. *Neuropsychologia*, *30*, 527–46, by kind permission Elsevier Science Ltd.

same or different in orientation. Control subjects showed a predictable advantage for the aligned (well structured) forms whereas HJA showed no such difference. However, HJA did show close to normal performance when the two items differed in terms of their global orientation (see right-hand side of figure 3.9).

Humphreys and Riddoch propose that visual perception involves a process in which the global form of stimulus is established and, independently of this, a second process deals with the individual features comprising that stimulus. In this second process the spatially-distributed elements of the stimulus undergo an integrative, 'binding', procedure – in the above experiment this was indicated by use of the shared orientation between stimulus elements (collinearity) as local grouping cues which enabled the well structured pictures to be dealt with more easily. In contrast HJA's lack of an advantage for aligned forms indicates that he is insensitive to these integrative local grouping cues. However, this does not lead to an inability to derive global shape because HJA was good at distinguishing items that did or did not differ in terms of global orientation. This indicates that the mechanism for deriving global shape, as suggested by Humphreys and Riddoch, is independent of more locally derived cues to perceptual structure.

If we devise a task in which a correct response can be derived from either global shape or local features it follows that HJA should do better using global shape. To test this an **object decision task** was devised in which real and unreal objects were devised – the latter being achieved by combining two components of different objects (see figure 3.10). Each object was presented twice, once as a drawing and once in silhouette, and HJA had to decide whether or not the object was real. According to prediction, HJA performed better on silhouettes while, as one would expect, controls found the task easier with line drawings.

The interpretation of HJA's agnosia as one involving the integration of local features has been sustained by further experiments involving him (e.g. Humphreys, Riddoch, Quinlan et al., 1992). In addition other investigators have pursued agnosia from a similar perspective. Butter and Trobe (1994) report a patient who, like HJA, shows superior naming of silhouettes relative to line drawings. Grailet, Seron, Bruyer, Coyette and Frederix (1990) report a patient, HG, with many similar characteristics to HJA and describe him as another case of integrative agnosia. Thus, when attempting to identify objects he appeared to use the same feature by feature strategy as HJA. However, HG's performance deviates considerably from HJA in that his tactile recognition of objects is affected as is his stored knowledge about objects.

Thaiss and DeBleser (1992) describe TK, a woman who developed object recognition difficulties in the context of dementia. Superficially

(a) Line drawings

(b) Silhouettes

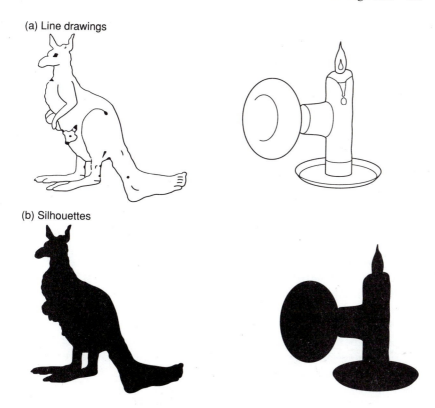

Figure 3.10   Items from the object decision task. From Riddoch and Humphreys (1995), *Birmingham Object Recognition Battery*. Reprinted by permission of Lawrence Erlbaum Associates Ltd., Hove, UK.

her deficit resembled that of HJA in that she would attempt piecemeal analysis of a stimulus in order to identify it. On closer inspection TK's deficit was rather different. When shown a large letter H made up of lots of small H's she was able to identify all the small letters but could not see the large letter. Whe HJA attempted this task he was able to name the global letter but not the individual letter elements. This is what we would expect from our earlier observations and confirms that HJA has relatively preserved global shape processing with an impaired ability to segment smaller elements of a stimulus effectively – a problem HJA describes as being unable to 'see the trees for the wood'. Returning to TK she obviously has defective global shape processing and it is this which interferes with her correct identification of objects.

Apperceptive Agnosia and Action

Goodale, Milner, Jakobson and Carey (1991) described a woman known as DF who developed a severe form of apperceptive agnosia due to carbon monoxide poisoning. Thus even when asked to distinguish between simple geometric shapes she was unable to do so. It was thus remarkable to discover that, despite this impairment, she was able to use information from objects to guide her hand movements when reaching out and grasping those objects. In one experiment she was presented with a large slot that could be placed in a variety of orientations. She was unable to describe the orientation or rotate her hand to match the position of the slot. However, when asked to place either her hand or a card in the slot she was able to do so quite accurately and analysis of her hand movements showed that her preparatory movements were appropriate for the task being demanded. In a further experiment she was asked to discriminate solid blocks of differing dimensions. This she was unable to do, but when asked to pick up the objects it was noticeable that the gap between her finger and thumb accurately reflected the size of the object to be manipulated.

These experiments indicated that DF retained the ability to calibrate normal aiming and apprehension movements towards objects for which she had little conscious visual information available. This finding indicates that there are separate brain mechanisms concerned with recognizing objects and directing skilled actions towards objects. However, further studies have indicated that this preserved control of action is rather limited. When asked to rotate a more complex object, a wooden T-shape, so that it fitted in a slot of the same shape, she was unable to do so above chance (Goodale, Jakobson, Milner, et al., 1994). This suggests that higher-level visual processes are required to direct action involving an object with two principal axes. Further experiments have also indicated that DF's movements are only accurate when luminance cues are available. Thus she can correctly orient towards a dark rectangle on black ground but is very inaccurate when identification of the rectangle requires more complex visual processing.

Associative Agnosia

Associative agnosia can be defined as a deficit in object recognition despite normal perceptual ability. The existence of this disorder is predicted by Warrington's model and by Marr's theoretical framework, both of which specify that knowledge about objects is represented independently of the perceptual processes that lead to their identification. However, as a deficit it is problematic for two reasons. First, demonstrating that a patient has no significant perceptual impairments can be very difficult. As Shallice (1988) notes, many of the early reports of associative agnosia lacked proper evaluation of possible visual impairments and must therefore be considered with caution. Another problem is that some patients with apparent visual agnosia may in fact be suffering from **optic aphasia.** This is a controversial disorder in which it is naming that is impaired rather than recognition itself. Thus the patient might be unable to name an object but nonetheless indicates its identity by gesture. It differs from anomia in that the deficit is only present in the visual modality. The distinction between associative agnosia and optic aphasia is not very clear, and some have argued that the latter is merely a milder form of the deficit. In addition a recent survey by Iorio, Falanga, Fragassi and Grossi (1992) indicates that patients may variably show elements of both disorders (see also Schinder, Benson and Schaure, 1994).

McCarthy and Warrington (1986a) reported a 77 year-old shopkeeper, FRA, who awoke following a left hemisphere stroke to realize that he could no longer read a newspaper. Further examination showed that he had developed a marked alexia being unable to make even simple discriminations between letters. Despite appearing to have normal visual abilities FRA reported visual problems such as being muddled when attempting to set the table. Further testing indicated that these visual failures did not have an obvious apperceptive origin. He could, for example, colour in individual objects contained within an overlapping figure despite being unable to name any of them.

Further tests, directed towards visual knowledge about objects did reveal severe difficulties. On one task he was asked to match physically dissimilar pictures of objects with the same function (e.g. two types of train) or to match pictures with a spoken name (e.g. 'train' with a picture of a train). He performed both tasks poorly and was worse on the picture/picture matching. As well as indicating his poor knowledge of object function per se his better performance on the spoken word/picture matching indicated that FRA's deficit was not complicated by optic aphasia – the latter deficit is assumed to reflect some difficulty in translating between visual and verbal representations and, if present, would be expected to affect the spoken word version of the task more.

In contrast to his poor visual performance, FRA was able to show normal knowledge about objects when tested in the auditory domain. In one study he either saw pictures or heard the names of three animals. His task was to decide which was the largest. With the spoken form his performance was perfect but he was badly impaired on the visual form.

A similar finding occurred when he was asked to decide which of three objects was heaviest.

Humphreys and Riddoch (1987a; 1993) have proposed that patients such as FRA have a form of associative agnosia which involves a failure to access structural descriptions. Essentially, it is proposed that we possess a visual, object-centred structural description of each object we know. Access to these structural descriptions depends on correct perceptual classification, thus failure on the unusual views test indicates an inability to map the content of a percept on to the correct structural description. These structural descriptions, in turn, have access to that object's functional properties. Knowledge of function, however, is not tied to any sensory modality and, as a result, can be addressed via any of the senses. It is for this reason that FRA, although unable to identify objects visually, can nonetheless describe their function when asked about them.

Given the above, it should be possible to observe instances where the deficit lies at the level of knowledge about objects rather than at the structural description level. Evidence for this type of impairment is provided by Stewart, Parkin and Hunkin (1992) in an investigation of HO. This patient developed marked object recognition difficulties as a result of herpes simplex encephalitis – a disease which causes necrotic lesions centred on the temporal lobes. Thus on naming tests which unimpaired subjects would perform normally she named around only 50 per cent of the objects. There was no evidence of visual impairment including 100 per cent accuracy on the unusual views test (see above). As part of her evaluation she was given the Object Decision Task (see above). HO got 85 per cent correct which is within normal limits. Further testing then examined whether she could show normal knowledge about objects when asked about them (e.g. 'What is the tool used to chop wood?'). On these tests she did very poorly and, in conjunction with her normal object decision performance, suggest that her deficit lies in knowledge about objects, regardless of how she is asked about them. Accordingly Humphreys and Riddoch have termed this form of deficit semantic access agnosia (for additional examples see Riddoch and Humphreys, 1987b; Sheridan and Humphreys, 1993).

Hierarchical Accounts of Agnosia – an Overview

In the preceding sections we have examined various explanations of agnosia which all assume that visual processing goes through a hierarchical series of stages and that different forms of object recognition impairment can occur depending on which stage of processing is affected. The accounts vary merely in the number of stages identified. Thus, in

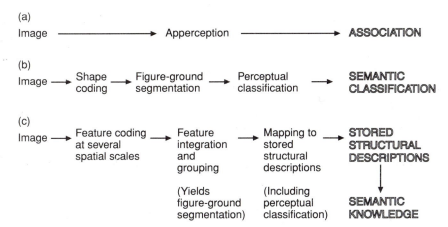

Figure 3.11 The relations between three hierarchical approaches to visual object recognition as derived from studies of visual agnosia (a) Lissauer, (b) Warrington, (c) Humphreys and Riddoch (from Humphreys and Riddoch, 1993a, reproduced with permission).

Lissauer's early account, deficits reflected merely impairments of apperception or association. Warrington's initial account distinguished perceptual classification from semantic classification and, in addition, regarded object recognition deficits linked to lower visual problems as pseudo-agnosia. Humphreys and Riddoch (1987a) offer the most detailed account of agnosia. They argue against the concept of pseudo-agnosia and propose that the interactive nature of visual processing means that even lower-level deficits (e.g. shape analysis) can reflect recognition difficulties rather than sensory impairment. Another distinction within the apperceptive domain is that between integrative processing and the mapping of a percept on to a stored structural description. At the associative stage a distinction is made between an agnosia in which structural descriptions are disrupted and one in which object knowledge itself has been lost. While the debate over pseudo-agnosia remains unresolved it is reasonable to see the latter two approaches as systematic developments of Lissauer's original idea (see figure 3.11).

Alternative Accounts of Agnosia

Farah (1990; 1991) has put forward an alternative account of agnosia which derives, initially, from a survey of cases involving alexia, visual object agnosia, and prosopagnosia – the latter is thought by many to

(a)   (b)   (c)

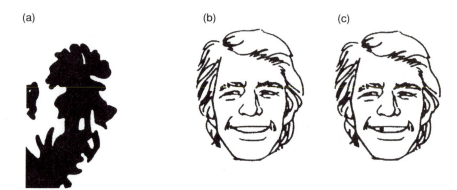

Figure 3.12   Wholistic versus featural processing. Deciding that stimulus (a) is a face depends on perceiving the relation between the fragments rather than the identity of any fragment itself. Deciding whether (b) and (c) are different depends on analysing individual features.

be a specific impairment in the ability to recognize faces and it is considered in detail in the next chapter. She notes that patients are found who have either all three deficits, alexia and object agnosia, or object agnosia and prosopagnosia. Alexia and prosopagnosia without object agnosia is not found, nor is object agnosia as an isolated deficit. From these findings Farah argues that object recognition is served by two parallel processes: one that deals with wholistic patterns and one which deals with the constituent features of objects (see figure 3.12). In addition, no distinction is drawn between apperceptive and associative forms of impairment.

It is assumed that faces are processed as wholes whereas words are processed in terms of their constituent features. Face recognition will therefore be impaired if wholistic processing is deficient and word recognition will be impaired if constituent features are poorly dealt with. Because objects depend on both wholistic and featural processes their recognition can be affected by damage to either process, although the nature of this impairment will of course vary.

Farah's theory makes some reasonable predictions about what should and should not be observable in the realm of object agnosia. Taking this point on, Humphreys and Riddoch (1993) claim many instances which cannot be accommodated by Farah's framework. First, they argue that the apperceptive/associative distinction is essential to explain patients such as HO (above) who show good performance on object decision but fail to recognize objects or know their function. Similarly the patient LH (Etcoff, Freeman and Cave, 1992) had a marked prosopagnosia and some object agnosia despite no obvious impairments on either tests of wholistic or featural processing.

Turning to the apperceptive disorders Humphreys and Riddoch argue from the much studied case HJA. They note that HJA has exceptionally poor face recognition ability, yet he reads short common words presented for short durations (100 msec) quite well. In Farah's terms this would imply a wholistic deficit. However, as we saw earlier, HJA does much better on the object decision task when it is presented in silhouette. This form of presentation largely excludes featural processing, so good performance by HJA must indicate good ability to deal with wholistic stimuli. Humphreys and Riddoch argue that an inconsistency as marked as this undermines Farah's case. Another difficulty with Farah's argument is the equation of facial memory with wholistic processing. While there seems little doubt that there is a right lateralized system sensitive to the wholistic quality of faces, there is also evidence for a left hemisphere system involved in the featural analysis of faces (Parkin and Williamson, 1986).

Category-specific Effects

Warrington and Shallice (1984) reported the case of JBR who had developed agnosia as a result of herpes simplex encephalitis. He was given pictures to name and the authors noted some very striking variations depending on the category from which the pictures were drawn. He performed well on pictures of non-living things and was also good at naming parts of the body. In contrast he did very poorly when confronted with living things and also musical instruments. This study stimulated a number of other studies, all of which appeared to show that agnosia could be selectively worse for living as opposed to non-living things (Pietrini, Nertempi, Vaglia, et al., 1988; Sartori and Job, 1988; Silveri and Gainotti, 1988). This led to the idea that our representation of knowledge in some way acknowledges the distinction between living and non-living things.

HO (Stewart et al., 1992), who we considered earlier, was tested on her ability to name living and non-living things. On initial testing she resembled the performance of JBR quite closely, even showing good identification of body parts and poor recognition of musical instruments. However, it was noted that experiments showing category-specificity had only ensured that the names of items comprising living and non-living categories were equally familiar. Stewart et al. pointed out that additional controls involving visual familiarity (e.g. the word camel may be more familiar than actually seeing a camel) and visual complexity (pictures may vary in their information content – a drawing of a cup would typically involve fewer lines than a drawing of a fly) should also be carried out.

In a subsequent experiment Stewart et al. controlled for all three relevant factors and found that HO no longer showed a category-specific effect in naming. The methodological criticisms of Stewart et al. were acknowledged by Sartori, Miozzo and Job (1993) who retested their category-specific patient Michaelangelo using additional controls. They again found poorer naming of living things. However, in a critique of this study, Parkin and Stewart (1993) argued that the controls employed did not adequately rule out other differences between living and non-living things (see also the reply of Sartori and Job, 1993).

Funnell and Sheridan (1992) also considered the role of stimulus artefacts in generating apparent category-specific effects. These experiments have typically used the picture database devised by Snodgrass and Vanderwart (1980). Funnell and Sheridan noted that, on average, pictures of living things sampled from this database were of lower familiarity than non-living things. Following this up they showed that a category-specific deficit observed in the patient ceased to exist when familiarity was controlled for. In addition they showed that the category-specific deficit shown by JBR (see above) was also removed when the familiarity factor was taken into account.

An additional factor that is crucial in understanding the origin of category-specific effects is **visual similarity**. Compare a typical array of objects from the category 'kitchen utensils' and those from the category 'insects'. It is immediately apparent that these items differ in visual similarity with insects sharing far more visual features. It is also the case that a comparison of body parts and musical instruments yields a similar difference. The implication of differences in visual familiarity is that more visual information will be required to discriminate categories such as insects and musical instruments than is needed for discriminating kitchen utensils and body parts. Thus, if there is damage to the processes underlying visual analysis, it is more likely that recognition of the categories high in visual similarity will be affected.

The role of visual similarity in generating category-specific effects was addressed in two experiments by Gaffan and Heywood (1993). In the first experiment human subjects were presented with pictures from different categories very briefly and asked to identify them. The results (see figure 3.13) showed that more errors were made to living things. In addition more errors were made to musical instruments than to tools. On its own this experiment does not necessarily mean that visual similarity is the key factor determining performance. Damasio, Damasio and Tranel (1990) have suggested that non-living things may have an advantage because of their tendency to be associated with kinaesthetic responses. In this context the superior identification of tools over musical instruments relates to the greater variation of movements associated with using the former.

To get round this problem the second experiment used monkeys as subjects. Here one can rule out any higher order factors because one can assume that monkeys know nothing about drawings other than what an experimenter decides to associate them with during an experiment. Gaffan and Heywood examined the ability of monkeys to discriminate living from non-living things using a paradigm in which some pictures were associated with reward and others no reward. It was found that monkeys learned much easier when pictures of non-living things were used. A particularly striking finding was the big increase in difficulty found when the number of animal pictures used was increased. In contrast there was a negligible effect of increasing the number of non-living pictures used (see figure 3.13).

The above studies suggest that many instances of apparent category-specificity involving poorer naming of living things may be an artefact of failing to control for factors such as familiarity, visual complexity, and visual similarity. However, some findings are not so readily dealt with in this way. Sacchett and Humphreys (1992) report a patient, CW, who consistently named pictures of non-living objects and body parts worse than living things. In addition, there are a number of studies in which a category-specific deficit for living things persists when knowledge is tapped verbally. Moreover, this deficit has tended to be more pronounced for sensory aspects of items rather than their functional properties, for example, is an apple round, oblong, or conical? versus is an apple eaten raw, dried or in both ways? (Basso, Capitani and Laiacona, 1988; Hart and Gordon, 1992; Silveri and Gainotti, 1988).

There are a number of points to make about these studies. First one must be sure that the questions asked about sensory and functional properties of living and non-living things are equivalent. Capitani, Laiacona, Barbarotto and Trivelli (1994) report that subjects find questions about non-living items easier, thus making any category-specific conclusions based on this form of questioning suspect. Laiacona, Barbarotto and Capitani (1993) report two cases in which they found normal performance (relative to controls) on questions about non-living items but impaired performance on questions about living things. However, performance of their controls on the questions is close to ceiling (94 per cent for non-living, 90 per cent for living) and so it is difficult to draw any firm conclusions as to whether the good performance by all subjects on non-living questions is due to the overall ease of

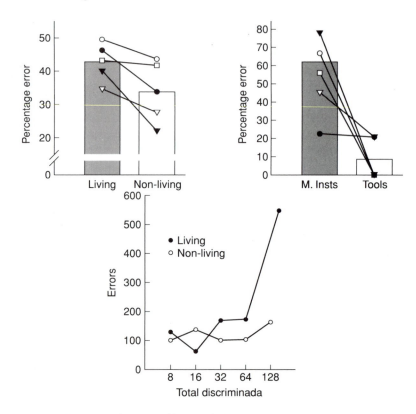

Figure 3.13 Data from Gaffan and Heywood (1993). (a) Results of an experiment in which human subjects attempted to identify different types of item. Lines superimposed on histograms show individual subjects' performance. (b) Ability of monkeys to learn discriminations between pictures of living and nonliving things as a function of the number of pictures in each set. Reproduced with permission of MIT Press.

these questions. It might be the case that harder questions could yield a different pattern of relative impairment. In asking questions about visual versus functional attributes one must also exercise care. Farah, Hammond, Mehta and Ratcliff (1989) found that all their control subjects performed worse on questions about visual attributes than they did about functional attributes.

Putting these difficulties aside there are other reasons to be careful about the interpretation of category-specific effects. Sheridan and Humphreys (1993) report a patient who had a severe naming difficulty which was most pronounced for foods. She was given a version of the object decision task (see above) in which she had to distinguish real from unreal

Figure 3.14   (a) Three animals. Each have the same component parts in the same places. We distinguish them by the relative differences in size and other aspects of those parts. (b) How different objects can be assembled by different spatial configurations of the same parts. Source (a) From Snodgrass and Vanderwart (1980), copyright © 1980 the American Psychological Association; (b) from Biederman (1987), copyright © 1987 the American Psychological Association, reproduced with permission.

animals and fruits. She performed the task remarkably well even though her naming ability for real fruits and animals was so poor. The authors suggest that the deficit lies at a point beyond structural description but stop short of arguing for specific categorial areas. Instead they suggest that different classes of item may depend on different encoding dimensions to differentiate them. Natural objects will tend to have the same parts in the same spatial configuration but differ in terms of the relative scale, width, etc. of these parts whereas non-living things can often involve the same parts in different configurations (see figure 3.14). Under these conditions disruption of an encoding system governing, for example, configural relations, would impair recognition of objects more than animals.

Connectionist Modelling and Category-specificity

Farah and McClelland (1991) have approached the issue of category-specificity from the perspective of connectionist modelling (see chapter 1). Like Humphreys and Riddoch they have rejected the idea that there might be a categorial distinction between living and non-living things and, instead, suggest that category-specific effects arise from differences in the encoding dimensions used to represent objects and living things. Following arguments put forward by Warrington and Shallice (1984), they took the view that the most plausible basis for category-specific effects is that living and non-living things vary in the extent to which they are represented in terms of visual and functional attributes. Thus a tiger, for example, is distinguished from related creatures by its colouring rather than its functional role as a predator. In contrast, a desk is distinguished from other forms of furniture by its functional role.

A network was devised in which living and non-living things were represented as combinations of visual and functional units. A semantic system comprising 80 semantic units was devised (40 visual and 40 functional). To capture the variation in types of attributes associated with each category, living items were, on average, associated with 11 visual units and 4 functional units whereas non-living things were represented by 6 visual units and 13 functional units. There were two input systems, one dealing with verbal inputs and the other picture inputs (see figure 3.15). Once the network had been 'trained' to identify 10 hypothetical living and 10 non-living things from both words and pictures it was 'lesioned' and its ability to perform re-examined. As one would expect, lesions of the visual units disrupted identification of living things more than non-living things and a lesion of the functional units only disrupted identification of non-living things.

A further experiment examined whether damage to visual units could disproportionately impair knowledge about the functional properties of living things. This was considered crucial because patients with category-specific problems involving animals can also have problems retrieving functional knowledge about animals. If poor naming of living things arises from loss of visual units it is reasonable to suppose that functional knowledge might survive. Accordingly the model was lesioned and it was found that damage to visual units reduced the availability of functional knowledge about living things. This indicated that the availability of functional knowledge about a living thing depended on an intact representation of visual knowledge. The simulation thus shows that loss of both visual and functional knowledge about a living thing can occur within a semantic system, which makes only a division between visual

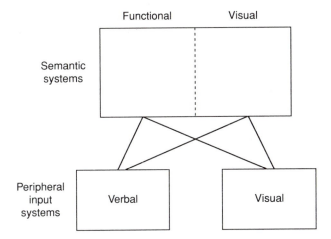

Figure 3.15 A schematic outline of Farah and McClelland's connectionist model of semantic memory. Copyright © 1991 by the American Psychological Association. Reproduced with permission.

and functional attributes. To the extent that we accept this model as reflecting the organization of the brain, we are not obliged to accept any further division such as that between living and non-living things (see also Small, Hart, Nguyen and Gordon, 1995).

Multiple Semantics?

While we must remember that connectionist models are just means of simulating aspects of human cognition, the similarities between the effects of lesioning these networks and the effects of real brain lesions make it compelling to believe that the network does shed some light on the organization of the real system. In this respect it is of some significance that the model has only one semantic system which can be addressed by both verbal and visual inputs. Thus, whether we see a picture of a fork or hear the spoken name 'fork' the knowledge made available to us (shiny, thin, cutlery, has a handle, used for eating) comes from the same semantic system. From a common-sense view this seems a good idea because it requires the development of only one semantic system (e.g. Marshall, 1988). However, neuropsychological evidence has now led some to suggest that more than one semantic system exists.

McCarthy and Warrington (1988) examined TOB's ability to identify living things and objects from either their spoken name or from a picture.

The results were quite dramatic; TOB had no problems identifying living things or animals from pictures but when spoken names were used he had a marked problem identifying animals. Thus when given a word 'rhinoceros' he replied 'Animal can't give you any functions' but when shown the picture of a rhinoceros he said 'Enormous, weighs over one ton, lives in Africa'. In response to the word 'pig' he replied 'animal' but for 'wheelbarrow' he replied 'The item we have here in the gardens for carrying bits and pieces'.

McCarthy and Warrington (1988) and Shallice (1993) have interpreted these findings as evidence for 'modality specific meaning systems' in which access to meaning from words and pictures involves separate semantic systems which have most commonly been referred to as **verbal** and **visual semantics**. This 'multiple semantics' idea has not gone unchallenged. Caramazza, Hillis, Rapp and Romani (1990) have suggested that the pattern of results shown by TOB can be explained in terms of a single semantic system which they have called the Organized Unitary Content Hypothesis (OUCH). According to their theory pictures have privileged access (see figure 3.16). Essentially their argument is that words and pictures differ in their relationship with representations of meaning. For words the association of a word with its meaning is almost always arbitrary (the exception being onomatopoeia) – thus a 'fork' could be called anything providing that the label was used systematically. With pictures, however, it is argued that some structural features of the object are perceptually salient. Thus the tines of a fork indicate an ability to spear things which, in turn, is one of the semantic features associated with our representation of fork.

Within this system pictures are easier to name (and hence less vulnerable to disruption of naming) because various elements of the picture have salient links with components of the semantic representation. However, why should TOB be worse at defining animal names than object names? Here we could use the argument we developed when considering the origins of category-specific agnosia. It can be argued that representations of animals share many common features whereas an average array of objects has far less featural overlap. Thus the spoken name of an animal would make contact with a representation of animals far less distinctive than that for a range of objects.

A problem for the single semantic system view is the existence of patients who have a greater problem defining pictures than words because, as Shallice (1993) argues, this difference is possible for a multiple semantics position but extremely awkward for the privileged visual access account. McCarthy and Warrington (1986) describe FRA who could define spoken words but could not name or mime the use of visually presented objects. In a case like this it is important to be sure

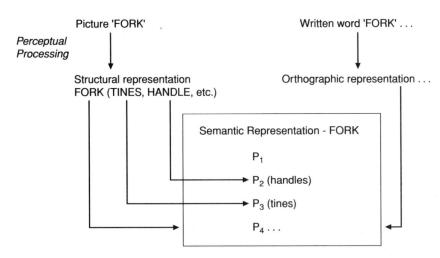

Figure 3.16   The OUCH model of unitary semantics proposed by Caramazza et al. P refers to the various properties of the object being processed. From Caramazza et al. (1990) *Cognitive Neuropsychology*, 7, 161–90. Reprinted with permission of Lawrence Erlbaum Associates.

that the patient did not have an apperceptive agnosia because, if so, failure with visual presentation could be perceptual. As we saw earlier McCarthy and Warrington (1986b) assert that FRA had normal perceptual abilities. However, Rapp, Hillis and Caramazza (1993) argue that the evidence for normal perceptual processes in this patient is not as strong as it could be.

Recently Warrington and McCarthy (1994) have described DRS as a patient with specific difficulty in accessing the meaning of pictures relative to spoken words. When asked to name objects from verbal descriptions he performed well but poorly when objects were depicted as pictures. When asked to mime the use of objects he performed perfectly when object names were spoken, but poorly when they were presented visually. Moreover, in this latter condition he tended to make semantic errors such as demonstrating a screwdriver as a hammer. This indicates that his problem is more than just name retrieval and must involve some aspect of semantics.

In order to counter explanations of DRS's picture naming problems in terms of defective perception he is shown to have adequate performance on tasks such as figure-ground and form discrimination. In addition, his ability to name object pictures did not improve when they were presented in usual views relative to unusual views – an improvement might well be expected if DRS had a visual deficit because usual views would be easier to deal with. A further finding was his normal performance on a demanding object decision task in which objects were drawn as silhouettes and depicted from unusual views. Added to this was an additional finding that DRS's picture naming problems were somewhat category-specific in that he could recognize pictures of animals and vehicles better than common objects. If a perceptual impairment were responsible for DRS's defective picture processing then we would not expect to see this degree of selectivity in the impairment. On these grounds, and the more direct evidence for intact perception, Warrington and McCarthy argue that DRS's poor picture naming cannot be due to a perceptual impairment and that their data therefore refute the OUCH model. They concede that some modification of Farah and McClelland's theory could account for their data but, on grounds of parsimony, they prefer an account in terms of separable visual and verbal semantics.

OUCH has also been challenged by Chertkow, Bub and Kaplan (1992; see also Shallice 1993) who provide results which they claim are inconsistent with the model. They show, for example, that pictures with lots of discernible parts are not named any more easily by patients than those having fewer parts. However, in a rebuttal to these results, Hillis, Rapp and Caramazza (1995), the authors emphasize that it is the salience of features rather than the absolute quantity that determines the accessibility of semantics from a picture. Two other arguments of Chertkow et al. are also dismissed and the authors remain confident that OUCH remains plausible and that there is no need to invoke the idea of multiple semantics.

Recognition and Mental Imagery

As well as being able to perceive things we can also imagine what they look like. Although shunned by the behaviourists as an abstract unobservable process, mental imagery is very much back on the scientific agenda with various models proposed to account for how it takes place. One key issue concerns the relationship between perceptual processes and those underlying imaging. One influential view is that perceptual and imaginal processes use common underlying mechanisms and that they may even share the same neural substrate. According to these views, therefore, the act of imaging very much depends on accessing processes required for perception.

Support for this idea comes from many studies demonstrating a functional equivalence between perception and imagery. Farah (1989), for example, found that decisions about visually presented letters could be facilitated by asking subjects to imagine those same letters just before seeing them. At neurophysiological level it has also been shown that instructions to form images activate the primary visual cortex (Kosslyn, Alpert, Thompson et al., 1993) and that regional cerebral blood flow increases in the visual cortex when subjects answer questions demanding imaginal processing (e.g. Goldenberg, Steiner, Podreka and Deecke, 1992). Neuropsychological studies also support the equivalence viewpoint by showing that patients with perceptual problems have corresponding problems when trying to form images (e.g. Ogden, 1993; Wilson and Davidoff, 1993).

Despite all these findings there is evidence for a dissociation between the mechanisms of perception and mental imagery. RM (Farah, Levine and Calvanio) was unable to draw or describe objects from memory and his dreams also lacked images. In contrast he performed normally on tests of picture and object identification. DW (Riddoch, 1990) was unable to generate image-based information from memory (e.g. does a particular letter have curved or straight sides?). The converse deficit, preserved imagery with impaired recognition, has also been observed. HJA (see above) appears to have preserved mental imagery given the detail of his drawings and a patient known as MD (Jankowiak, Kinsbourne, Shalev and Bachman, 1992) also presents a similar pattern. Thus MD performed well on drawing from memory and on other tasks addressing mental imagery. A difficulty, however, is the extent to which his visual perception was impaired. On tests requiring the identification of line drawings his performance was poor but he had little difficulty with real objects.

The most compelling instance of preserved mental imagery in the presence of impaired perception comes from Behrmann, Moscovitch and Winocur (1994). CK had a profound integrative agnosia which caused him extreme problems when attempting to identify line drawings. Despite this, his ability to draw objects from memory was remarkably preserved and his knowledge about the visual appearance of objects was preserved on a range of mental imagery tasks. Interpreting these and related findings Behrman et al. suggest that, although imagery and perception share common mechanisms, they have additional independent components which can become dissociated from one another.

Summary

Visual agnosia is an impairment in the ability to recognize objects in the absence of any sensory or intellectual impairment. At the simplest level agnosia has been described as either apperceptive or associative. However, more detailed investigation of agnosia indicates different types of deficit within each of these broad categories. In particular apperceptive agnosia is now considered to include a range of deficits. Accounts of agnosia now square neatly with modular accounts of vision in which perception proceeds from a viewer-centred to an object-centred representation. However, studies of agnosia have not yet indicated how this transition occurs. The concept of category-specific agnosia remains controversial as does the idea that there are multiple semantic systems. While evidence indicates that visual perception and mental imagery share common underlying mechanisms there is also evidence for a dissociation between the mental processes.

4

Impairments of Facial Recognition

There is an apocryphal story about the famous English conductor, Sir Thomas Beecham. He was shopping in an exclusive London store when he saw a woman who seemed vaguely familiar. She smiled at him and in order to say something he said 'How is your husband nowadays' to which she replied 'Oh, still being King'. Although not as extreme as failing to recognize the Queen, errors in facial identification are common and have been useful in building up our ideas about how the facial memory system is organized. The above example, for instance, suggests that the ability to find a face familiar is distinct from information about identity. Young, Hay and Ellis (1985) collected a large number of slips of facial memory and these were instrumental in developing the model of face memory we shall shortly consider. However, the principle data upon which models of facial memory have developed have come from people suffering a variety of facial memory impairments.

The Variety of Facial Memory Impairment

Our discussion will be aided by some brief classification of the types of impairment that arise. Perhaps the most well known impairment of facial recognition is **prosopagnosia** in which the patient exhibits a profound inability to recognize familiar people. Although described in the nineteenth century the term prosopagnosia was introduced by Bodamer (1947; see Ellis and Florence, 1990, for a summary translation). He described two patients who had no difficulty perceiving that a face was a face but were unable to identify people they knew. Instead, identification relied on other cues such as clothing, gait, voice and other distinctive features. One patient, for example, was shown a photograph of Adolf Hitler and recognized it instantly:

'What do you recognise it by?'
'The moustache and the parting.'
'Would you have recognised the face?'
'No I'd not have recognised it by the face, the face itself I don't actually
    see, for me it's just a mass, everything is the same, and a face should
    really be differentiated and it's by the very differentness that you
    recognise a face.'

(Ellis and Florence, 1990, p. 93)

Other deficits in facial recognition have also been identified. Thus patients have been identified in whom the primary difficulty involves deciding whether two unfamiliar faces are the same or not (e.g. Malone, Morris, Kay and Levin, 1982) whereas others seem to have particular difficulty analysing expression (Shuttleworth, Syring and Allen, 1982). Palinopsia is a rare disorder in which visual images, often of people, persist after a stimulus has disappeared. Kinsbourne and Warrington (1963b) describe a patient:

'One day I was watching my wife gardening, through the window in bright
    sunlight. Returning to my chair I saw her in a corner of the room, set in
    the window frame. I looked away but she appeared wherever I looked.'

Sometimes images return much later

'One Sunday morning I was watching a church service on television. I was
    watching the expression of faces of members of the congregation as the
    roving camera picked them out. In bed that night I saw them all again very
    clearly.' (p. 469)

At present there is no clear explanation of this disorder (see Stagno and Gates, 1991) although one suggestion is that it reflects some exaggeration of normal visual processes – a fact supported by its common association with visual impairment.

There is overwhelming evidence that problems in identifying faces arise from lesions to the right hemisphere. Palinopsia also seems exclusively linked with right hemisphere dysfunction and there are many studies, both from normal and brain damaged subjects, that the right hemisphere has a particular role in different aspects of facial identification (e.g. Benton, 1990). More problematic is prosopagnosia. Early accounts suggested that prosopagnosia was also linked only to right hemisphere damage (e.g. Damasio, Damasio and Van Hoesen, 1982). Recently DeRenzi, Perani, Carlesimo et al. (1994) have collated neuro-imaging and neurosurgical evidence from known prosopagnosic cases and argued that the impairment is restricted to the right hemisphere. They note, however, that right hemisphere damage of the kind giving rise to prosopagnosia is common yet the disorder is very rare. They attribute this to varying patterns of lateralization in our memory for familiar faces. In most people this function is present in both left and right hemispheres and only in a very few is it restricted to the right hemisphere.

A second set of facial recognition memory impairments are known collectively as **delusional misidentification** and these will be considered in a later section.

A Model of Facial Recognition

The pattern of facial memory impairments found following brain injury has formed an important basis of the functional model of facial memory proposed by Bruce and Young (1986; see figure 4.1) although observations of normal facial memory and its failures have also been instructive. This model identifies four separate routes by which different forms of information can be derived from a face. In the model the only processing stage held to be common to all routes is that involved in producing a **viewer-centred description** of a face.

The first distinction that is made is between the processing of familiar and unfamiliar faces. Familiar faces undergo **expression-independent structural processing** with the output making contact with **facial recognition units** – these are units which identify specific facial configurations. These units in turn access **person identity nodes** which provide information about who the person is and allow access to their name as well as other information about them stored in the **cognitive system** – it is the dissociation between these two modules that allows someone to be familiar but unrecognized. The processing stages identified in this aspect of the model square nicely with various failures of recognition we observe in everyday life. We may, for example, fail to recognize someone completely – this corresponds to a failure to get from the structural description to the face recognition unit. Failure to get from the activated

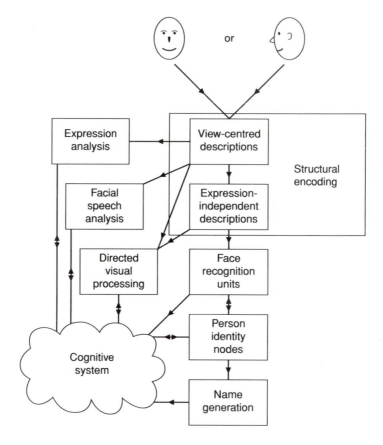

Figure 4.1   The Bruce and Young (1986) model of facial recognition. Reprinted with permission of the British Psychological Society.

unit to its associated person identity node gives rise to the experience of finding someone familiar but not knowing who they are. The ability to know who someone is (e.g. occupation) but being unable to name them is attributable to a failure at the **name generation stage**. The model also predicts, correctly, that we never seem to know the name of someone if we do not know their identity.

Other aspects of the model are largely proposed on the basis of various double dissociations that have been observed. The distinction between routes for processing familiar and unfamiliar faces comes from a number of studies. Benton and Van Allen (1972) reported a prosopagnosic patient who performed well within normal limits on an unfamiliar faces matching task. In contrast, patients with problems matching unfamiliar faces often fail to show prosopagnosia (Benton, 1980). Malone et al.

(1982), for example, reported two patients: one was unable to match unfamiliar faces but able to recognize familiar faces while the other showed the reverse pattern of impairment. On this basis the model assumes that unfamiliar faces are dealt with by a directed visual processing module which is separate from that involved in dealing with known faces.

Evidence for distinguishing between expression analysis and the processing of familiar faces has been shown by Tranel, Damasio and Damasio (1988) who found intact recognition of expression in a patient with severely impaired facial recognition ability. Similarly Shuttleworth et al. (1982) described a patient who was able to interpret facial expressions despite complete failure at identifying familiar faces. Conversely, Kurucz and Feldmar (1979) reported that their patient was unable to identify the expressions of faces he nonetheless recognized. The additional dissociation of expression analysis from unfamiliar face processing comes from a study by Bowers, Bauer, Coslett and Heilman (1985) in which patients with either right or left hemisphere lesions and controls received a battery of tests involving perceptual, emotional and identity judgement tasks. As expected the right hemisphere group performed worse on all the tests. However, an additional analysis showed that the impairment on tasks involving expression could not be accounted for solely in terms of a basic problem in facial processing (as shown on tasks involving identity judgements) and that an additional deficit had to be specified to account for all the patients' difficulties with expression.

Another set of dissociations has involved expression analysis and the ability to lip-read speech. Campbell, Landis and Regard (1986) found two patients, one of whom could lip-read phonemes despite an inability to recognize faces or judge expression and a second who had intact recognition and expressions analysis but no ability to lip-read. From this it has been argued that a separate route dealing with facial speech analysis exists.

Refining the Evidence

The evidence considered so far provides reasonably good evidence for the Bruce and Young model but there are a number of difficulties with the evidence. These have been formally identified by Young, Newcombe, De Haan et al. (1993):

> Most of the evidence for double dissociation involves comparison of single patients from separate studies conducted in different laboratories using non-standard procedures.

Many of the double dissociations do not meet Shallice's criterion of a classical dissociation in that a dissociation is inferred from relatively better or worse performance on given tasks rather than normal performance on one and a deficit on the other (see chapter 1).

Supporting the existence of more than two routes on the basis of pairwise double dissociations may not be valid (see Farah, 1991).

In some studies a deficit has been inferred from failure on just one test considered to reflect a specific ability. However, patients may fail tests for reasons other than the hypothesized functional deficit (e.g. they may just feel unco-operative that day).

There may be some bias towards sampling those patients showing the appropriate pattern of impairment.

Patients with a deficit may nonetheless achieve normal performance by abnormal means (e.g. HJA's laborious copying of pictures – see last chapter).

Young et al. attempted to avoid the above shortcomings using the following procedure. A group of 34 men who had suffered penetrating head wounds of either the right or left hemisphere were recruited. They were concerned with three of the key abilities – unfamiliar face matching, familiar face identification, and expression analysis – and devised two different tests for assessing each function. For four of the tests they also measured reaction time as a means of ruling out any patient who was using an unusual strategy – the argument being that any abnormal strategy would take longer to carry out. For a deficit to be identified a patient would have to show deficient performance, compared with controls, on both tests testing a particular function and normal performance on each pair of tests addressing the other two functions. In addition performance speed for the unaffected tasks would have to be within normal limits.

The results of the study were a qualified success. Based on just test accuracy there was evidence of selective impairment on all three abilities – one subject showed impairments in recognizing familiar faces, one was selectively impaired on matching unfamiliar faces and five had a difficulty restricted to expression analysis. However, when response latency data were taken into account only evidence for a selective deficit in expression analysis remained.

Face recognition impairments are most commonly associated with right hemisphere damage so it was not surprising that the subjects impaired on familiar face recognition or unfamiliar face matching had right hemisphere lesions. However, a surprising finding was that all five patients with a deficit in expression analysis had *left* hemisphere damage. Generally studies have shown that right hemisphere damage is more likely to impair expression analysis. Young et al. resolve this by pointing out that there were subjects in their study with right hemisphere lesions who also showed problems with expression analysis. However, these patients also failed on other types of task. Thus the role of the left hemisphere in expression analysis appears emphasized, or perhaps exaggerated, when the classical dissociation procedure is used.

Young et al.'s study thus suggests some caution in accepting some of the modular distinctions embodied in the Bruce and Young model. In particular the authors note that the data do not fully support the distinction made between familiar and unfamiliar face recognition. With expression analysis the authors claim a clear demonstration of a selective problem in dealing with facial expression. However, the Young et al. study does not examine how these patients fared on other tests involving non-facial emotional expression and so the question of a more general deficit underlying performance is not ruled out. A separable mechanism underlying facial expression analysis is shown by Rapcsak, Comer and Rubens (1993) in their study of OK. This patient could produce appropriate verbal labels in response to pictures of emotional scenes where expressions on faces had been erased, but was unable to name expressions directly from facial information. In addition there is recent evidence that problems with the processing of facial expression may be linked to part of the medial temporal region known as the amygdala (Young, Aggleton, Hellawell, et al. (1995)).

Apperceptive versus Associative Prosopagnosia

In the previous chapter we saw that agnosias can divide into those that are primarily apperceptive and those that are associative. It is thus plausible that prosopagnosia might yield a similar distinction. Case 2 of Bodamer's (1947) study provides a good instance of impaired perception giving rise to a recognition impairment. When presented with a face he could pick out the individual features easily enough but could not integrate them into a perceptual whole.

Levine and Calvanio (1989) investigated the perceptual abilities of a prosopagnosic patient LH. In addition to face naming he was given a series of general perceptual tests to perform. These included a Gestalt completion test, a concealed word test, and a 'snowy pictures' test. In all these tests a degree of 'closure' is required in that some wholistic configuration must be imposed on the stimulus so as to identify the object. LH performed very poorly on these tasks and, on this basis,

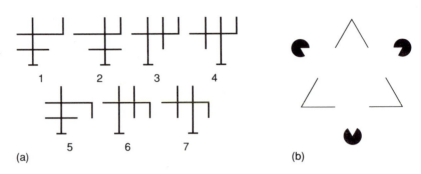

(a)   (b)

Figure 4.2 Tests of perceptual ability on which LH performed normally. (a) Rectilinear objects each composed of the same parts. Distinguishing them can only be achieved by remembering the different configurations. (b) A Kaniza illusory contour figure. From Etcoff et al. (1991). Reproduced with permission of MIT Press.

Levine and Calvanio argued that LH's facial recognition impairment was due to a more fundamental apperceptive deficit involving configural processing.

LH has been further investigated by Etcoff, Freeman and Cave (1991) and their conclusions about the nature of his deficit are rather different. They point out that the configural tasks used by Levine and Calvanio were difficult for control subjects so their relevance for understanding LH's deficit is questionable. In addition they gave LH a range of other perceptual tasks including an illusory contours test and a task involving memory for rectilinear objects (see figure 4.2). LH performed well on these tasks and the authors argued that, although his perceptual abilities were not totally intact, his prosopagnosia was more associative in nature.

DeRenzi, Faglioni, Grossi and Nichelli (1991) gave three prosopagnosic patients a range of tasks to perform including the unusual views test (see previous chapter), a Gestalt completion test, unfamiliar face matching and a famous faces test. The patients' performance on these tests was compared with control values and it was shown that one patient, GD, performed much more poorly on perceptual tests (e.g. unusual views) than those involving memory (famous faces) whereas the reverse deficit was found in patient VA. On this basis De Renzi et al. argued for a separation between prosopagnosia that was primarily perceptual in nature and associative agnosia in which the problem mainly lies in retrieving information about a face that has been adequately perceived. In addition the authors argued that face-specificity in prosopagnosia (see below) is most likely to occur when the deficit is associative in nature.

Bruyer, LaTerre, Seron, et al. (1983) present a particularly clear example of prosopagnosia in the absence of any significant perceptual ability. Mr W had no difficulty distinguishing human faces from animal faces, he could copy animal faces accurately, identify sex and age, and correctly classify expressions. He was also able to match faces across different expressions even when obvious distinguishing features (e.g. hairstyle) had been obscured. However, Mr W did not have completely normal perception in that his performances on some tests were slightly below average.

These findings clearly indicate that prosopagnosia can occur in the presence of varying degrees of perceptual impairment. For some patients, such as GA (DeRenzi et al., 1991), these perceptual impairments seem to underlie the patient's face recognition difficulties but for others like LH it has been argued that perceptual difficulties are insufficient to account for prosopagnosia and that the deficit must arise from deficit in accessing stored knowledge about faces.

Is Prosopagnosia Face-specific?

An obvious assumption of the Bruce and Young model is that the brain has a specific system for identifying faces as opposed to other types of stimuli. The assumption of face-specificity is often made on intuitive grounds: faces are very special to humans so it is likely that the brain has evolved a specific mechanism for dealing with them. It is claimed, for example, that new-born children have an innate ability to recognize facial configurations and that the development of facial recognition has a unique course. However, each of these lines of evidence is controversial and proponents of face-specificity commonly cite prosopagnosia as a key line of supporting evidence, e.g. Ellis (1989).

However, it is an issue as to whether face-specificity has been unequivocally demonstrated because prosopagnosic patients tend to have associated impairments affecting other types of stimuli. Bodamer's original Case 1 had marked problems identifying animals. Shown a dog with long hair he identified it as a 'human but with funny hair' and looking at a cockerel he said 'Going by the body, it could be a cockerel, but the head . . . I don't know' (Ellis and Florence, 1990, p. 88).

Many other prosopagnosic patients also have associated recognition problems and typically these involve distinguishing between exemplars of categories in which all members share the same basic characteristics (e.g. birds, cars). LH, reported by Etcoff et al. (1991) performed poorly on recognizing faces but also failed to identify 15 out of 30 four-legged animals. PH (De Haan, Young and Newcombe, 1992) was poor at recognizing cars and flowers. However, others have reported face-specificity in prosopagnosics. Case VA (De Renzi et al., 1991, see above) is often cited as pure prosopagnosic. In line with De Renzi's claim that face-specificity is most likely in patients with an associative agnosia, VA appeared free of any significant perceptual deficit. However, data relevant to face-specificity are presented very informally:

> [having established prosopagnosia] The investigation of his recognition of a familiar exemplar within a category was extended to other classes of objects. For this purpose neckties, milk cups, alarm clocks, combs, shaving brushes, watches, shoes were presented in a number from five to seven and always including a personal item and the patient was requested to point to his own belongings. His choice was always correct and occurred without hesitation. The same occurred when he was asked to name the makes of 15 cars seen in a parking lot and to discriminate Italian or German coins from those of another country. (p. 219)

Without information about the relative discriminability of these items relative to faces it is difficult to evaluate evidence such as this as unassailable grounds for assuming face-specificity.

In arguing for face-specificity it is therefore essential that the classes of stimuli used in comparison with faces should be, at least on prima facie grounds, of comparable discrimination difficulty. Sergent and Signoret (1992) report a prosopagnosic patient RM whose deficit encompassed all types of facial processing. Thus he could not match identical views of the same face, estimate age, or comprehend emotion. RM did, however, possess a 'quasi-encyclopaedic' knowledge of cars and had a collection of over 5000 miniatures. RM was shown pictures of 210 different cars. He named 172 correctly, giving the company, the model and the approximate year of manufacture. For the remainder he gave at least the company name. In contrast, the best of six controls who were interested in cars scored 128 correct. Sergent and Signoret argue that if the processing deficits underlying RM's prosopagnosia were relevant to the processing of other objects then he should have experienced difficulty on the cars task because, like faces, these items all have the same basic characteristics and only differ in terms of their specific details.

Evans, Heggs, Antoun and Hodges (1995) describe a woman known as VH who had a progressive form of prosopagnosia. Of most interest here is the authors' claim that her impairment 'confirms the hypothesis that faces are indeed special' (p. 1). The claim rests on her extremely poor naming of famous faces (even though she could identify people when given names) in the presence of an ability to name famous places (e.g. Eiffel Tower, Big Ben, Statue of Liberty) at the same level as controls. Unfortunately there are problems with this claim. First DF may have found the famous places task easier. However this is difficult to rule out because control performance was extremely good on both tasks. Second, and linked with this argument, pictures of landmarks contain far more cues to identity than faces and thus could have allowed VH greater scope for a compensatory strategy.

It is also noticeable that VH did have problems naming flowers. The authors dismiss the importance of this by showing that she could pick out the correct flower picture from an array of 20 when given a name. It would thus have been interesting to see how she would have performed in a similar task involving faces but this was not carried out. Finally, the progressive nature of her disorder allowed retesting and it is clear that her performance on both facial and non-facial tests deteriorated significantly – a finding that is equally consistent with two mechanisms declining in parallel or a single underlying deficit.

McNeil and Warrington (1993) studied WJ who, following a series of strokes, was found to have a profound prosopagnosia. On a test involving the selection of a famous face from an array of three faces he performed at chance. Following his stroke WJ acquired a flock of 36 sheep and these proved invaluable in the further investigation of WJ's prosopagnosia. WJ reported that he had learned to recognize the sheep despite his continuing face recognition difficulties. The authors set out to investigate this by devising a yes–no recognition test involving sheep from his flock and a second recognition test involving sheep from a different breed. As a control McNeil and Warrington also tested two other men who had recently retired and taken to sheep-farming and five other men matched for profession and age. In order to help learn the sheep and faces all subjects were asked to rate each sheep as either pleasant or unpleasant (a manipulation that is known to enhance facial memory). The results showed that WJ outperformed both sets of controls on both sheep tasks despite chance performance on the familiar faces task.

McNeil and Warrington thus show that WJ performs well above average on a non-facial task which controls find hard and well below average on a facial task which controls find easy. One cannot, therefore, attribute his preserved memory for sheep as simply better performance on a simpler task. However, what exactly do we make of WJ's enhanced memory for sheep? It does not seem to be a routine consequence of sheep-farming because the two sheep experienced men performed no better than the five 'sheep naïve' controls. The issue of high levels of animal recognition ability is addressed by Bornstein, Sroka and Munitz (1969) who emphasize that the identification of many individual animals is a rare skill and may thus have a very special status. They also note that few artists are able to paint an array of animals so as to give each member an individual identity, even though the same artists have no difficulties with faces. It is possible, therefore, that WJ has an unusual cognitive ability that is unrelated to facial processing ability. However, does this in turn mean that his prosopagnosia is only face-specific? Here we must return to how he performs on more routine tests involving items from confusable categories. Here he was found to perform normally but the number of items used in each test was very small and there is no means of being certain that the items were equally discriminable when compared with faces.

Recently Moscovitch and Behrmann (1996) have reported data on case CK. This patient had a severe intergrative agnosia (see chapter 3) being unable to name most simple line drawings. However, on a test of recognizing famous faces he performed better than the control average. Farah, Levinson and Klein (1992) report further data on patient LH (see above). The authors tackled the commonly held view that the apparent face-specificity of prosopagnosics arises simply because faces are harder to recognize. To get around this they devised two experiments comparing object and face recognition in which an attempt to match for difficulty was undertaken. In the first study controls did not differ in their ability to identify pictures of objects and faces whereas LH was disproportionately impaired on facial memory. However, Farah et al. note that the comparison with objects may not be valid because each object came from a different class of item whereas faces all come from within the same class. They report a second study in which memory for faces was compared with different sets of spectacles. LH did not differ in his ability to recognize the two classes of stimuli but control subjects showed a distinct advantage for faces.

Farah et al. argue that, collectively, the above data indicate a selective deficit in facial processing for case LH. However, they are cautious in assuming that this reflects face-specificity. They suggest, somewhat enigmatically, 'that prosopagnosia is an impairment of a specialized form of visual recognition that is necessary for face recognition and is not necessary, *or less necessary* [italics added], for the recognition of common objects' (p. 661). They go on to suggest that this visual processing might involve 'the encoding of complex shapes with relatively little decomposition into parts' (p. 673). This idea seems rather similar to the conclusion reached by Levine and Calvanio (1988) in their study of LH.

The issue of face-specificity in prosopagnosia thus remains an open question. There is little doubt that most examples of the disorder have associated impairments involving an inability to discriminate between other classes of confusable items. Cases of apparent face-specificity have come to light. Of these, RM (Sergent and Signoret, 1992) appears more compelling but, even here, the argument for face-specificity depends on the parallel preservation of what can be considered an unusually well-developed skill (as with WJ) – thus raising the difficult issue of assuming typicality about normal performance in a patient who may have developed abnormally within the domain in question (see chapter 1). CK also appears to have face-specificity. However, the objections raised by Farah, that facial recognition involves a more generalized visual recognition process that is also used in some forms of object recognition, can still be raised. The answer to face-specificity thus depends on the development of a paradigm in which facial recognition is compared to recognition of stimuli that are similar to faces in every respect except that they are not faces. It remains to be seen how easy that is to achieve.

Covert Facial Recognition

One of the most interesting discoveries about patients with face recognition difficulties is the phenomenon of **covert recognition** – the demonstration that, despite conscious denial of any recognition, other aspects of the patient's behaviour indicate that the face has been recognized (see Bruyer, 1991, for a review). There are two basic sources of evidence for covert recognition, **behavioural** and **psychophysiological**.

One line of behavioural evidence involves face–name associations in which subjects are asked to learn names associated with famous faces they have failed to consciously identify. A comparison is made between the learning of faces compared with their correct name and those paired with an incorrect name. The typical finding from these studies (e.g. Bruyer et al. 1983; DeHaan, Young and Newcombe, 1987) is that correct pairings are learned more easily than incorrect ones. This suggests that some residual memory for the face–name associations exists even though the patients cannot consciously access it.

Greve and Bauer (1990) presented a prosopagnosic patient with some unfamiliar faces and then re-presented him with pairs of faces comprising one face he had been shown and one unfamiliar face. When he was asked which of the two faces he had seen before he performed at chance but when asked which of the two faces he preferred, he consistently chose the face he had previously been shown. DeHaan et al. (1987) used a name classification task with the prosopagnosic PH. On this task the subject was presented with stimuli comprising a name written in a speech bubble, and this was usually accompanied by a face. The task was to classify the name in the bubble as belonging to a politician or not. There were four conditions: name and face the same, name only, face and name from different occupational categories, face and name from same occupational categories. Normal subjects showed an interference effect in that response times were slower when the face came from a different category to the name. This indicates that the identity of the face is having some influence on task performance. PH also showed this effect indicating that he also had identity-based information about the faces even though he could not identify them consciously.

Psychophysiological evidence comes initially from a study by Bauer (1984) using a skin conductance monitor. This measure exploits the fact that skin conductance increases when subjects are presented with information they are familiar with. While viewing photographs of familiar faces a prosopagnosic patient also heard a list of names including that of the person in the photograph. It was found that, in line with controls, skin conductance increased when the correct name was presented irrespective of whether the patient overtly recognized the person. Similar findings are also reported by Tranel and Damasio (1988).

On the basis of this evidence Bauer (1984) suggested that there were two neural systems underlying facial recognition but that only one was associated with conscious awareness. Further, using available neuro-anatomical evidence, he argued that conscious facial recognition was mediated by areas in the ventral cortical visual areas (the 'ventral route') whereas recognition not involving awareness, i.e. those processes allowing affective judgements and moderating changes in skin conductance, went via the dorsal cortical visual areas (the 'dorsal' route). A similar idea is embodied in the facial recognition model proposed by DeHaan, Bauer and Greve (1992).

Earlier we noted that prosopagnosia can be considered as either apperceptive or associative. It has been suggested (e.g. Bruyer, 1991) that covert recognition of faces only occurs in patients with an associative disorder and that prosopagnosia due to perceptual problems will not show these effects (see also Young, Humphreys, Riddoch, et al. 1994).

Covert Recognition and Connectionism

Farah, O'Reilly and Vecera (1993) devised a connectionist network which comprised name units and associated hidden units, semantic units (which included units designating particular occupations) and face input units associated with hidden units (see figure 4.3). The network was trained on forty individuals, ten of these were designated as actors, ten as politicians, and the remaining twenty were not assigned a profession. Training involved re-presentation of each face, name or identity until the

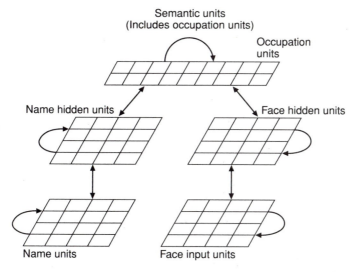

Semantic units
(Includes occupation units)

Occupation units

Name hidden units

Face hidden units

Name units

Face input units

Figure 4.3 Outline of Farah et al.'s connectionist model of face recognition. Reproduced with permission of the American Psychological Society.

network could reproduce the other two with high levels of accuracy. The model was then subjected to various lesions and the resulting performance on various tasks observed.

Damage to the face and face-hidden units was shown to have a similar and marked effect on the network's ability to identify faces it had previously known with disruption of only 12.5 per cent of the units causing almost a 40 per cent drop in naming ability. Once in its damaged state the model was given the task of relearning either facename pairs in their original pairings or previously incorrect pairings – a manipulation analogous to the procedure used by DeHaan et al. (1987, see above).

Figure 4.4 shows how the model performs following 50 per cent damage to face hidden units or the face input units. In all three cases there is considerable learning of previously correct face-name pairs but no comparable learning of incorrect pairs. These findings can only be explained by arguing that, despite an inability to overtly identify facename pairs at the outset, the network had sufficient residual knowledge of those pairs to facilitate relearning at a rate faster than that for previously incorrect pairs.

Farah et al. go on to show that their damaged network exhibits other phenomena analogous to covert recognition in prosopagnosia. They stress, however, that these phenomena arise from a single network for overt identification, not one in which separate routes for overt and

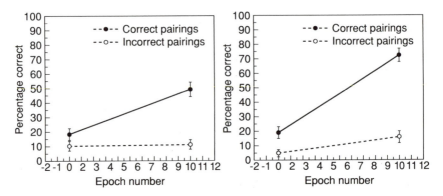

Figure 4.4   Performance of Farah et al.'s connectionist network after 50 per cent lesioning of either its face hidden units (left) or face input units (right). Reproduced with permission of The American Psychological Society.

covert recognition are identified. Thus, if connectionist models are a valid means of modelling cognitive processes, these data suggest that covert recognition in prosopagnosia might be more easily explained in terms of damage to a single face recognition system rather than one in which two separate routes are specified.

Delusional Misidentification

Delusional misidentification (DMI) disorders, as their name might suggest, have typically been considered to be of psychiatric origin. However, there is now increasing interest in the idea that at least some components of these disorders might have a neuropsychological basis. Most well-known of the delusional disorders is **Capgrass Syndrome** (Capgrass and Reboul-Lachaux, 1923) in which the patient believes that a familiar person has been replaced by a double. Often the patient protests that there are subtle differences between the impostor and the real person, such as differences in skin texture and personality. There are now many reports in the literature and this example is typical of what has been observed:

> The 'substitution' first occurred on their wedding day, when her husband went to the men's room and an impostor took his place. As evidence, she produced snapshots from the wedding, comparing pictures of her husband and his 'twin'. When the pictures failed to be convincing she claimed that the best ones had mysteriously disappeared. (Spier, 1992, p. 280)

A condition probably related to Capgrass Syndrome is **reduplicative paramnesia** (Pick, 1903). Typically this involves the belief that a familiar place such as a home or hospital has been replaced with a replica but duplication of persons is also observed. There is considerable debate as to whether this disorder exists separately from Capgrass Syndrome or whether the two disorders are basically the same, but with reduplicative paramnesia having less psychiatric involvement.

Other delusional disorders include **Fregoli Syndrome** in which the patient believes that a certain person can assume different physical appearances. In the original case report (Courbon and Frail, 1927) the patient believed that she was being persecuted by two famous actresses who could take the form of people she knew. In **intermetamorphosis** familiar people change identity – thus A becomes B, B becomes C and C becomes A. Thus in the first report of this disorder (Courbon and Tusques, 1932) the patient believed that her husband had taken on the appearance of a neighbour and that the neighbour had come to look like her husband (see Ellis, Whitley and Luaute, 1994).

An early study by Joseph (1986) demonstrated widespread organic involvement in DMI. More recently Forstl, Almeida and Owen et al. (1991) examined 260 cases of DMI. Capgrass Syndrome was the most prevalent disorder and was reliably associated with either psychiatric illness, mainly paranoid schizophrenia, or organic brain disease such as Alzheimer's Disease. Reduplicative paramnesia was reliably associated with organic injury particularly within the right hemisphere (see also Jocic and Staton, 1993).

Ellis and Young (1990) have attempted to account for DMI in terms of the model of face recognition developed by Bruce and Young (1986) and its subsequent development by DeHaan et al. (1992). It will be recalled that Bauer proposed that conscious facial identification occurred via a dorsal route and that non-conscious affective processing occurred via the ventral route. According to Ellis and Young, Capgrass Syndrome could arise from damage to the dorsal route. Under these conditions information about facial identity, which is conveyed by the ventral route, would be preserved but no affective information would be available. Capgrass Syndrome might then represent an attempt to reconcile indentity information in the absence of affective information (see also Young, Reid, Wright and Hellawell, 1993). In the case of Fregoli Syndrome it was suggested that some deficit in the person identity nodes could explain the disruption and, for intermetamorphosis, the deficit could lie at the level of face recognition units.

If Ellis and Young's approach is valid then it should be possible to demonstrate face recognition impairments in patients with DMI. Ellis, dePauw, Christodoulou, et al. (1993) used a split-field task (see chapter

6) to examine facial recognition abilities in Capgrass patients and controls. The controls showed the normal left visual field advantage for faces indicative of right hemisphere specialization for facial processing. Patients with Capgrass Syndrome showed the reverse effect. These results were seen as confirming Cutting's (1990) proposal that Capgrass Syndrome stems from some deficit in the right hemisphere processes that enable variations within categories such as faces to be distinguished.

Young, Ellis, Szulecka and dePauw (1990) examined the facial recognition abilities of four patients with DMI, one with Fregoli Syndrome and three suffering from intermetamorphosis. The Fregoli patient showed a number of impairments including, as one might predict, difficulty in recognizing the same person in disguise. Two of the intermetamorphosis patients also showed face memory impairment but a third, JS, was free of impairment despite a history of bizarre beliefs and behaviour in which he believed that a woman he loved appeared wherever he went.

Interpreting these data Young et al. urge a more cautious approach concerning the relation between face memory impairments and DMI. With specific reference to their case JS, they argue that a long-standing face memory impairment may not be a necessary feature of DMI. Instead they suggest that the presence of organically-related facial memory impairments may play a role in allowing delusions arising in other ways to dominate the patients' lives. This idea is consistent with the recent study by Fleminger and Burns (1993). They surveyed 100 cases of DMI and found that paranoid delusions, preceding the onset of DMI, were more common in patients who did not show organic impairment. As Fleminger (1992) suggests, these data are consistent with the idea that misidentification can arise from an interaction between organic impairment and delusional beliefs with the former tending to undermine reality in some general sense. At one end of the spectrum a disorder may be entirely driven by delusions (e.g. case JS) while at the other, as in cases of reduplicative paramnesia, the deficit may depend entirely on the presence of brain injury. This approach also deals more satisfactorily with the co-occurrence of more than one DMI simultaneously and the frequent association of DMI with non-face related delusions (e.g. lycanthropy – belief that one is an animal; Cotard's delusion – belief that one is dead; erotomania – abnormal sex drive).

Summary

Facial memory impairments take a number of different forms. The nature of these impairments has led to the modular account of facial memory devised by Bruce and Young. Experiments have shown various dissociations in facial processing such as that between expression analysis and the processing of personal-identity information. Prosopagnosia – the inability to recognize once familiar faces – has been central to the claim that faces are dealt with by a special system. However, the evidence for this is not very strong. Prosopagnosia exists in both apperceptive and associative forms and it is only in the latter that covert recognition of faces may be seen. A two-route model has been put forward to account for overt and covert recognition but a recent connectionist account indicates that this model may be inaccurate. Recently delusional misidentification has been subjected to a cognitive neuropsychological analysis but an account based solely on this type of explanation now seems unlikely.

5

Neglect

So far we have been concerned with deficits that interfere in some way with the processes of perception. Thus in blindsight we encountered patients who experience fundamental problems in establishing a percept that they can access consciously, while those with agnosia experience problems at higher stages of perceptual analysis. In this chapter we explore the phenomenon of neglect. Here, as the name suggests, the problem is not one of perceiving. Instead the person fails, for some reason, to notice or respond to things that occur on one side of the world. Most commonly neglect arises from damage to the right hemisphere, usually in the region of the parietal lobe, and a consequent neglect of the left side.

My experience of neglect involved a woman known as Thelma. She suffered a head injury in a road accident and this left her with multiple difficulties. She cannot speak very well due an inability to control her mouth muscles (dysarthria). Her comprehension abilities and memory function have been affected to some extent. Thus she finds it hard to follow instructions and often has to be reminded about what she is supposed to be doing. She also has marked problems in moving around and holding things (apraxia).

Perhaps the most notable and frustrating of Thelma's condition is that she ignores things that appear on her left-hand side. This is not due to a field defect because she will notice things if they are very important.

(a)

(b)

Figure 5.1 Thelma's performance when asked to (a) cross out all the zeros on the page and (b) draw a flower.

However, when she reads a magazine she starts reading halfway in from the edge of the page. If she is shown a word comprising two smaller words (e.g. address) she will only read the right-hand part of the word. If asked to cancel all the zeros in an array she misses most of those on the left. When asked to draw a flower her drawing lacks a left side (see figure 5.1).

Thelma presents a very clear case of neglect. In line with most instances she neglects the left-hand side of the world so we can attribuite her disorder to some form of damage to the right hemisphere. At this point it will be useful to introduce some basic terminology commonly used in accounts of neglect. It is usual to consider the visual field as being divided into left and right **hemispaces**. The hemispace on the same side as the patient's lesion is referred to as **ipsilateral** and that on the opposite side as **contralateral**. Neglect is most commonly seen in patients who have had strokes but can be associated with a range of other neurological injuries. For most patients neglect is a relatively transient disorder but in a considerable number of cases it can persist for months or even years.

It is now evident that neglect is not a single disorder but a range of disorders which can occur in varying degrees within any patient. Perhaps the classic symptom is **hemispatial neglect** which can be shown easily using simple drawing tasks. In some instances a stimulus presented to the neglected side will not be ignored but reported as if it occurred on the other side – a phenomenon known as **allesthesia**. In visual allesthesia a stimulus might appear on the left but the patient points to it having occurred on the right.

Another phenomenon frequently found in neglect is **extinction of double simultaneous stimulation** or, more simply, **extinction**. This can be demonstrated by asking the patient to close their eyes and then touching them on either both hands simultaneously or on just one hand. When either hand is touched in isolation the patient can indicate that they have been touched but when both hands are touched simultaneously the hand corresponding to the neglected side is not reported as touched. Extinction can also be shown in the visual modality: the patient is asked to fixate centrally (following the standard procedure of perimetry – see chapter 2) and two stimuli are presented one to the left and one to the right. The detection of either stimulus can be accomplished in isolation but that on the neglected side is ignored when both are presented simultaneously.

Recently Baylis, Driver and Rafal (1993) have explored visual extinction in more detail. They noted that one of their patients only reliably showed extinction when an object shown to the left was the same as that shown to the right; thus, if presented with two pens he would not notice the pen of the left but, if this was a comb, he would notice it. They explored this systematically and confirmed that in an extinction procedure neglect patients show **repetition blindness** – a failure to detect an item in the left if an identical item is presented in the right visual field.

Neglect can also occur in motor tasks in which the patient is required to initiate a movement. In **hypokinesia or pre-motor neglect** the patients have difficulty initiating movements with either limb into the neglected space. They may also show a reluctance or inability to use limbs on the neglected side known as **motor neglect**. Thus when asked to raise both hands a typical patient might just raise their right hand. In extreme cases neglect patients can also exhibit an unawareness of their bodies on the neglected side. This is apparent in patients with hemiplegia (limb weakness) who will often deny that they have any problem – a deficit known as **anosognosia**.

Distinguishing between Perceptual and Pre-Motor forms of Neglect

One attempt to distinguish different forms of neglect has drawn a fundamental distinction between **perceptual** and **pre-motor** neglect. Briefly these theories postulate a system responsible for devising a representation of external space and a second which is involved in the programming of movement within that space. The term perceptual neglect does not presuppose that neglect occurs as a consequence of poor perception because, as we shall see, neglect may well arise from a failure in processes that occur subsequent to perceptual analysis. The term perceptual merely defines a deficit that occurs prior to the execution of movement.

One implication of these differing forms of neglect is that it may often be difficult to decide why a patient shows neglect on a particular task. In the line bisection task, for example, neglect might arise because there is some impairment in perceiving, attending to or representing the left side of space or because the patient has difficulty in initiating movements into the left side of space. Coslett, Bowers, Fitzpatrick, et al. (1990) set out to distinguish these two explanations using apparatus that prevented direct visualization of the line to be bisected. Subjects sat facing an opaque screen above which was a TV monitor. A curtained gap between the screen and a table allowed subjects to place their hands into the area where the line to be bisected was presented. The line was made visible to the subject on the TV via a video camera suspended above the apparatus. The subject's task was to try and bisect the line using the visual feedback from the TV. There were four experimental conditions:

A – Line Right TV feedback Right
B – Line Right TV feedback Left
C – Line Left TV feedback Right
D – Line Left TV feedback Left

Coslett et al., reasoned that if errors in line bisection were attributable to some failure to attend to or represent the left side of space then performance should be consistently poorer when the visual feedback was on the left (B, D). However, if failure were due to left-sided hypokinesia, performance should be poorest when the line was placed to the left for bisection (C, D). Four subjects with neglect were tested and for two (Cases 1 and 2) the pattern indicated hypokinesia whereas for the other two the deficit appeared due to problems with attending to or representing space.

The Complexity of Space

Typically neglect is demonstrated in terms of a right/left dichotomy but recent investigations indicate that the phenomenon is more complex than that. Patients with left neglect have, for example, been shown to misbisect vertically presented lines above their midpoint, so called altitudinal neglect (Rapcsak, Cimino and Heilman, 1988), and the reverse, systematic bisection below the vertical midpoint has also been noted (Shelton, Bowers and Heilman, 1990). Patients have also been shown to misbisect radially-oriented lines (Marshall and Halligan, 1990).

There have been many suggestions that the brain may distinguish between 'near' (peri-personal) and 'far' (extra-personal) space (e.g. Mennemeier, Wertman, and Heilman, 1992). Peri-personal space refers to the area around an individual in which objects could be grasped whereas in extra-personal space objects can only be pointed at. Animal studies have given weight to this distinction and, more recently studies of neglect have also suggested two different forms of space. Halligan and Marshall (1991) described a patient who exhibited typical hemispatial neglect when assessed using the line bisection task. However, they devised a second task in which lines were presented about 2.5 metres away and the patient was asked to indicate the midline using a light pen. In this, and a subsequent condition in which the patient indicated the midline by throwing a dart (he was a good darts player), evidence of neglect was either abolished or markedly reduced.

Recently Cowey, Small and Ellis (1994) tested five patients with marked left-sided neglect on two line bisection tasks, one presented in peri-personal space and the other in extra-personal space. Contrary to Halligan and Marshall they found that line bisection was worse in the extra-personal condition even though the lines used in this condition subsumed the same degree of visual angle as those used in the peri-personal condition. On the basis of these data and other earlier studies Cowey et al. make a strong case for dissociated systems dealing with peri- and extra-personal space.

Perceptual Deficit Theories

By now it should be evident that neglect is not a unitary disorder but one that comprises many different forms. For this reason we cannot expect to find one theory that fits all the data. However, we can examine and evaluate some theories and come to some interim conclusions as to how this puzzling phenomenon occurs. Principally, theories of neglect have addressed hemispatial neglect of the type demonstrated by failures on tasks such as line bisection.

Perhaps the most straightforward explanation of visuo-spatial neglect is that it arises from some form of sensory loss. At the lowest level it could be that neglect patients suffer some form of hemianopia. There can be no doubt that many neglect patients have field defects and these may interact with the extent to which neglect is observed. Disentangling neglect from hemianopia was addressed in a study of the neglect patient BQ by Walker, Findlay, Young and Welch (1991). They used a task in which the subject first fixated on a central cross, after this a digit appeared either to the left or right. There were three conditions:

Overlap: fixation point remains on while digit is also visible

0 Gap: digit displayed immediately after fixation point is extinguished

+100 Gap: digit displayed 100 msec after fixation point is extinguished

These manipulations greatly affected the probability of BQ reporting the left digit correctly in that performance was much better in the +100 Gap than the other two conditions. We will return to the explanation of this later but, for the moment, we will simply conclude that these data are incompatible with a field defect interpretation of BQ's neglect because this would predict equally poor performance in all conditions.

A more subtle argument, still linking the deficit to a lower stage of the perceptual process, is that there is some internal deficit in the representation of the visual field. Nichelli, Rinaldi and Cubelli (1989), for example, attempted to explain neglect in terms of a 'representational amputation'. Here the idea is that space is represented in terms of some internal medium and that the percept is 'projected' on to it. The effect of the brain lesion is to delete part of this medium, usually the leftward side, and thus prevent part of the world being seen. Marshall, Halligan and Robertson (1993) point out that these theories are incompatible with basic observations of neglect. Chattergee, Mennemeier and Heilman (1992), for example, have shown that letter cancellation in the neglected side is determined by the number of targets in the array. If the left side were amputated it is difficult to see how the number of stimuli on the left side could influence performance. Another problem are findings such as the repetition blindness effect observed by Bayliss et al. (see above).

Given the complexity of neglect, it remains possible that some form of sensory processing deficit might account for some phenomena. Marshall et al. (1993) suggest that impairments in figure-ground discrimination might impede performance on cancellation tasks. The same authors also suggest that the striking omissions seen in works of art completed by artists with neglect (see front cover) might stem from some 'misinterpretation of degraded left-sided information'. To amplify this point they cite Mesulam's (1985) strange observation of a patient who, when drawing a clock, produced the typical pattern of neglect. However, when asked to repeat the task with his eyes closed, all 12 numbers were drawn and placed in approximately the correct position.

Representational Deficit Theories

Up until now we have largely been concerned with demonstrations of neglect when subjects are looking at stimuli. However, there are a number of demonstrations signifying that neglect can occur for stimuli subjects just have to think about. Bisiach and Luzzatti (1978) asked two patients with neglect to describe the Piazza del Duomo in Milan from two perspectives; imagining themselves looking at the cathedral from the opposite side of the square or looking at the square from the front doors of the cathedral. In both cases subjects only described landmarks that were on the right. In a similar investigation Marshall et al. (1993) asked a patient with neglect to describe a walk from the south coast of England to the Scottish Highlands. On the way up she named only towns in the east and on the way back she named only towns in the west.

More objective evidence that neglect patients can ignore the left side of objects they are only thinking about comes from two studies by Bisiach, Luzzatti and Perani (1979) and Ogden (1985). In the former study subjects viewed cloud-like shapes that moved in a horizontal plane. Viewing took place through a vertical slit so that subjects could only see part of the shape at any point in time. Subjects had to decide whether two successively viewed shapes were same or different. On different trials the feature contributing the difference occurred equally often on either the right or left. For control subjects performance was similar irrespective of side of difference but for neglect patients they were much better when the critical difference was on the right-hand side.

Both these sets of findings suggest that the origin of neglect is not in the availability of information but in some deficit in expressing that knowledge in a spatial dimension. Thus, in the Bisiach et al. experiment the subjects would have perceived all the components of the stimulus, but fail because, for some reason, they cannot express that information in a spatial domain. Similarly, the imagery-based experiments demonstrate that the subjects know about the entire scene but they choose only to describe the right-hand side. Findings such as these have been the basis of a representation theory of neglect. This proposes that neglect patients have a fundamental inability to construct internally the left-hand side of the world. We will return to this theory later.

Neglect as a Deficit in Attention

The most widely held theory of neglect is that it is a deficit in attention that results in the left-hand side of the world being inadequately explored. The basis of this idea is that each hemisphere has a bias to orient attention to contralateral space and that in an intact individual an equilibrium exists between these two opposing biases (Kinsbourne, 1987). Animal studies, for example, show that a lesion to the right hemisphere results in 'circling' behaviour with the animal continually turning to the right while the opposite occurs when a left-sided lesion is made. This is not a motor-bias problem but one due to inappropriately biased attention to environmental cues. Neglect is seen to be a naturally occurring version of this deficit with a right-sided lesion causing an inability to shift attention to the left and a predominance of the intact left hemisphere attention system which orients to the right side (Kinsbourne, 1993).

Support for an attentional deficit theory came from Posner, Cohen and Rafal (1982). They examined the speed at which patients with right parietal lesions could switch their attention to the right or left. In the experiment subjects were asked to fixate and a cue was exposed either 10 degrees of visual angle to the left or right of fixation. This was followed, after a variable interval, by a target stimulus which appeared briefly either on the same side or the opposite side to the target. Subjects were simply asked to respond to the target's appearance as quickly as possible. On 80 per cent of the trials the target appeared on the same side as the cue thus making the cue a valid predictor of where the target will appear.

The most important finding concerned stimuli presented to the left-neglected field under invalid cueing conditions (i.e. when the cue appeared on the right). When there was a very short delay between the cue and the target (less than 200 msec) a good proportion of the targets were missed completely and for the remainder the reaction times were exceptionally slow (see figure 5.2). However, when a longer interval between cue and target was used, subjects were better at detecting the invalidly cued left-side targets.

It might be argued that the poor performance to the invalidly target on the left arose from poor sensory processing but this cannot be the case. Figure 5.3 also shows the performance of subjects when the target was validly cued on the left with only 50 msec elapsing between cue and target presentation. The very small amount of time elapsing between cue and target is critical because it allows insufficient time for subjects to initiate an eye movement and fixate centrally on the stimulus. The subject's response under these conditions therefore indicates perception in the left-neglected field. Performance with valid cueing is close to that achieved under the same conditions with presentation in the good field. If there were some basic sensory problem with the left side then one would expect bad performance regardless of cueing.

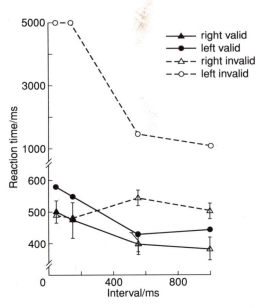

Figure 5.2 Median reaction times of a right parietal patient to respond to targets presented either to the left or right in both valid and invalid cueing conditions. Note long reaction times to targets presented on the left under invalid cueing conditions. The median reaction time of 5 sec at very short intervals between cue and target indicates that most targets were missed. Data from Posner et al. (1982), reprinted with permission of the Royal Society.

Posner et al. suggested that the primary problem of neglect was one of **disengagement** from the current attentional focus when moving towards the target, and engaging the novel target. On this basis one can expect performance to be poorest when there is very little time elapsing between the invalid cue and the appearance of the target on the other side. A longer interval allows more time for disengagement and reorientation. A theory of this kind might also explain the findings from BQ (Walker et al., see above) we considered earlier where it was shown that her target identification on the left improved markedly when an interval was introduced between fixation and target appearance.

Recently it has been suggested that not only disengagement leads to neglect but that a 'magnetic attraction' of initial gaze to the right also plays an important role (D'Erme, Robertson, Bartolomeo, et al. 1992). In perhaps the most important experiment the investigators repeated Posner et al's original conditions but included a second condition. Here no cueing was used, but instead two empty boxes, one on the left and one on the right of fixation, appeared on the screen on every trial.

Despite the fact that the boxes had no cue validity, it was found that subjects took longer to respond to targets on the left under these conditions than in the standard invalid cueing condition. It was thus proposed that the box on the right exerts some form of 'attentional capture' which ensures that attention is initially oriented to the right.

The idea that neglect involves some form of attentional deficit helps us to understand a variety of other phenomena associated with the disorder. It is known, for example, that line bisection deficits can be reduced if a stimulus is placed at the neglected end of the line (Humphreys and Riddoch, 1993b). Attentional theories also seem the best way to explain another series of phenomena demonstrated in visual neglect. Marshall and Halligan (1988) repeatedly presented two drawings of a house to a patient with severe left-sided neglect. The houses were identical except that the house on the left had bright red flames coming out of a window on the left-hand side. The patient failed to report any differences in the appearance of the two houses, but when asked which one she would prefer to live in she consistently chose the one without flames. This finding appears to suggest that the meaning of the picture is somehow influencing performance at a subconscious level. However, Bisiach and Rusconi (1990) repeated the experiment and found that two of their neglect patients consistently favoured the burning house!

The 'burning house' studies indicate that subjects do attend at some level to information they fail to report from the neglected field. It is not clear, however, whether this information is processed at a meaningful level. Subjects could, for example, be responding to the greater visual complexity of the burning house. In order to establish whether meaning can be processed in the neglected field Ladavas, Paladini and Cubelli (1993) briefly presented a word in the neglected field followed by a letter string. The subject's task was to decide whether the letter string was a word or not. On trials where there was a real word target it was either preceded by a related word (e.g. DOG CAT) or unrelated word (e.g. DRESS CAT) projected into the neglected field. Ladavas et al. found a significant priming effect – faster identification of the target word when preceded by a related word – even though subsequent testing showed that the subject was unable to identify or extract any semantic information about the words presented in the neglected field. The data thus suggest that meaning can be extracted in the neglected field and this places the level of attentional failure at a rather late stage in stimulus processing (see also Berti and Rizzolatti, 1992; McGlinchey-Berroth, Milberg, Verfaellie, et al., 1993; D'Esposito, McGlinchey-Berroth, Alexander, et al., 1993).

Neglect dyslexia – the finding that neglect patients tend to read only the rightward portions of words also seems most easily accommodated within an attentional theory. Behrmann, Moscovitch, Black and Mozer (1990) reported two patients showing different types of neglect dyslexia. One patient was more affected by relatively low-level features of words (e.g. reading of letter strings was increasingly less accurate as words increased in length), whereas the other was more influenced by higher-order factors such as lexical status (e.g. neglect was more evident when nonwords rather than words were pronounced). Behrmann et al. argued that these seemingly different types of impairments could be accommo-dated within a single attentional deficit theory. The basis of their theory is that perception involves an interaction between 'top-down' infor-mation and the information being attended to. They suggested that the impairment in neglect involves an attentional deficit which increased in severity from right to left. In addition, this attentional deficit can differ in gradient. In cases where the gradient is steep, top-down information, such as whether or not a string of letters is a word, will not be relevant because of the very low level of attention possible in the left. However, when the gradient is shallower, and a higher level of attention is avail-able, sufficient information may be extracted by the left-sided system to enable some interaction with top-down information.

Young, Hellawell and Welch (1992) have suggested that the attentional gradient theory might be extended to embrace visual neglect in general. To illustrate this point they gave their patient BQ objects to name. These were chosen so that the critical defining feature (e.g. a hammer head) fell in either the left or right of the object when depicted in the horizontal plane. Under these conditions she always named the object correctly and they attribute this to the featural information on the left side being sufficiently salient to engage the defective attentional mechanism.

The concept of an attentional gradient must be combined with other factors before a comprehensive account of attentional deficits in neglect can be produced. It is now accepted that the left and right hemispheres differ in terms of the spatial scale over which their attentional mechan-isms operate. The left hemisphere primarily allocates attention at the level of individual detail whereas the right hemisphere is concerned with more global aspects of attention (see Robertson and Lamb, 1991). This differential involvement can be seen when patients with either right or left hemisphere damage attempt to remember the Rey Complex Figure (see figure 5.3).

Under normal conditions the combination of these two processes provides a balanced level of attention. In neglect, however, it is thought that right hemisphere damage disrupts the global mechanisms of atten-tion and that attention develops a rightward bias towards more detailed aspects of stimuli because of the dominant left hemisphere. If this

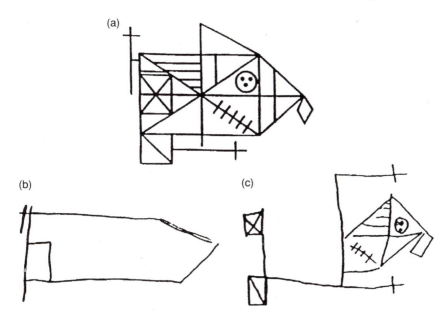

Figure 5.3 Attempts at drawing the Rey Figure (a) by a person with left hemisphere injury (b) and right hemisphere injury (c). Note that left hemisphere injury impairs the ability to attend to detail in the figure whereas right hemisphere injury interferes with the ability to appreciate global shape. From Robertson and Lamb (1991) reproduced with permission of Academic Press.

account is correct then it might be possible to reduce neglect by taking active steps to engage the defective global processing mechanisms of the right hemisphere.

As we have seen a cardinal feature of neglect is that patients show a rightward bias on the line bisection task. However, when squares of the same magnitude as the lines are used the patients will bisect them in the centre (e.g. Tegner and Levander, 1991). Halligan and Marshall (1994a) have shown that the critical aspect of this **figural configuration effect** is a large vertical line in the right side of space. They have suggested that this line serves to boost the ability of the damaged right hemisphere to employ global processing and thus overcome the rightward bias in line bisection.

Is Neglect Viewer-centred or Object-centred?

An important observation is that left-sided neglect is not always co-extensive with ignoring the left hemispace. Young, De Haan, Newcombe and Hay (1990) presented a neglect patient KL with chimeric stimuli (see plate 5.1). These comprise a single face made by the fusion of two halves. When shown a single chimera comprising the faces of two famous people KL (Young et al., 1990) named only the face depicted on the right. However, in a subsequent study in which two chimeric stimuli were shown together his ability to name the left part of the chimera was just as likely when the chimera occurred on the right as when it did on the left. In addition Marshall and Halligan (1993) have devised a new test of visual neglect which demonstrates a similar phenomenon. Here the patient has to copy the flower and in the illustration you can see that the patient copies the right side of each component of the flower irrespective of whether it is on the left or right of the picture (see also plate 5.1). These findings thus suggest that neglect is occurring at a level where objects have been segregated from their background.

Recently, Driver, Baylis and Rafal (1992) have demonstrated that left-sided neglect at the object level occurs preattentively. CC was presented with stimuli of the type shown in figure 5.4. These stimuli comprised a large red rectangle with a small irregularly defined green area at either the far left or right end. When shown stimuli such as these, subjects report a green shape superimposed on a red background. On each trial one of these shapes was presented followed by a probe which either did or did not match the contours of the green shape and CC was asked to decide whether the two contours matched. If CC's neglect were determined by hemispatial position then he should perform better when the green shape is on the right. However, if his neglect is object-centred then he should do better when the green shape is presented on the left. This follows because, from an object-centred perspective, the critical feature of the shape, its outline, lies on the right. The results supported the object-based prediction with responding being more accurate with left presentations.

Findings such as these indicate, in a loose sense, that neglect is 'object-based' – that is neglect is occurring at a level of analysis where individual objects have been identified within the visual field as opposed to their position within right or left hemispace. However, this is not equivalent to arguing that neglect can be object-centred in the more precise sense we encountered in the previous chapter.

Briefly, you will recall that theories of object recognition now identify a transition between recognition based on viewer-centred and object-centred representations. In a viewer-centred representation left and right are defined in terms of how the subject is looking at the object. In an object-centred representation the left and right of an object are defined in terms of the object itself rather than the perspective of the viewer.

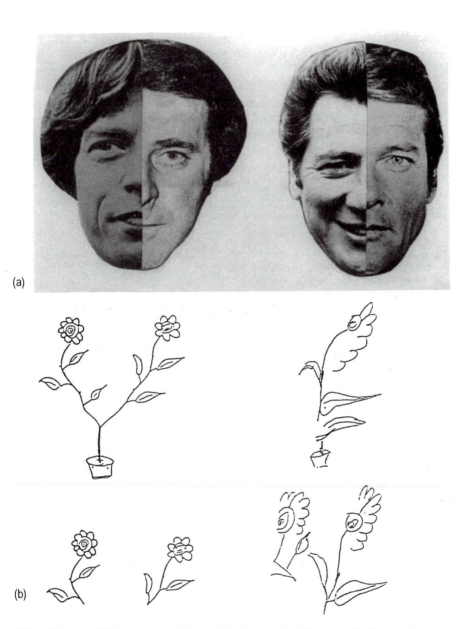

Plate 5.1 (a) Chimeric stimuli formed by fusing the left and right halves of two different famous faces. From Young et al. (1990). (b) Flower copying test devised by Marshall and Halligan (1993) and patient's copy. Note that the left side of each component is neglected regardless of its position in the visual field. Reprinted with permission.

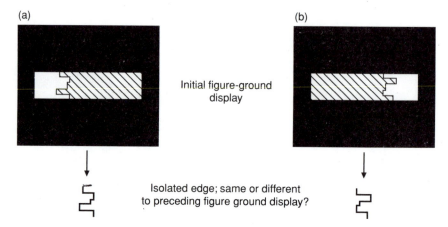

Figure 5.4 Stimuli and procedure used by Driver et al. (1992.) Hatched area red, blank area green. Illustration kindly supplied by Jon Driver.

Thus if a rectangle is tilted by 30 degrees, its left and right, as defined by its principal, vertical axis, remain unaltered even though part of the left now falls in the right visual field and vice versa.

Young et al. (1990) wished to establish whether their patient BQ's neglect arose from problems at the viewer-centred or object-centred level of representation. To evaluate this she was presented with chimeric faces and asked to name the persons depicted. As before, she failed to name virtually all the facial halves depicted on the left. The faces were then rotated by 180 degrees and the task repeated. Performance was poorer given the difficulties of identifying things upside down but it was still the case that it was the stimuli to the left that she was unable to report even though she had named them when presented on the right. In addition an intermediary level of responding was obtained when the stimuli were rotated through only 90 degrees. Young et al. argued that if her neglect was object-centred she should continue to ignore the left side of the stimulus regardless of its viewer-centred orientation. Instead her responses seemed linked to the chimeras as she viewed them.

Recently, Driver and Halligan (1991) have examined the possibility of object-centred neglect. They devised pairs of stimuli which differed in one critical respect. The difference between each pair was varied systematically as being on either the right- or left-hand side of the subject. A further assumption was that the principal axis of elongation for each stimulus ran through the vertical midline – as would be the case with a rectangle placed on its end. There were also additional sets of

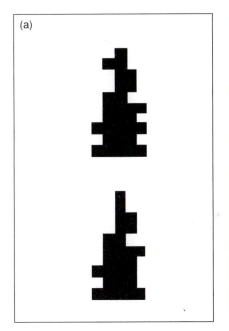
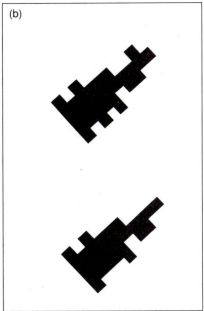

Figure 5.5 Stimuli used by Driver and Halligan. Note that in (b) the feature distinguishing the two shapes falls to the right of the midline but lies on the left in terms of the object-centred vertical axis. From Driver and Halligan (1991) *Cognitive Neuropsychology* 8, 475–96. Reproduced by permission of Lawrence Erlbaum Ltd.

stimuli in which the pairs were identical. The stimuli were presented in the vertical midline (see figure 5.5) and a patient with neglect was asked to decide whether the stimuli were the same or different. Under these conditions she performed well when the critical difference occurred on the right but very poorly when the critical difference was on the left-neglected side.

The experiment was then repeated except that the stimulus pairs were tilted. This manipulation created conditions in which the critical difference between pairs could be on either the left or right side of the objects independently of whether the differences were presented in the left or right hemispace. Under these conditions it was found that the subject was consistently unable to detect differences on the left side of objects even when the differences were presented in the right hemispace.

This experiment appeared to indicate that neglect is occurring at the level of object-centred rather than viewer-centred representation and that the left and right of an object is determined by principal axis of

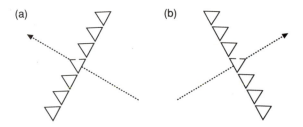

Figure 5.6 Stimuli originally devised by Attneave (1968) and employed by Driver et al. From Driver et al. (1994) Axis-based neglect of visual shapes. *Neuropsychologia*, 32, 1353–66. Reproduced by kind permission of Elsevier Science Ltd.

elongation. However, Driver, Baylis, Goodrich and Rafal (1994) have pointed out an alternative explanation of the results. They argue that neglect is not necessarily operating in terms of the left and right as defined by the absolute egocentric midline, i.e. everything to the patient's left ignored, everything to the right attended to. To emphasize this point they cite a study of letter cancellation, which showed that neglect was not determined by the patients' midline; each patient had their own 'attentional boundary' which in some cases extended to the right of the midline (Marshall and Halligan, 1989).

If the attentional boundary can extend to the right of the midline then it was possible that poor detection of anomalies on the left of Driver and Halligan's rotated figures could reflect the fact that the critical feature appeared relatively leftwards of any shifted right-left boundary (see figure 5.5). In order to rule out explanations of this kind it was therefore necessary to devise an experiment in which the location of target information in terms of an object-centred framework was manipulated while keeping the viewer-centred position of the object constant. Figure 5.6 shows two rows of equilateral triangles. One row (a) is 'base aligned' so that the triangles appear to point towards the top left of the display whereas the other row of triangles (b) is base-aligned so as to point to the top right of the display. The direction in which the triangles point is indicated by the dotted arrows and this also indicates the principal axis of the triangles. You will notice that the triangle in the middle of each row has a small gap in exactly the same place. However, because of the differing orientation of the triangles, the gap lies to the right of the principal axis in (a) but to the left in (b). Three neglect patients were asked to decide whether or not there was a gap in the middle triangle and they missed far more when the gap appeared to the left of the triangle's principal axis (b) than on the right (a). This result cannot be explained in terms of viewer-centred representation of the triangles.

While the above studies indicate the existence of object-centred neglect other studies have failed to support this conclusion. Behrmann and Moscovitch (1994) required neglect patients to name the various colours associated with the edge of a common object which was either presented in its normal orientation or tilted through 90 degrees. Under these conditions neglect was entirely viewer-centred with no evidence of neglect being determined by which side of the animal the colours were associated with. However, a second experiment used letters and stimuli. For symmetrical letters (e.g. A, X) there was no evidence of object-centred neglect but with asymmetrical letters (e.g. B, F) there was increased neglect of the left side of the letters even when these were rotated into the right side of viewer-centred space.

Behrmann and Moscovitch suggest that object-centred neglect may depend on the objects having intrinsic handedness, as is the case with asymmetrical letters. For most real objects, however, there is no intrinsic handedness and thus no basis for object-centred neglect. As yet these findings have not been reconciled with those of Driver and his colleagues. Driver et al. prefer to argue that object-centred neglect can therefore arise in different ways – where objects have clear principal axes or where objects have intrinsic handedness. Alternatively one might hope for a single explanation that explains the intermittent demonstration of object-centred neglect. It is notable that the phenomenon seems largely associated with the use of abstract stimuli. These stimuli might be inherently more difficult to deal with and thus evoke a strategy of assigning a left and right. This might be easier to do when there is an asymmetry to exploit or where the overall configuration allows left and right to be easily established.

Theories of Neglect – An Overview

From the above you can see that neglect is a complex topic offering up a wide range of phenomena and theories about why it occurs. Of the various theories it seems unlikely that ones proposing a deficit at a relatively low level of perceptual processing can accommodate the data. The suggestion that neglect patients may have some representational amputation of the left hemispace seems implausible given many of the findings. The idea of 'amorphosynthesis' – some deficit in the quality of the perceptual process – may have some relevance but, on its own, fails to give a convincing account of phenomena such as performance in Posner et al.'s valid and invalid cueing procedure.

At the present moment the most convincing class of theories concerning neglect are those that propose some form of attentional deficit. Essentially these theories suggest that there is an imbalance in the amount of attention allocated to left and right and that, due to right-sided damage, the left hemisphere dominates attentional processing with a resulting bias to the right side. Furthermore, this bias may be observed in terms of either viewer-centred or object-centred frames of reference. In addition it is now thought that the forms of attention carried out by the left and right hemispheres are different with the former emphasizing local detail and the latter global form.

Earlier we considered a class of theories which suggest that neglect patients have problems constructing a spatial representation of the world. It is not easy to see how this type of theory could be easily distinguished from attentional theories because the outcome of defective attentional processing will, in effect, provide an impoverished view of the world. However, Shallice (1988) has pointed out that the data used to support the representational account (e.g. the inability to imagine the left side of a familiar public place) do not cause problems for attentional theories. He points out that modern theories of mental imagery (e.g. Kosslyn, 1994) assume that images are processed within some form of spatial medium (e.g. the visuo-spatial scratch pad of Baddeley and Hitch's (1977) working memory model). It is proposed that these images can be scanned and it is thus perfectly feasible to suppose that an attentional deficit manifest in the neglect of exterior space could cause similar problems when an internal spatial medium is the basis of responding.

Attentional theories seem, at present, to provide the best account of findings. They do, for example, provide a more ready explanation of 'disengagement' phenomena, and repetition blindness, subliminal influences from the neglected field. However, the idea that a single theory of neglect will emerge is highly unlikely because of the diversity of deficits being discovered (for a recent overview of theories attempting to explain neglect see Halligan and Marshall 1994b).

Summary

Neglect is a phenomenon in which, for some reason, a person ignores one side of the world. Most commonly this is the left side following damage to the right side of the brain. Neglect can be manifest in several ways. Most common is hemispatial neglect which is easily demonstrated with tasks such as line bisection. Neglect can also be either perceptual or pre-motor and, in the case of perceptual neglect, it may involve neglect of peri-personal or extra-personal space. Perceptual deficit theories attempt to account for neglect as a deficit of perception but there is abundant evidence that this type of theory is wrong. Most favoured is the attentional deficit theory because this accounts for many phenomena (e.g. attentional disengagement effects). Theories based on a defective internal representation of space can account for most of the data but if one assumes that attentional mechanisms operate on internal representations of space the representational theory cannot be distinguished from the attentional theory. Neglect can be demonstrated as occurring at either the viewer-centred or object-centred level of object recognition.

6

The Split Brain

Because of its conspicuous nature the function of the corpus callosum[1] or central commissure (see figure 6.1) has long been a matter of speculation and scientific debate (Bogen, 1993). During the Renaissance period it was widely believed that the corpus callosum served only the mechanical role of supporting other brain structures – this was not particularly surprising because this was the era of ventricular localization in which it was assumed that mental functions were subsumed by the fluids of the ventricles rather than by the brain tissue itself. However, with the realization that brain tissue itself was at the heart of mental function, anatomists of the eighteenth century began to ascribe a more important role to the corpus callosum. Viq d'Azyr (1784) suggested that:

> The commissures are intended to establish sympathetic communications between different parts of the brain, just as the nerves do between different organs and the brain itself.

The idea that the corpus callosum was involved in communication between brain regions continued along with more fanciful notions that

[1] Callosus in Latin means 'hard' and refers to the fact that the corpus callosum is considerably harder than other areas of the brain. It was this hardness which suggested its mechanical role.

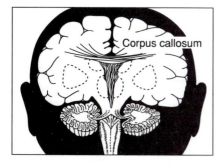 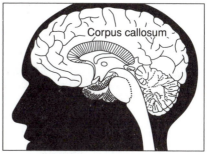

Figure 6.1 The corpus callosum. From Lindsay and Norman (1972). Reprinted with permission of Academic Press.

it was the seat of the soul. The corpus callosum came to the attention of the 'classical neurologists' of the nineteenth century. Liepmann (1908) described a right-handed man with a callosal lesion who showed left-handed apraxia and left-handed agraphia. Thus, with his left hand, he was unable to obey verbal commands (e.g. pick up the pencil) or write anything. Liepmann correctly interpreted this deficit as a disconnection syndrome. This can be defined as a disorder arising from some interruption of the communication pathways between brain regions. Liepmann proposed that only the left hemisphere was able to comprehend language and that for the left hand to follow a verbal command some transmission of information via the corpus callosum to the right hand was necessary.[2]

Leipmann's account of his patient's deficit was esssentially correct. However, at the time, many argued for a different interpretation suggesting that the impairments observed following callosal lesions were not pure and that associated damage to other brain regions could account for the observed deficits. A second factor was a growing body of evidence from animal studies which appeared to show that a section of the corpus callosum had no adverse effects on behaviour. This led Lashley (1929) to suggest half-jokingly that the role of the corpus callosum was simply to hold the two cerebral hemispheres together. On a similar basis Dandy (1936) pronounced:

> no symptoms follow its division. This ... puts an end to all of the extravagant hypotheses on the functions of the corpus callosum.

[2] In this chapter it is vital to remember that, for most functions, the cerebral cortex is cross lateralised – i.e. the right cerebral hemisphere controls the left and vice versa.

Human Commissurotomy

An important development in the debate about the corpus callosum was the neurosurgical procedure of **commissurotomy** (Bogen and Vogel, 1965). This was devised as a treatment for intractable epilepsy in which the corpus callosum is completely divided along with, in some cases, an additional interhemispheric tract known as the **anterior commissure**. The idea of the surgery was to alleviate epilepsy by preventing the spread of seizures from one hemisphere to the other. The operation proved successful and, in addition, provided neuropsychologists with a unique opportunity to answer fundamental questions about brain organization: first and foremost did the corpus callosum actually do anything?

Early neuropsychological testing of these **split-brain** patients (e.g. Akelaitis, 1944) confirmed the conclusions reached from the animal work. Thus one commentator (Tomasch, 1957) remarked: 'the corpus callosum is hardly connected with any psychological functions at all.' However, these conclusions were reached on the basis of relatively unsophisticated testing and a rather different picture emerged when more refined methods were used.

Modern Research into Commissurotomy

The modern view of callosal function owes its origins to the work of Roger Sperry and his associates (e.g. Gazzaniga, 1970; Sperry and Gazzaniga, 1967; Zaidel, 1983a) who showed that, under appropriate testing conditions, split-brain patients had a number of processing impairments. At this point it is useful to outline the basic testing procedures that were used. Figure 6.2 shows the standard tachistoscopic procedure used to investigate hemispheric functions. The technique exploits the normal organization of the human visual and tactile sensory systems. Thus, if a point is fixated, all information to the left of that point is projected initially to the right hemisphere, and for information presented initially to the right it projects initially to the left hemisphere. This technique, often referred to as the **split-field** technique, can only achieve localized presentation of stimuli if presentations are brief – less than 200 msec. If any longer presentations are used an eye movement is possible and the laterally-presented stimulus can be centrally fixated and thus processed by both hemispheres.

First, and returning to the pioneering work of Leipmann, Sperry and his colleagues were able to show the classic symptoms of disconnection. In addition to left-handed apraxia and agraphia the patients also showed

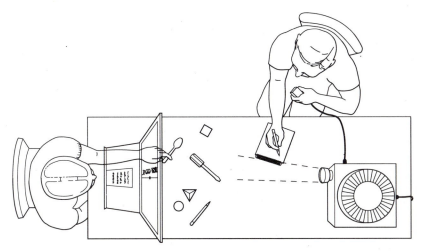

Figure 6.2   General purpose testing system for using the split field technique with split brain patients. From Gazzaniga (1983). Copyright © 1983 by the American Psychological Association. Reproduced with permission.

an inability to identify objects with their left hand (**astereognosis**). Also, when asked to draw in three dimensions with their right hand, the pictures lacked depth (see figure 6.3).

These classic signs of disconnection confirmed that the corpus callosum did play a functional role and supported a view of hemispheric organization in which language functions were largely mediated by the left hemisphere. Astereognosis thus arose from failed right to left transmission of sensory information, and agraphia from an inability to pass information about graphic motor movements from left to right. Apraxia was attributed to interrupted transmission of verbally-determined arm movements to the right hemisphere. Failure to draw in three dimensions with the right hand suggests disconnection of right-sided spatial centres from the left hemisphere centres controlling hand movements.

Right Hemisphere Language

One consequence of commissurotomy was that it allowed psychologists to explore the language capabilities of the isolated right hemisphere. When these studies began the prevailing view was that the right hemisphere was 'word deaf and word blind' (Geschwind, 1965; Gazzaniga, Bogen and Sperry, 1962). However, further investigations of some

Figure 6.3   Drawings by the right hand of split brain patient MP (Parkin and Barry, 1991). Note the lack of a third dimension in all drawings.

patients indicated that there was some right hemisphere capability for understanding language even though speech was not possible. Gazzaniga showed that two split-brain patients, NG and LB, were, on hearing the name of an object, able to pick it out from a hidden array of objects. This ability extended beyond the recognition of simple nouns to include functional definitions, for example, 'pick up the object that is used to drive nails'. Also when the printed names of objects were presented to only the right hemisphere (i.e. via the left visual field) the patients were able to point to the appropriate object.

These early observations suggested considerable linguistic ability in the right hemisphere. However, as more split-brain patients were studied it became evident that right hemisphere language, as shown by NG and LB, was not a typical occurrence. In addition, it was also thought that right hemisphere language may have been overestimated. It was also discovered that, with repeated exposure of the same set of items, the left hemisphere can become implicated in the matching of objects presented in the left hand. As a result apparent comprehension of an object name by the right hemisphere might actually be mediated by the left hemi-sphere (Gazzaniga, 1983a).

The early split-brain studies were based on the 'West Coast' series of patients but a second 'East Coast' group subsequently became available (Wilson, Reeves, Gazzaniga and Culver, 1977). Of particular interest were three patients, JW, VP and PS because out of 28 these were the only three to show evidence of right hemisphere language. For two of these patients, PS and VP, right hemisphere language ability was remarkably good.[3] Left visual field presentation of verbal commands produced the correct response even though the patients could not report verbally (using their left hemisphere speech system) why they had performed the acts. Reuter-Lorenz and Baynes (1992) provide new data on JW which suggests the right hemisphere may be less efficient at reading because it employs a serial encoding process in lexical access compared with a parallel process in the left hemisphere. More recently Baynes, Tramo and Gazzaniga, (1992) have reported a fourth East Coast split-brain patient (DW) with evidence of right hemisphere language ability.

The question of right hemisphere language in split-brain patients has remained controversial (see Gazzaniga, 1983a, b; Gazzaniga and Smylie, 1983; Levy, 1983; Zaidel, 1983a, b). Gazzaniga's view is that the rarity of right hemisphere language in split-brain patients makes it difficult to accept that the phenomenon is relevant to right hemisphere function in general. Others (e.g. Zaidel, 1990) have argued that language representation is more widespread in the right hemisphere. Reasons for the variability in the occurrence of right hemisphere language are not that clear. An undoubted problem concerns contamination of split-brain findings by the effects of extra-callosal damage. One source of damage are the lesions responsible for the epilepsy which, in turn, might provoke an atypical pattern of language lateralization. Thus a left-sided lesion experienced early in life might provoke greater representation of language in the right hemisphere. A problem, however, is that those patients showing most evidence of right hemisphere language have little evidence of extra-callosal damage.

---

[3] These three patients differed from the West Coast series in that the anterior commissure was left intact and, in two cases (JW and VP) commissurotomy was performed in two stages. It might therefore be argued that this represents a crucial difference and that some interhemispheric transfer remained in these patients. This point is rejected by Gazzaniga (1983a) on the grounds that JW has a similar profile of right hemisphere language to NG and LB even though the latter had their anterior commissures sectioned.

Inter-Manual Conflict and the 'Alien Hand'

One of the more puzzling and bizarre symptoms associated with split-brain patients is that of inter-manual conflict or alien hand (Brion and Jedynak, 1972). This symptom most commonly involves situations in which the left hand is seen to be deliberately interfering with the actions of the right hand. My own experience of this disorder involved a woman known as MP who suffered a ruptured aneurysm which caused complete destruction of the anterior part of the corpus callosum known as the genu (Parkin and Barry, 1991):

> She was swimming up and down quite normally, got out of the pool, dried herself, and then handed the towel to an assistant. At this point trouble started because her left hand reached out and tried to grab the towel back from the assistant. A tug-of-war continued between the two hands until finally the assistant pulled the towel away . . . Other examples . . . included the left hand closing doors and drawers as soon as the right hand had opened them; the left hand undoing buttons that had just been done up . . .; the left hand removing pieces that the right hand had just placed in a collage; the left hand removing items that the right hand had just packed (left unaided MP took several hours to pack a suitcase), and so on. Her husband reported instances of conflicting emotion between the hands. Thus she would pull him towards her with her right hand while the left hand simultaneously tried to push him away . . . On occasions the left hand caused mayhem by appearing to try and co-operate. In living skills MP was making good progress with an omelette when the left hand 'helped out', first by throwing in a couple of additional uncracked eggs, then an unpeeled onion and a salt cellar into the frying pan. There were also times when the left hand deliberately stopped the right hand carrying out a task. In one instance I asked her to put her right hand through a small hole. Nothing happened and then she said 'I can't the other one's holding it'. I looked over and saw the left hand firmly gripping the right hand at the wrist. (Parkin, 1996a)

Can we explain the alien hand sign as being another consequence of disconnection? The answer would appear to be 'no' because this sign, unlike the other disconnection symptoms, is only a permanent feature of split-brain patients who have cortical damage in addition to a split brain. Because of this Della Salla, Marchetti and Spinnler (1991) have proposed that two forms of alien hand sign need to be distinguished: An acute form due solely to callosal damage and which disappears fairly quickly, and a chronic form which arises from damage to both the anterior corpus callosum and the supplementary motor area (SMA) located in the mesial frontal cortex. The acute form is attributed to temporary disturbance to the SMA that might arise by retraction of the hemispheres during commissurotomy.

Some examples of chronic alien hand lend weight to this theory. Della Salla et al. describe the relatively rarer instance of right-sided alien hand arising in a right-handed person where there was both callosal damage and a lesion affecting the left mesio-frontal cortex. Trojana, Crisci, Lanzillo, et al. (1993) report a man with a right mesio-frontal lesion and anterior callosal damage in which many aspects of alien hand behaviour were present 11 months after a right anterior cerebral artery ischemia. There are even claims that the alien hand sign can arise without callosal involvement. Both Goldberg, Mayer and Toglia (1981) and McNabb, Carroll and Mastaglia (1988) have argued that mesio-frontal damage alone can account for the alien hand sign but these studies do not provide convincing evidence that callosal damage was not implicated (see Leiguardia, Starkstein, Nogues, et al., 1993, for possible examples of non-alien hand without callosal involvement).

It thus seems certain that chronic alien hand depends critically on some disruption of the mesio-frontal structures, specifically the SMA, involved in the planning of movement with, additionally, some lack of inter-hemispheric connection. With this in mind can we produce some explanation of why the alien hand behaves the way it does? In particular why is the alien hand so apparently anarchic?

In my interactions with MP I was struck by how relatively infrequent alien hand incidents were. I viewed with some trepidation her offer to pick me up at the station but was surprised by a smooth driving performance ... during my first meal with her, I half expected her aberrant left hand to start flicking peas at unsuspecting patients. This never happened and it soon became apparent that alien hand behaviour was almost always restricted to two types of situation. The two categories of task were either those in which only one hand could be employed to achieve the goal and where a range of options was possible (e.g. go vs. no go; do-up vs. undo; pull up vs. pull down; select A vs. select B) or where tasks involving a number of components but where these components were not overlearned (e.g. planning a meal).

Physiological studies show that both left and right SMA's are active even when only one hand is initiating and carrying out a task (Tanji and Kurata, 1982). Under these conditions movements planned in the hemisphere ipsilateral to the activated hand must be suppressed either by some direct action within the hemisphere or inter-hemispherically via the callosal pathway. However, if this suppression mechanism is faulty, as might occur in alien hand, then the other hand may become active and become involved in the task. If a task is simple – 'open', any attempt by the alien hand to contribute positively is problematic because the right hand is fully capable. However, unsuppressed and with the need to contribute, the next best movement – 'close' is carried out. Behaviour thus appears anarchic when, in fact, it is the next best response given the general-action context.

The above explanation offers an explanation of some alien hand behaviour but is not complete. Above we noted MP's alien hand behaviour associated with omelette making. Lack of suppression cannot be the sole answer, some deficiency in planning must also be present. Even then there are still puzzles. Why, for example, do alien hands always want to undo buttons rather than do them up? or grab trouser legs repeatedly? The most likely possibility is that alien hand is not due to a single deficit but arises from various impairments that are present in different degrees. There is no clear answer, but one possible complication, also associated with frontal damage, is utilization behaviour (LHermitte, 1983) in which the hand can spontaneously and involuntarily grab nearby objects (see chapter 10). Case 1 Goldberg et al. (1981) suggests this possibility:

> In the fifth week after onset (of alien hand), the patient began to walk alone. The right arm would, however, tend spontaneously to reach out and grasp objects (e.g. door knobs) that she passed, thus interfering greatly with her progression. (p. 684)

Finally, how do patients feel about having an alien hand? Some are clearly frightened and may even be scared to go to sleep in case the hand strangles them. Others, like my own case MP, learn to live with it and can sometimes show bemusement. De-personalization of alien hand activities varies considerably. Like many, MP regards her alien hand as 'it' but accepts that it is part of her. In more extreme instances patients deny the hand is theirs and believe it to be controlled by someone else. They shout at it as it goes out of control and may even give it a name (Doody and Jankovic, 1992). Interestingly, de-personalization of the alien hand is just as common when the lesion is in the hemisphere dominant for language thus indicating that denial is not linked with an absence of verbal expression.

Commissurotomy and the Subcortical Pathways

Although commissurotomy interrupts the major connections between the hemispheres the disconnection is not total. Running between the hemispheres are a large number of subcortical fibres which remain intact after the operation. Conducting experiments which examine the extent to which one hemisphere can communicate with another when the corpus callosum has been sectioned thus provide a basis for discovering the kinds of information that can be transferred by these subcortical pathways.

Holtzman (1984) showed split-brain subjects two 2×2 matrices of X's, one in each visual hemifield. Next, one X was briefly surrounded by a circle in order to specify a specific location and subjects were required to direct their eyes to the same location in the other matrix. The subjects were able to do this task easily thus indicating that information about visual location had been transferred between the hemispheres. However, the subjects could not do this task if they were probed to look at a particular symbol in the other hemifield. Thus if a cross were highlighted in the left visual field they could not move their eyes to look at the same cross in the right visual field. This finding thus suggested that information about spatial location could be transferred but not information concerning item form.

If two spots of light appear sequentially at different points in the visual field you can, providing the interval is short enough, observe a phenomenon known as apparent motion. Ramachandran, Cronin-Golomb and Myers (1986) have demonstrated that split-brain subjects can also show apparent motion even when the two spots of light are presented to different hemifields. Although there have been criticisms of this study more recent evidence confirms the Ramachandran et al. findings (Corballis, in press).

Sperry, Zaidel and Zaidel (1979) used a specialized contact lens technique to show the split-brain patients NG and LB arrays of four pictures (see figure 6.4). In one test LB's right hemisphere was shown four pictures, one of whom was the then current President Richard Nixon, and asked to pick out the famous person:

Ex: 'Out of these four, do you recognise any?'
LB: looked at the 4 items for 5 sec, then pointed to the face of Nixon. He then asked hesitantly 'Is it yourself?' But this vocal guess was quickly rejected when heard by the right hemisphere and LB corrected himself. 'No, not either of you.' In making an evaluative thumb signal he hesitated between the thumb-up position and thumb-down and finally settled on a definite neutral horizontal position with the added comment to himself 'It's okay, not that good.' (The date was May, 1973, prior to the full Watergate disclosure.)
Ex: 'This is neutral, eh?'
LB: 'Yeah.'

Ex: 'Who do you think it is?'

When LB could not answer examiner asked 'One of your family? . . . from TV . . . or screen?'

LB started to write with his left forefinger on the back of his right hand.
Ex: 'No don't write. Historical?'
LB: 'No.'
Ex: 'Somebody here?' When subject didn't answer, examiner asked again 'Historical or personal?'
LB: 'Historical.'
Ex: 'Federal government, . . . or state?'
LB: 'State, no federal.'
Ex: 'Minister of defence, of commerce, foreign minister, president?'
LB: 'President.'
Ex: 'Who is it then?' (long pause) 'Present, . . . past, . . . future?'
LB: 'In between.'
Ex: 'What do you mean in between? Present or past?'

LB again didn't answer for a long period, then said 'Goldwater.'

Ex: 'Goldwater?'
LB: 'No, it's *not* Goldwater; I'm going through who it is *not*, now.'
Ex: 'Tell me, liberal or conservative?'
LB: 'Don't quickly know.'
Ex: 'Democrat-Republican?'
LB: 'Republican.'
Ex: 'Senate-House of Representatives?'
LB: 'Neither.'
Ex: 'Any names?'

LB was not given further cues on this showing and remained unable to state vocally the name of the president.

In this example there seems to be reasonable contextual information being transmitted to the left hemisphere but nothing precise. In other cases, such as when LB's right hemisphere was shown a photograph of Hitler, a mental 'aura' appeared to reach the left hemisphere and result in a negative response.

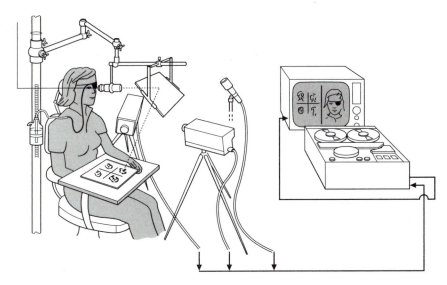

Figure 6.4   Apparatus used to enable extended presentation to a single hemisphere by restricting presentation to one visual half field. From Sperry et al. (1979), self recognition and social awareness in the deconnected hemisphere. *Neuropsychologia*, 17, 153–66. Reproduced by permission of Elsevier Science Ltd.

Higher-level Subcortical Transfer?

Findings such as those above led Myers and Sperry (1985) to conclude that the information transmitted via subcortical pathways was 'largely connotative, contextual or orientational' but too vague for stimulus identification. Inability to transmit information about form is also consistent with split-brain subjects' failure to name words or objects presented to the left visual field and their chance performance on same – different judgements when stimuli have to be compared across hemifields.

However, a number of authors have challenged this conclusion and argued that the subcortical pathways can convey higher-level information such as that specifying form. Cronin-Golomb (1986) used a 'lateral limits' technique, which allows prolonged viewing by only one hemisphere. In the experiment one hemisphere was presented with a single picture and the other with an array of three pictures. The subject's task was to decide which of the three pictures was conceptually related to the single picture. Both concrete and abstract overlaps between stimuli were explored and it was found that accuracy was remarkably good

Figure 6.5 Examples of stimuli used by Sergent (1990). Reproduced with permission of Oxford University Press.

irrespective of which hemisphere was used for presenting the single picture and which one used viewing for the array. This was particularly impressive given that the links between the abstract concepts were quite difficult.

Cronin-Golomb's results suggested that stimulus associations, including those at a categorial and functional level, could be transmitted subcortically. Further support for this view came from a series of experiments by Sergent (Sergent, 1986, 1987, 1990). In one experiment (Sergent, 1990) two digits were briefly presented in parallel either side of a fixation point (see figure 6.5) and the subject was required to make a decision. When asked whether they were the same or different all three subjects performed at chance. However, all three subjects could decide whether the same two stimuli were both odd, both even, or different. All three subjects were also able to decide which stimulus was higher. In a further experiment a digit was presented on one side and the word 'odd' or 'even' on the other. The task was to decide whether the number matched the word and on this task only LB performed above chance.

Sergent's findings, along with others (e.g. Cronin-Golomb, 1986; Lambert, 1991) thus challenged the established view of subcortical integration between disconnected hemispheres and suggested that the level of information exchange was at a more complex level than previously proposed. Seymour, Reuter-Lorenz, and Gazzaniga (1994) explored the generality of Sergent's findings by carrying out similar experiments to hers on three East Coast split-brain patients, JW, VP and DR. Despite trying a range of tasks the authors found no evidence that the separated hemispheres of JW or DR could share information. VP, who is now known to have some sparing of callosal fibres, did perform above chance on one task.

Seymour et al. discuss the discrepancy between their studies and those of Sergent. First, they note that much of Sergent's data are derived principally from LB and that here are considerable grounds for viewing this patient as atypical and that his performance profile is closer to normals than other split-brain cases. An additional suggestion is that Sergent's data may reflect a 'response readiness' strategy. Here each hemisphere has a response readiness which varies in strength systematically with the size of the digit presented. As digits are presented simultaneously two patterns of response readiness are available and the one that is strongest suppresses the other. In this way the hemisphere with the highest digit could reliably respond even though it had no idea what digit was shown to the other hemisphere. Unfortunately this explanation seems ad hoc and it is not clear how it would explain evidence such as that produced by Cronin-Golomb (1986).

Corballis (1994) replicated Sergent's findings but noted that the response accuracy achieved by the patients (68%) was lower than that found when Sergent tested the same subjects (93.5%). However, he concludes that the data do not support inter-hemispheric transfer because response accuracy obtained by the patients was no greater than would be expected from a strategy based on using the information available from a single hemisphere. For example, attending to only the right digit and responding 'right greater' if higher than three and left otherwise would achieve 79 per cent accuracy.

Corballis and Trudel (1993) also considered Sergent's findings and in a careful analysis they note that procedural factors could explain the apparently high level of inter-hemispheric communication obtained. In one instance they argue that sophisticated guessing could explain some of her results. They carried out two studies comparing the commissurotomy patients LB and DK with controls. In the first task lines were presented simultaneously in both hemifields and subjects had to decide whether they were aligned (see figure 6.6a). LB performed this task normally but DK was at chance. In a second experiment subjects had to decide whether a string of letters was a word or not. Words were presented either to the right or left visual field or bilaterally by straddling the visual fields (see figure 6.6b). LB and DK performed like normals with right visual field and also above chance with left visual field presentation – the latter being another indication of right hemisphere language. However, when half of the word fell in each visual field performance was at chance. Discussing this result in the light of Sergent's (1987) study in which she showed that two split-brain patients (one of them LB) could achieve 75 per cent accuracy on the same task when words were presented bilaterally, Corballis and Trudel suggest that Sergent's procedure, which involved presenting each string of letters many times, enabled subjects to build up sufficient knowledge of the word set so as to guess a word's identity from only its initial letters. This was avoided in the authors' own study and no evidence of subcortical transfer was found.

Corballis and Trudel also highlight one other methodological problem that can lead to an exaggerated view of subcortical inter-hemispheric

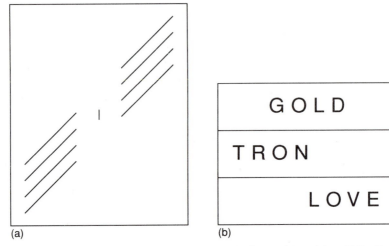

(a)   (b)

Figure 6.6   Examples of stimuli used by Corballis and Trudel (1993). Reproduced with permission of the American Psychological Association.

transfer – **cross cueing**. This involves one hemisphere being able to initiate cues which the other hemisphere can pick up and use as a source of information. Sometimes these cues are rather obvious (e.g. the left hemisphere whispering to the right hemisphere) but in the case of patients like LB it has been suggested that the cues could be very subtle involving, for example, movements of the tongue.

On the basis of the above evidence, as well as that from other studies (e.g. Reuter-Lorenz and Baynes, 1992; Corballis, 1995) it would seem that Sergent's studies overestimated the degree of subcortical information transfer possible in split-brain patients. Overall it seems that only the subcortical transmission of lower level information (e.g. location, emotional tone) can be detected reliably and that higher level transfer of information about stimulus form (e.g. letter identity, number size) does not occur. Where higher level transfer has been demonstrated it may have arisen from sophisticated guessing or cross cueing.

Attention and Commissurotomy

The available evidence indicates that each cerebral hemisphere appears to have a number of discrete functions and that the level of communication between the hemispheres via subcortical pathways appears to be rather limited. An additional issue, however, is whether attention is also divided or whether a single set of attentional processes, mediated by intact subcortical pathways, controls the activities of both hemispheres.

One idea of visual attention is that it takes the form of a 'spotlight' in that information processing at a particular location can be enhanced by the allocation of additional processing resources. Experimentally this can be shown in experiments where subjects are first cued to expect a stimulus at a specific location and then measuring the difference between reaction time to the stimulus when it appears at the expected location as opposed to an unexpected one. In normal subjects reaction times are faster to stimuli in expected locations and this has also been shown in two split-brain subjects. Holtzman Sidfis, Volpe et al. (1981) displayed two 3×3 grids, one in each hemifield, and a cue appeared in one location to indicate where a target would appear. In one condition the cue appeared in the same hemifield as the location cue and in the other the cue and target appeared in different hemifields. In both conditions the typical advantage for expected location was found, thus indicating that the mechanisms responsible for shifting attention were being mediated subcortically.

On the basis of these studies Gazzaniga (1987) concluded that 'the attentional system remains unified in the split-brain patient' (p. 131). However, other evidence has now indicated that the disconnected hemispheres may have separated attentional processes. Levy, Trevarthen and Sperry (1972) presented split-brain patients with chimeric faces (see chapter 5) ensuring that each half-face was presented to each hemifield. When naming, subjects tended to favour the face on the right, but when pointing, the one on the left was favoured. On some trials, just as the subject was about to point, the chimeric face was removed and the subject asked to name the face while on other trials the reverse change was made. Under these conditions naming still favoured the right and pointing the left. The fact that subjects were able to switch response modes rapidly suggests that independent attentional resources were operating in each hemisphere that enabled both halves of the face to be attended to simultaneously. Under a unified attention system account one would not expect this on the grounds that attention would have been allocated to performance of the aborted task.

More recently Luck, Hillyard, Mangun and Gazzaniga (1994) asked subjects to search for a single target item that differed from distractors in terms of the spatial layout of its features (see figure 6.7). On some trials the array was divided with half being shown in the left visual field and the other half in the right. On other trials the entire array was shown either on the left or right. Luck et al. reasoned that if there is a single attentional resource mediating both hemispheres then processing should be no quicker with bilateral presentation than when all the items

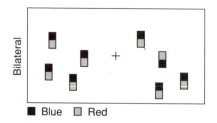
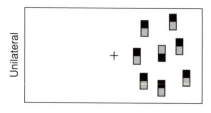

■ Blue □ Red

Figure 6.7   Examples of Bilateral and Unilateral search arrays used by Luck et al. (1994). Reproduced with permission of MIT Press.

are presented to one visual field. However, if the two hemispheres can search their arrays separately, one could expect bilateral arrays to be dealt with faster than arrays restricted to one visual field.

Four split-brain patients were compared with controls and in both cases search times lengthened as the number of items in the array increased. The controls showed a small advantage in the speed with which they located targets in bilateral compared with unilateral arrays. The split-brain patients also showed this effect but it was significantly larger, that is, the split-brain patients dealt with bilateral arrays significantly quicker than controls. If a single attentional resource were being allocated to the task regardless of hemisphere then one would not predict an advantage for bilateral presentation. The observed advantage thus suggests that separate attentional mechanisms were dealing with each half of the array thus enabling a total search of the array to occur more quickly. This is an unusual finding because it is a rare instance of a brain lesion enabling a task to be performed better than by an intact brain (for a similar recent finding see Mangun, Hillyard, Luck, et al., 1994).

While the evidence on attention in split-brain patients remains somewhat complex (see, for example, Corballis, in press) one means of resolving discrepancies is to reconsider the distinction we raised earlier between information about location and that concerning form. In those studies involving information about spatial location there is good evidence for a unified attentional system. Moreover, it is reasonable to suppose that this attentional mechanism is directly related to the processing system that allows inter-hemispheric transfer of location information to direct eye movements. In contrast, studies indicating separate attentional processes have tended to involve the processing of form. From work we considered in chapters 2 and 3 it is known that the perception of form is centred on cortical processes and so it is not surprising that attentional processing at this level is not unified in split-brain subjects.

Dual or Single Consciousness?

The demonstration of separate attentional systems leads us inevitably to consider whether the two hemispheres contain separate conscious entities. This was certainly the view of Sperry who, from his frequent observation of right hemispheres producing superior performance on a range of tasks, found it inconceivable that the right hemisphere was not conscious. However, compelling though they may be, these observations are subjective. In the absence of being able to communicate a state of conscious awareness others, such as Eccles (1965), have argued that the right hemisphere is merely a non-conscious automaton.

Shallice (1988) has attacked the automaton position along the following lines. He notes a study by Zaidel, Zaidel and Sperry (1981) in which NG and LB were asked to carry out Raven's Progressive Matrices separately with the left and right hemispheres. The task is not easy yet in both instances the patients performed similarly with both hemispheres. Considering this result he argues:

> If this level of performance could be obtained unconsciously, it would be really difficult to argue that consciousness is not an epiphenomenon. *Given that it is not* (italics added), it is therefore very likely, if not unequivocally established, that the split-brain right hemisphere is aware.

Shallice's argument thus depends crucially on the assumption that consciousness plays a causal role in cognitive performance. However, this view is not universally accepted (e.g. Velmans, 1991) and the issue of consciousness as a causal entity is far from resolved. Even if we put that issue aside can we use the split-brain data to infer that two separable states of consciousness exist in all of us? First the atypicality problem that mars the interpretation of split-brain data in other domains applies here as well – two conscious entities may be an exception. However, if it were not, it can still be argued that the split-brain data are not relevant because, when the system is intact, consciousness reflects a co-ordination between the two forms of consciousness which we fail to detect. This arises because the hemispheres usually interact in a complementary way. This is not the case in a split-brain patient and it may be this lack of complementarity that underlies their particular manifestation of consciousness.

Summary

Testing of individuals who have undergone commissurotomy or 'split-brain' operations indicate that the two cerebral hemispheres have very different functions. In particular it is well established that the left hemisphere is specialized for language and the right deals with spatial processing. There are, however, some indications that the right hemisphere may possess some ability to comprehend language even though speech production is not possible. However, this remains controversial and it is possible that right hemisphere language in split-brain patients may reflect abnormal development. Split-brain patients can also exhibit alien hand sign which appears to be a higher-order deficit in motor planning. Split-brain patients have provided considerable evidence about the nature of subcortical transfer. Some studies have suggested that information about stimulus form can be transferred, but other studies suggest more limited transfer, such as information about stimulus location and the connotative, emotional aspects of stimuli. The issue of whether each hemisphere has its own attentional system is complex. When attention is applied to lower-level information such as spatial location it would appear that a unified attentional system is at work. However, when attention is directed towards the form of stimuli each hemisphere appears to have its own attentional mechanism.

7

Spoken Language
Impairments

'What regiment is your son with?' a lady was asked. She replied: 'With the 42nd Murderers.'

The above slip of the tongue is taken from Freud's classic work *The Psychopathology of Everyday Life* and in the above instance the woman has mistakenly used the German word Mörder (murderer) instead of the intended word Mörser (mortars). Freud believed that speech errors provided an important window on people's unconscious motivation. This may or may not be true, but what is certain is that the analysis of speech errors has played an important role in trying to understand the nature of speech production. Errors produced by normal people have, for example, shed considerable light on the nature of sentence production (e.g. Levelt, 1993). However, in developing models that deal with more fundamental aspects of language, data from brain damaged subjects has been of prime importance.

Pathological Language

Figure 7.1 shows the well known 'cookie theft' picture (Goodglass and Kaplan, 1972) and given below are three attempts to describe it by

Figure 7.1   The Cookie Theft Picture (Goodglass and Kaplan, 1972). Reproduced with permission.

patients with different forms of **aphasia** – a term used to describe any impairment in the ability to understand or produce language (all taken from Goodglass and Kaplan, 1983).

Patient 1:   'This is a boy and that's a boy an' that's a thing! An this is going off pretty soon. This is a . . . a place that is mostly in [examiner suggests bathroom] No . . . kitchen. An' this is a girl . . . an' that something that they're running an' they've got the water going down here.' (p. 86)

Patient 2:   'Well this is . . . mother is away here working her work out o' here to get her better, but when she's looking, the two boys looking in the other part. One their small tile into her time here. She's working another time because she's getting to. So two boys work together and one is sneakin' around here, making his work an' his further *funnas* his time he had.' (pp. 81–2)

Patient 3:   Cookie jar . . . fall over . . . chair . . . water . . . empty. (p. 76)

Although all three descriptions are difficult to follow they are so for different reasons. Patient 1 produces sentences with a reasonable grammatical structure but has obvious word-finding problems. As a result there are many hesitations and indefinite terms such as 'thing' substituted. Patient 2 speaks reasonably fluently but the content comprises complex sentence structures involving meaningless phrases. In addition it also contains a nonsense word or neologism. Patient 3 has a very different problem in that speech comprises just nouns and verbs with a complete absence of grammatical structure.

Within clinical neuropsychology these patients would be classified as suffering from different aphasic syndromes. Patient 1 would be considered an anomic aphasic, Patient 2 a Wernicke's aphasic, and Patient 3 would be classed as a Broca's aphasic – the latter two terms refer to the nineteenth-century neurologists who first described these disorders and attributed them to specific regions of the left hemisphere known as Wernicke's and Broca's Areas respectively. These three syndromes are part of a broader classification scheme applied to all aphasic disorders (e.g. Benson, 1993). Schemes of this kind are not, however, without their critics and cognitive neurophsychologists, in particular, have argued against the syndrome-based approach to the classification of aphasias. It has been argued that attempts to group patients into distinct syndromes is impossible because of the individual variability and that the only way to proceed is to consider individual cases which manifest specific functional deficits. Proponents of the syndrome-based approach have counter-attacked and we discussed some of these views and those advocating single-case designs in chapter 1. However, the study of aphasia has provided the principal arena for this debate and we will thus consider it again at a later point in this chapter.

In devising this chapter I have decided to side with the cognitive neuropsychological approach rather than one based on different aphasic syndromes. Partly this is because the type of theorizing produced by this approach is more in tune with theories I have discussed elsewhere. However, it is also clear that syndrome concepts may mask important functional differences between patients. It is established, even within the syndrome-based approach, that anomic aphasia may reflect at least two functionally-distinct impairments. Similarly, a category like Broca's aphasia might contain a range of distinct impairments.

A Framework for Understanding Language Impairments

In this and the following sections I will describe how cognitive neuropsychologists have used experimental data to build up a modular account of language function. This account is my attempt to distill the work of a number of eminent cognitive neuropsychologists who have operated primarily within the single-case approach. It might be useful, therefore, to remind yourself of some of the methodological issues surrounding this form of investigation and remind yourself about the concepts of neurological specificity and modularity.

Our account starts with figure 7.2 in which a modular system, or 'functional architecture' for identifying and producing spoken words is shown. The acoustic analysis module is responsible for converting the speech signal of a word into a phonemic code which can then access that word's entry in the auditory input lexicon – this corresponds to a store of information about the sound of each word that we know. From here the meaning of the activated word can become available within the semantic system. You will notice that the arrows are two-way in this route. This acknowledges the ability of information to feed down the system so that higher levels can facilitate lower levels of analysis (e.g. semantic context can aid word identification). Both the auditory input lexicon and the semantic system have links with the phonological output lexicon. This comprises information about how to say all the words that we know and its output goes to a phonemic response buffer. The link between the phonological output lexicon and the phonemic response buffer is also two-way thus enabling the two modules to become interactive in the generation of speech. There is also a direct link from the acoustic analysis system to the buffer via an acoustic to phonological conversion system. This enables us to repeat back nonsense words such as BLIG and SPONE. You will also see that information can flow from the phonemic response buffer back to the acoustic analysis module. This enables phonemic information to be recycled in the system and provides the basis for what is often termed 'inner speech' – the tendency to hear things in our heads when we are reading or thinking. Recycling can also occur, of course, by means of speaking and rerouting this via acoustic analysis.

Pure Word Deafness

Neuropsychological evidence for a separable acoustic analysis module derives principally from pure word deafness. In this disorder the patient is unable to understand spoken words despite being able to read, write and speak normally (Bauer, 1993; Takahashi, Kawamura, Shinotou, et al. 1992; Yaqub, Gascon, Alnosha and Whitaker, 1988). In addition patients with pure word deafness are unable to repeat back words that they cannot understand. This latter deficit gives an important clue about the underlying deficit and suggests that it may be due to some specific problem in perceiving speech-like sounds. Patients' observations confirm this with comments such as 'voices come but not words' and the descrip-

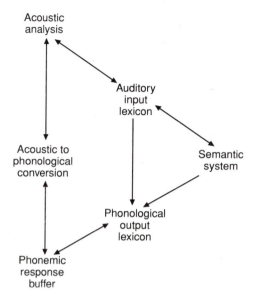

Figure 7.2 A functional architecture for hearing and speaking words. After Ellis and Young (1988).

tion of speech as an 'undifferentiated continuous humming noise without any rhythm' (Klein and Harper, 1956). A perceptual deficit is also suggested by demonstration that pure word deafness is less severe when contextual cues about word identities are provided (e.g. Okada, Hannada, Hattori and Shoyama, 1963) and where lip-reading is allowed (e.g. Auerbach, Allard and Naeser et al., 1982). Comprehension can also be improved by slowing down the rate at which speech is presented (Auerbach et al., 1982) and by the maintenance of a specific context. Okada et al., for example, found that their patient understood questions quite well when they were all on the same topic but then became much worse when the topic changed.

Explanations of the perceptual deficit responsible for pure word deafness have centred on the idea that it involves a deficit in phonemic processing – that is the ability to segment a string of speech sounds into its constituent phonemes. Phonemes are not all equally discriminable from one another. In particular, vowels are easier to discriminate than syllables comprising a single consonant followed by a vowel. The easier discrimination of vowels is attributed to their greater time duration in speech. Vowel durations typically range between 100 and 400 msec whereas consonants preceding vowels have very brief durations of around 40 msec. Accurate speech recognition thus depends critically on the ability to make fine temporal discriminations between acoustic signals that are changing very rapidly.

An influential theory of perception is that both hemispheres have the ability to make auditory discriminations but that only the left hemisphere is capable of the fine discrimination required for efficient phonemic analysis. In experiments using a dichotic procedure – this involves the simultaneous presentation of speech sounds to both ears using headphones – it has been shown that words presented to the right ear (and hence to the left hemisphere) are recognized better than those presented to the left ear. This **right ear advantage** for words is attributed to the left hemisphere's greater ability at making fine discriminations. This is confirmed by experiments showing that no right ear advantage can be found when just vowels are presented (e.g. Shankweiler and Studdert-Kennedy, 1967). Evidence from pure word deafness is consistent with a left hemisphere specialization for fine phonemic processing: The disorder is only associated with left hemisphere lesions and patients have been shown to be capable of discriminating vowels but not syllables (Denes and Semenza, 1975).

The selectivity of pure word deafness is emphasized by the relatively normal performance of these patients on the recognition of environmental sounds and music. Certain 'paralinguistic' aspects of speech also survive. Patients may recognize the identity of a spoken voice and be able to use intonation cues to decide the affective tone of sentence. At this juncture we should also note evidence that impairments in recognizing environmental sounds can occur in the absence of aphasic symptoms. Fujii, Fukatsu and Watabe et al. (1990) report a truck driver who suffered a right hemisphere lesion that produced only a very mild impairment of language. However, when attempting to name familiar environmental sounds he initially did very poorly. This, and other similar cases (see Bauer, 1993), indicate that knowledge about environmental sounds is represented separately from linguistic ability and, its consistent association with right-sided lesion indicates that it is primarily a capability of the right hemisphere.

Pure Word Meaning Deafness

In pure word meaning deafness the patient is unable to understand what a word means even though words can be repeated and written accurately to dictation.[1] Ellis (1984) has revived the early anecdotal

---

[1] For simplicity I have not yet included how the model accounts for spelling, this follows in the next chapter. All we note for the moment is that accurate writing to dictation indicates that a word has been heard correctly.

case of Bramwell (1897) who, when asked 'Do you like to come to Edinburgh?' said she could not understand it until she had written it down and read it. More recently Berndt, Basili and Caramazza (1987) described a patient who had intact repetition of spoken words despite severe comprehension problems. However, the apparent purity of the disorder in Bramwell's case was not present because the patient also had difficulties comprehending written words. Nonetheless the authors believed that the deficit lay beyond the auditory input lexicon because the patient performed normally on an auditory lexical decision task – this involves deciding whether spoken words are, or are not, real words in English and normal performance is assumed to reflect an intact input lexicon. More recently additional cases of this rare disorder have been reported. Schacter, McGlynn, Milberg and Church (1993) describe JP, who developed a severe problem in comprehending spoken words despite a relatively intact ability to repeat words and write to dictation.

Perhaps the clearest case of word meaning deafness is described by Franklin, Turner and Morris (1994). Dr O suffered a stroke which initially left him with a global disturbance of language. However, his condition improved and it became clear that, along with a spelling problem, Dr O had very marked problems with comprehending spoken words. On one test Dr O had to decide whether two words shared the same meaning or not. When presented in written form his performance was perfect but when spoken, many errors occurred. Dr O was also affected by **imageability** in that he found abstract words (e.g. gist, justice) more difficult to define than words that readily evoke a mental image (e.g. door, bicycle) – this is one of many instances where imageability has a significant influence on the pattern of an impairment. We will consider the underlying nature of imagery effects more in the next chapter.

A further test explored Dr O's auditory lexical decision ability by asking him to discriminate between real words and nonwords that differed from real words by just one phoneme. His accuracy was 94 per cent. This suggests that there is an internal representation of each known word but, given the lack of comprehension, this must be distinct from the semantic system – hence an auditory input lexicon. Preservation of this module can also be implicated in preserved repetition and writing to dictation. The preserved comprehension shown with written material also indicates that the semantic system is intact and that the deficit in word meaning deafness lies in the connection between the auditory input lexicon and the semantic system.

A key feature of pure word meaning deafness is intact repetition. Dr O was asked to repeat and define words and, as before, he was less able to comprehend words of low rather than high imagery. However, he had little difficulty repeating both types of words. Good examples of repetition without comprehension are:

Slow: 'slow, slow, slow, I know what it is but I can't get it, slow, slow – you'll have to write it down for me' [word is written down] 'Oh slow, well slow is the opposite of fast.'

Soul: 'soul, soul, soul, I don't know what it is – I should that' [word is written down] 'Oh soul, it's a religious concept, is the soul.' (p. 1161)

Studies of word meaning deafness thus show that it is possible to have a marked inability to understand spoken words while having preserved ability to comprehend written words. An important characterisitic of these cases is their preserved ability on auditory lexical decision. This provides a strong indication of a separable auditory input lexicon. Moreover, demonstrations of intact repetition of spoken words in the absence of comprehension indicates that there are no problems in hearing words accurately.

Auditory Phonological Agnosia

Earlier we argued that logic dictated the existence of a direct route between the acoustic analysis module and the phonemic output buffer because, without an arrangement like this, it would not be possible to repeat unfamiliar words and nonwords. Neuropsychological support for this route comes from cases of auditory phonological agnosia. Beauvois, Dérousné, and Bastard (1980) report JL who presented an unusual and very specific language problem. He was able to read aloud well and there was no problem with his writing. He did, however, complain that he had difficulty with new words such as scientific terms and place names. When tested it was found that JL had no problem repeating familiar words, but his ability to repeat nonwords was extremely poor. Since he could repeat real words normally JL cannot be word deaf. Instead it appears that he has lost the specific ability to translate acoustic inputs into speech – this being the only potential means of repeating nonwords. For JL, therefore, the only route for repetition is via the auditory input lexicon.

Anomia

Anomia, as illustrated by Patient 1, is a condition in which the patient has problems finding the right word and analysis of this disorder has been the primary basis for proposing an auditory output lexicon. TOB, a man with a progressive language disorder, had very marked anomic problems and would often resort to quite elaborate circumlocutions in order to communicate. Thus a 'doll' would be described as a 'solid representative of a baby'. His speech also had an empty feel to it and there was an overreliance on stock phrases such as 'take on board' and 'all the rest of it' as a means of covering up word-finding problems. Here TOB explains his word-finding problems:

> No there is one or two serious points I can draw your attention to. You see, again, having been so much into industry and all the rest of it the complete integration that is necessary with education and all the rest of it is that I have always known different companies, their names and what have you. This is the one serious problem that I now cannot recall. I can still teach students but I cannot now draw their attention to specific companies where I have been and already had discussions with respect to these functions to the basic functions that I want them to take on board. (Parkin, 1993a, p. 202)

Benson (1979) made a fundamental distinction between semantic anomia and word selection anomia. In semantic anomia the patient has problems finding words because of a semantic disturbance. On the assumption that there is a single semantic system, a patient with this disorder should have problems finding words under any circumstance. A good example of this is provided by KE (Hillis, Rapp, Romani and Caramazza, 1990) who performed poorly on a wide range of word-finding tasks involving reading, word/picture matching, spoken comprehension and naming from tactile exploration. On all these tasks he tended to make semantic errors, substituting a word of similar meaning for the correct word. Analyses of these errors indicated a strong interdependence in that failure to retrieve a word on one task tended to predict retrieval failure for that word on other tasks (for an additional example of anomia arising from a semantic impairment see case JCU reported by Howard and Orchard-Lisle, 1984).

KE's anomia appears to arise from a semantic impairment in which a defective semantic code attempts to specify a word in the auditory output lexicon. In word-finding anomia the semantic input appears intact and the defect lies within the auditory output lexicon itself. A deficit of this kind thus requires evidence that the semantic system is intact. A recent instance of this is provided by a psychologist called Mark Ashcraft who suffered a transient ischemic attack which gave rise to a temporary linguistic disturbance. Later, Ashcraft (1993) wrote about his experience:

> I turned on the computer on the table opposite my desk. The message on the screen indicated that I was still logged on .... As I positioned my hands at the keyboard, I realized that I could not remember the command to log off – the command of course, is simply logoff, a command I issue with great regularity. I stared at the screen for a few moments, still could not remember the command, and at that point I realized something unusual was happening. (pp. 50–1)

This, and similar events, all occurred even though Ashcraft could understand what people were saying to him.

Although of great interest, transient neurological disorders are hard to study and firmer evidence for word selection anomia comes from studies of permanent disorders. A clear example is RGB described by Caramazza and Hillis (1990a). When asked to name things he made many semantic errors such as 'celery' → 'lettuce' and approximate answers, for example, 'pajamas' → 'what we wear at night'. However, when RGB was asked to define written or spoken words he performed extremely well. Thus, although naming a picture of a volcano as 'Hawaii' he defined the word volcano as follows: 'looks like a mountain but instead of rocks it has lava'. Similarly a 'quill' was named as 'feather' but defined as 'they're long and have a point . . . animals, porcupines have them'.

An interesting feature of anomia is that the loss of vocabulary is systematic. TOB's loss of words was directly related to their frequency of use in the language: the less frequent the word the more likely it was to be lost. This suggests that word frequency is a salient feature in the representation of words. However, Hirsh and Ellis (1994) point out that word frequency is often confounded with another factor: age of acquisition – more frequent words tend to be acquired earlier in life. They conducted a study on their anomic patient and found that the latter factor was the primary determinant of his word-finding problems. Hirsh and Funnell (in press) again demonstrated that age of acquisition was a primary determinant of word-finding problems but also showed that the familiarity of the concept represented by the word was also an important factor.

While it remains that word frequency may be an important factor in determining the extent of anomia the above studies suggest a more complex picture. This is an important issue because the explanation of word frequency effects has been a central task in modelling word recognition (e.g. Monsell, 1991). It is thus important to understand the extent to which correlates of word frequency also contribute to word recognition and to incorporate these factors into any resultant model.

Anomia for Proper versus Common Nouns

In everyday life we tend to forget the names of people far more frequently than the names of other things. This suggests that there may well be a difference between our representation of proper nouns and common nouns. Neuropsychological investigations of anomia support this idea. MP (Hittmair-Delazer, Denes, Semenza and Mantovan, 1994) had only a mild impairment in producing common nouns on a naming task. However, he had markedly poor memory for people's names despite clear evidence that he knew who those people were. The study illustrated that MP's anomia arose at the word selection level because MP had intact semantic knowledge of people he could not name. Shown Kevin Costner, for example, he mentioned 'Dances with Wolves' but could not retrieve his name. As a salesman he had many clients but, despite being able to say in detail what he had sold them, he could not provide their names. Interestingly, other cases of proper name anomia also appear to occur at the word selection phase (e.g. Carney and Temple, 1993; Luchelli and De Renzi 1992; Semenza and Zettin, 1989).

The above data suggest that proper names have a distinctive representation but to be sure of this a parallel preservation of proper nouns relative to common nouns needs to be shown. An early report by McKenna and Warrington (1980) describes a patient in which there was a selective preservation of geographic names. In part of the study the patient was shown items from different categories and asked to name them. Here, only countries (illustrated by map outlines) and parts of the body showed preservation. However, when the task was matching a spoken name to a picture he performed well across all five categories chosen. This would suggest a problem with word selection rather than comprehension. More recent studies have also indicated the relative preservation of proper nouns (e.g. McNeil, Cippolotti and Warrington, 1994; Semenza and Sgarmella, 1993).

Why should proper nouns be represented differently to common nouns? One suggestion is that proper nouns are 'referring expressions' (e.g. Kripke, 1980) which in themselves are devoid of meaning. The role of proper nouns is to identify individuals by acting as pointers to the representation of an individual in memory. This contrasts with common nouns which specify only types and do not refer to individuals. As such common nouns map directly onto semantics. It is for this reason, perhaps, that we observe the 'Baker – baker paradox' – the demonstration that Baker is harder to recall when presented as a name than as an occupation (e.g. Cohen and Faulkner, 1986).

Neologistic Jargonaphasia

In the introduction we encountered Patient 2 whose speech was fluent but meaningless and contained neologisms. This was termed Wernicke's aphasia but within cognitive neuropsychology it is now common to describe this disorder as neologistic jargonaphasia.

Ellis, Miller and Sin (1983) described the case of RD. He was asked to describe a picture and this is an extract of his response (intended words are shown in parentheses):

> A *bun, bun* (BULL) ... a *buk* (BULL) is *cherching* (CHASING) a boy or *skert (SCOUT) is by a bone poe* (POST) of pine. A ... post ... *pone* POST) WITH A, ER, *tone toe* (LINE?) WITH *woshingt* (WASHING) HANG-ING ON INCLUDING HIS SOCKS *saiz*(?). A ... A *nek* (TENT) IS BY THE WASHING. A B-BOY IS *sw'ing* (SWINGING) ON THE BANK WITH HIS HAND (FEET) IN THE *stringt* (STREAM). A TABLE WITH *orstrum* (SAUCEPAN?) AND ... I DON'T KNOW ... AND A THREE-LEGGED *stroe* (STOOL) AND A *strane* (PAIL) – TABLE, TABLE ... NEAR THE WATER. A ER *trowlvot* (TRIVET), THREELEGGED ER ER MEANS FOR HANGING A *tong, tong* (PAN?) ON THE *fiyest* (FIRE) WHICH IS BLOWED BY A BOY-BOY. A BOY *skrut* (SCOUT) IS UP A TREE AND LOOKING AT ... THROUGH ... *hone* (?) GLASSES. A MAN IS KNOCKING A PAPER ... PAPER WITH A *notist* (NOTICE) BY THE ER T-TENT, TENT ER *tet* (TENT) ER TENT.

How can neologistic jargonaphasia be expained? RD had a good understanding of written words being able, for example, to group words into meaningful pairs (e.g. exhaustion – fatigue) and classify sentences as sensible or not. A similar pattern is reported for the patient JS (Caramazza, Berndt and Basili, 1983) who could categorize word and pictures correctly despite producing high levels of neologisms in speech. Results such as these rule out some form of general semantic impairment. Another possibility might be an articulation problem but this seems unlikely. Both RD and JS demonstrated word frequency effects in that they were much more likely to produce a neologism when the word they were searching for was low frequency. This effect had nothing to do with articulation because they could retrieve longer high-frequency words such as 'cigarette' but be unable to produce simpler less common words like 'frog'.

Ellis et al. noted that RD's neoglisms most commonly occurred when he was searching for a **content word** – these are words that convey meaning (i.e. nouns, verbs, adjectives). In contrast it appeared that RD made few neologisitic substitutions when function words were required – function words are articles, conjunctions etc. (e.g. a, the, and, but, of) which play essential grammatical roles but have no inherent meaning in themselves. This might suggest that the deficit underlying neologistic jargonaphasia has some specific involvement with the generation of content words. However, function words tend to be very common so the selective problem with content words could just be a word frequency effect. Ellis et al. subsequently confirmed this by showing that RD had equal degrees of reading difficulty for content and function words when matched for frequency.

A frequent observation in neologistic jargonaphasics is that they are often unaware that they are producing nonsense words. Ellis and Young (1988) suggest that this is because patients like RD may have an additional word deafness problem – RD could only understand written material – which meant that he was unable to comprehend spoken material and thus detect neologisms. On this basis neologistic jargona-phasia would be a form of word selection anomia exaggerated by a failure to monitor the lexical status of words they produced – something that has been termed 'phonological derailment'.

While the above account may suffice for RD it cannot explain other instances of neologistic jargonaphasia. AS, reported by Maher, Rothi and Heilman (1994) had preserved auditory comprehension of words. He was able to follow conversations, obey commands and answer questions appropriately. Yet when asked to describe the cookie theft picture he said: 'on the left hand side, the oldest, fernest is the boy who is standing up on the char stealing a back of ockebells . . .' (p. 408) and so on.

Further experiments showed that he recognized more of his errors when listening to his own voice than when speaking, and that he noticed even more errors when someone else was speaking. Moreover, he experienced disruption when auditory feedback from his own voice was delayed – thus suggesting that he was experiencing auditory feedback. Maher et al. note that no single account is capable of explaining all of the error patterns generated by AS. They suggest that an attentional factor may have a significant role but that, in addition, a more abstract concept of **denial** is needed to explain failure in detecting neologisms.

Before moving on we should also note another form of jargon aphasia known as **semantic jargon**. EF (Kinsbourne and Warrington, 1963a) produced the following utterance: 'Tape recording and automatic wind-ing voice and the very very recording the typewriting and memorandum

and tensioning and dialling to winding and balancing very very good.'
Few cases of this have been investigated and the nature of the underlying
deficit is not clear. Ellis and Young (1988) have, however, suggested that
it may reflect an inability to set up an appropriate input into the linguistic
processes, i.e. there is some deficit in the high-level process which plans
the content of sentences at a prelinguistic level.

How Many Routes for Word Repetition? – Deep Dysphasia

The model shown in figure 7.2 allows three ways for a spoken word to
be repeated. The first of these involves the acoustic to phonological
conversion system and this mechanism applies equally to words and
nonwords. A second route, via the semantic system, involves the
activation of meaning and the specification of pronunciation in the
phonological output lexicon. The third route, which we will term the
direct route, proposes a direct link between auditory input lexicon and
phonological output lexicon – with this route, therefore, pronunciation
is achieved lexically without the activation of meaning.

   Evidence for the third route comes from patients such as GE (Patterson, 1986). This aphasic patient could not speak, repeat, read aloud,
name objects, write the names of objects or write spontaneously.
Remarkably, however, he could write to dictation quite impressively.
Most importantly he was as good at spelling irregular words correctly
(e.g. PINT see chapter 1 and next chapter) as he was regular words (e.g.
LINE). This finding immediately indicates that GE is relying on specific
lexical information when writing, otherwise he would have no way of
knowing the irregular spelling patterns. However, he could be accessing
the correct spelling via the semantic system and its connections with
word-specific representations of spelling (see next chapter). This seems
unlikely. Patterson required GE to match words with pictures, for
concrete (high imagery) he was 80 per cent accurate, but for abstract
(low imagery) words he was 60 per cent accurate. Nonetheless his ability
to spell these words was 92 per cent and 88 per cent respectively. GE is
thus able to spell words he does not know the meaning of and thus
cannot be using the semantic route. This could reflect a direct route
between the auditory input lexicon and the mechanisms governing
spelling but, given other evidence implicating the phonological output
lexicon in spelling, it is more parsimonious to assume that this is the
case here (see p. 185).

   The existence of these three routes is relevant to the interpretation of
deep dysphasia. This is a rare form of aphasia characterized by both the
production of semantic errors when repeating real words and an inability

to repeat nonwords. Repetition is also more difficult for abstract words than concrete words. First, to account for the inability to repeat nonwords one must assume that the acoustic to phonological conversion system is inoperative. To account for semantic errors it has been suggested that there is a deficit in the direct route as well which requires all repetition to go via the semantic system. This reliance on the semantic system also accounts for imageability effects. The reason why semantic errors should appear is not so clear. Katz and Goodglass (1990), for example, have suggested that failure of the semantic route is due to a deficit in retaining the phonological form of the word during the semantic access process (for a recent discussion of deep dysphasia and an alternative account see Martin and Saffran, 1992).

The evidence we have considered so far provides the basis for the model outlined in figure 7.2. As you will have seen, the evidence has been primarily concerned with deficits manifest at the level of producing single words so the model itself must be considered limited in that respect. There is of course much more to explain in language, in particular the manner in which we produce and comprehend sentences. This topic has received much less attention, within cognitive neuropsychology, because of its undoubted complexity and the difficulties of dissecting out clear dissociations. Nonetheless one area, the debate over 'agrammatism' has led neuropsychologists to consider sentence production.

Broca's Aphasia and the Agrammatism Debate

From the example we saw earlier (Patient 3), Broca's aphasia appears to be a disorder in which speech lacks essential grammatical components. This had led some to describe this disorder as essentially one of agrammatism in which the patient is reduced to short utterances which tend to lack function words (e.g. articles and prepositions) and **bound morphemes or inflections** (e.g. -s, -ed, -ing). Luria (1970) gives this example of an agrammatic patient recounting a recent film he has seen.

> Odessa! a swindler! down there ... to study ... the sea (gesture of diving) ... into ... a diver! Armenia ... a ship ... went ... oh! Batum a girl ... ah! Policeman ... ah ... I know! ... cashier! ... money ... ah! ... cigarettes ... I know ... this guy.

With additional recovery the speech of these patients may become telegraphic in that the structure resembles the economical form of expression used in telegrams: 'Joan and I ... coffee' (Goodglass, 1993).

Agrammatism was first studied at the beginning of this century in Germany. These studies were based on the single-case approach, but the first modern attempts at investigating agrammatism used group studies – the idea being that there was a reliable syndrome of agrammatism into which patients could be placed. These studies have been reviewed by, among others, Howard (1985) and Ellis and Young (1988), thus only a brief summary will be given here.

Although the omission of inflections is a predominant feature of agrammatism not all inflections are equally likely to be omitted. The inflection -s, for example, is much more likely to be omitted when it serves as a possessive (e.g. Al's) than when it indicates a plural. Similarly the present participle -*ing* may be omitted less than the past participle -*ed* and the plural -s left out more often when it does not form a syllable (e.g. goats) than when it does (e.g. horses). Sentence position also seems important, with function words being omitted more often from the beginning of sentences and when they were unstressed. Content word omissions also occur, particularly for verbs that specify actions.

Agrammatic patients also have difficulty with phrases such as 'large white house' or 'give friend dollar'. These sequences are perfectly good telegraphic speech and do not require any function words or inflections for enhanced comprehension. Thus some additional deficit must be present. Other aspects of speech comprehension are also affected although these might be less noticeable because patients can use various cues to determine the meaning of what is said to them, even though their linguistic comprehension may be compromised. Thus they can understand sentences such as 'The bicycle that the boy is holding is broken' because this can be comprehended just from the order of the content words (bicycle . . . boy . . . hold . . . broke). When an analysis of this kind does not allow an obvious interpretation, for example, 'the man that the woman is hugging is happy' – (man . . . woman . . . hugging . . . happy) – comprehension is badly affected.

Group investigations of agrammatism led to an attempt at specifying a single underlying deficit responsible for the disorder. Caramazza and Zurif (1976), for example, argued that agrammatism arose from damage to a single language processing mechanism that affects both production and comprehension of speech. These, and other attempts to specify a single deficit (e.g. Kean, 1985) depend on one crucial assumption – that all patients classified as agrammatic are suffering from the same disorder. If it were the case that averaging in group studies masked important individual differences between patients, then the notion of a single deficit explaining all patients' symptoms would be invalid.

Badecker and Caramazza (1985) published an influential and highly controversial critique of aphasia research in which they argued that the idea of agrammatism as a specific neuropsychological deficit was fundamentally flawed, and that patients defined as agrammatic suffered from a range of distinct primary deficits that could vary in their extent within individuals (see also Howard, 1985). Thus although groups of 'agrammatic' patients might, on average, appear to have the same characteristics, a more refined analysis would show that there were important qualitative variations across patients.

To illustrate their point Badecker and Caramazza took some examples of agrammatic speech from a paper by Saffran, Schwartz and Marin (1980). Five patients were each asked to describe a picture in which a girl is presenting flowers to a woman in a classroom:

(a) The young . . . the girl . . . the . . . little girl is . . . the flower.
(b) The girl is flower the woman.
(c) The girl is . . . going to flowers.
(d) The girl is giving . . . giving the teacher . . . giving it teacher.
(e) The girl is . . . is roses. The girl is rosin'.

The authors point out that although omission of function words and inflections does characterize the utterances there are important additional differences. Thus (b) appears to have no main verb, (c) appears to be semantically ill-formed, and in (e) the verb is replaced by a nominal stem. Badecker and Caramazza conclude that facts such as these suggest that agrammatism is not just a problem with producing function words and inflections. Additonal independent deficits for each individual must also be specified in order to explain the observations fully.

Following up this issue Miceli, Silveri, Romani, and Caramazza (1989) made a detailed analysis of the speech output of 20 aphasic patients considered to be agrammatic. Their argument was that, if agrammatism had a single underlying cause, there should be some kind of consistency in the pattern of errors shown across the group. Instead the authors found many extreme variations. One patient, for example, omitted 83 per cent of prepositions but only 23 per cent of definite articles whereas another had scores of 19 per cent and 64 per cent for the same categories. Analysis of the patients' production difficulties with inflections also showed considerable variation. It was also shown that the omission of main verbs from sentences varied greatly across the patients.

For some the arguments against agrammatism as a theoretical entity, and indeed the idea that data from any group of patients cannot be meaningfully combined, is won. Thus Caramazza (1988) writes: 'Surely the time has come to put an end to vague claims about clinical categories of aphasia. . . . When is enough, enough? Why is it still possible to publish papers which purport to make theoretically coherent claims about patient categories such as. . . . Broca's aphasia?'

The answer to Caramazza's final point is that many researchers in the aphasia field and beyond still value the syndrome concept and the idea of group studies. We have been over some of the arguments favouring this position in chapter 1 so here I will restrict us to the continuing debate about agrammatism. Caplan (1986) argues that far more of agrammatic speech can be accounted for if attempts are made to use linguistic and psycholinguistic theory to interpret the speech of agrammatic aphasics (see also Caplan, 1992). In addition, he argues that much of the variation emphasized by Caramazza and Badecker could be due to variations in severity and interactions with other language impairments – verb selection, for example, might be a deficit that is sometimes associated with agrammatism. Also Caplan suggests that differences in agrammatic speech can reflect patients' varying adaptive strategies to their disorders.

Another supporter of agrammatism is Grodzinsky (1984, 1990, 1991) who has taken particular issue with the data presented by Miceli et al. His primary argument is that agrammatism has never been defined in quantitative terms. Grodzinsky has developed his own account of agrammatism based on Chomsky's government and binding (GB) theory of grammar (Chomsky, 1981). In GB theory grammar is organized on a series of levels. The lexicon comprises information about the meaning and phonological form of all known words. At the D-structure level sentences exist in their basic form which are then transformed by a move-alpha component into an S-structure which corresponds to a spoken utterance taking a particular grammatical form. Thus in the sentence 'John was hit by Bill' the items would be selected from the lexicon and placed in the D-structure as 'Bill hit John' then by move-alpha rules a passive might be created as the spoken output. Within this system the lexical items have further specifications in which distinctions are made between lexical components – nouns, verbs, adjectives, and non-lexical components – function words and inflections. Grodinsky's account is that agrammatic patients cannot identify non-lexical components and that this affects both their ability to produce and comprehend certain types of sentences.

Initially Grodzinky's theory was a parallelistic one in that it attempted to account for the co-occurrence of production and comprehension problems in agrammatic aphasics via a single underlying deficit. However recent evidence has led to this position being untenable (see Grodzinsky, 1990, p. 107). Caramazza and Hillis (1989), for example, describe ML whose language comprehension was found to be within normal limits. However, when asked to describe the 'cookie theft picture': 'Mother washing sink . . . water flowing floor . . . running water . . . dishes, slopping . . . cookie jar . . . stealing cookies . . . toppling stool.' This pattern of impaired production with spared comprehension has also been reported by Kolk, Van Grunsven and Keyser (1985); Berndt (1987) and Druks and Marshall (1991).

Returning to Miceli et al.'s experiment, Grodzinsky notes that the defective S-structure theory, like other accounts of agrammatism, makes no predictions as to the rate at which omissions and substitutions of various types will occur. As a result, Miceli et al.'s attempt to use variations in the relative frequencies of different types of errors is misleading. Grodzinsky also notes that Miceli et al.'s data show clearly that every patient omitted and substituted words in their speech and that these errors were restricted to particular grammatical types. He argues that it is the similarities between the patients that should be emphasized rather than the differences because the latter could originate from variations in severity, from factors such as the relation between the properties of the words involved in the errors and the words themselves. On this basis only very fine grained analyses of agrammatic speech could reveal whether or not agrammatic patients shared some fundamental deficit. However, these analyses need to be specified in strong theoretical terms so as to avoid potential criticisms that awkward differences are being explained away in terms of poorly-specified additional deficits. Grodzinsky thus proposes that the idea of agrammaticism remains a useful one while acknowledging that other factors can colour and complicate interpretation of agrammatic responses.

The debate over agrammatism is obviously not over. This is perhaps unsurprising given the entrenched positions that still exist concerning the more general issue of single-case versus group-based designs (see chapter 1). Caramazza's plea seems largely unheeded. Journals are still publishing papers which attempt to model agrammatism as a syntactic disorder (e.g. Mauner, Fromkin and Cornell, 1993) and recent texts on aphasia contain accounts of agrammatism as a specific theoretical entity (Goodglass, 1993). Nonetheless it remains to be seen whether a theory of agrammatism can be produced which overcomes the inter-patient variability at the heart of Badecker and Caramazza's argument. At present this seems a long way off. There are already, for example, a number of studies arguing against Grodzinsky's theory of agrammatism (e.g. Badecker, Nathan and Caramazza, 1991; Druks and Marshall, 1991). However, other attempts at a general theory of agrammatism derived from Grodzinsky are being proposed (e.g. Hickok, Zurif and Canesco-Gonzalez, 1993).

Prosody

An important property of language is that the same sequence of words can have different meanings depending on the way it is said. Consider the sentence 'You're not going': with a falling intonation at the end it is a command whereas a rising intonation turns it into a question. Intonation is one aspect of prosody and other aspects involve **stress** patterns on syllables, **pauses**, and **affective prosody**. In the latter case a sentence like 'Come over here' could be a command or an enticement depending on how it is said.

Initial studies identified selective problems in dealing with affective prosody and, contrary to all the language impairments we have considered so far, these deficits were associated with damage to the right hemisphere. Heilman, Scholes and Watson (1975) found that right hemisphere patients performed reasonably well at understanding the content of sentences but could not tell the difference between happy and sad tones of voice. This contrasts nicely with the case of pure word deafness we considered above. Here a patient with a left hemisphere lesion could not understand the words spoken to him but could judge affective tone.

Tucker, Watson and Heilman (1977) demonstrated that right hemisphere lesions were associated with deficits in the comprehension and production of affective prosody. This might suggest a common mechanism underlying both abilities, but further work, concentrating on the characteristics of individual cases, has suggested that there may be dissociations. Notably, a study of ten patients by Ross (1981) presented dissociations between the production and comprehension of prosody.

Weintraub, Mesulam and Kramer (1981) investigated the effects of right hemisphere damage on the ability to distinguish between non-emotional **propositional** prosody (e.g. statements, commands and questions). Patients performed far worse than controls and this led to the view that the right hemisphere mediated all aspects of prosody. However, this conclusion lacked evidence from comparing right with left hemisphere damage. This was done in a subsequent study by Heilman, Bowers, Speedie and Coslett (1984) and it was found that right hemisphere damage particularly impaired affective prosody but that both patient groups were equally impaired at comprehending non-emotional prosody. In a further study Emmorey (1987) required brain damaged subjects to distinguish between noun phrases (green house) and compound nouns (greenhouse). This requires an ability to detect different patterns of stress and it was found left hemisphere damage was associated with poorest performance. Following on from this Hird and Kirsner

(1993) showed that right hemisphere patients employed proper use of duration differences to distinguish between compound nouns and noun phrases.

If affective and propositional prosody are lateralized differently then one should expect to find dissociations between these abilities. Heilman et al. asked subjects to listen to speech that had been made unintelligible but had preserved tone and intonation patterns. In one condition they had to decide whether an utterance was a statement, command, or question and in a further condition decide whether utterances were happy, sad or angry. A range of impairment was found and, commenting on these results, Ellis and Young (1988) note that some patients found emotional prosody more difficult whereas others found non-emotional prosody more difficult – one must note, however, that no patient was observed showing difficulty with only one form of prosody.

The above results suggest that there is a dissociation between the processes governing affective and propositional prosody. Furthermore, affective prosody itself dissociates into separable production and comprehension disorders. As for the underlying mechanisms affected not a great deal is known. Bowers, Coslett, Bauer, et al. (1987) have suggested that right hemisphere damage may lead patients to be more distracted by the semantic content of utterances and thus pay less attention to the intonation patterns. To test this they examined the comprehension of emotional prosody using sentences that were either appropriately or inappropriately intoned. Thus subjects might hear the sentence 'all puppies are dead' said in either a sad or a happy voice. Right hemisphere patients made more errors with inappropriate sentences, whereas patients with left hemisphere lesions were not affected by making the semantic content inappropriate. This provides some support for the distraction theory but it cannot be the complete explanation. In the same study it was shown that the right hemisphere patients continued to show a deficit in understanding affective prosody even when the speech was made unintelligible. This suggests that the right hemisphere contains some more basic representation of affective tones of voice which may interact with higher levels of language processing.

At present our understanding of prosodic deficits does not go much beyond identifying dissociations. It should be hoped that future research into prosodic deficits might become more linked to theories of prosody in normal subjects (e.g. Ladd and Cutler, 1983). Partly this has reflected the inability to analyse dysprosodic speech in sufficient detail. However, this situation no longer exists (e.g. Hird and Kirsner, 1993) and a more fruitful interaction between normal theory and neuropsychological observation should be possible.

Deficits in Auditory Verbal Short-term Memory

In chapter 1 we briefly considered the working memory model put forward by Baddeley and Hitch (1977) and subsequently developed by Baddeley (1990). A key feature of this model was that STS had two slave systems, an articulatory loop and a visuo-spatial scratch pad. The latter is thought to be specialized for the storage of spatially represented information but our interest centres on the articulatory loop.

Warrington and Shallice (1969) reported the case of KF, a young man who suffered a closed-head injury after falling off his motor bike. KF developed a number of deficits as a result of his brain damage but we shall concentrate on how this injury affected his memory span. In a typical memory span experiment subjects hear a sequence of digits and have to repeat them back in the same order as they heard them. A normal person has a span of 7 plus or minus 2 but KF's span was only 1! At this point you might expect that KF would have a poor memory overall but this was not the case. On a test of paired associate learning, for example, his performance was comparable to normals.

Since this report a number of patients have been reported who appear to have a selective deficit in **auditory verbal short-term memory.** Baddeley (1990) has argued that this deficit is best interpreted as an impairment of the articulatory loop. This reasoning is based on various lines of experimental evidence indicating that verbal span tasks make specific use of a articulatory coding system and that performance on these tasks declines when use of this system is impeded. One example is the well known **word length effect** in which memory span is higher for words with a shorter spoken duration even when syllable length is controlled for. However, if this comparison is made using a task in which subjects are required to recite 'the' repeatedly as they try to remember the words, the word length effect disappears – a finding attributed to the articulatory task clogging up the articulatory loop (Baddeley, Thomson and Buchanan, 1975).

Experiments have then been carried out on patients with defective memory span in order to establish the role of the articulatory loop in normal cognition. One such patient is PV (Vallar and Baddeley, 1984; 1987). PV was asked to classify as true or false simple sentences such as *Plants grow in gardens,* verbose simple sentences, *There is no doubt that champagne is something that can certainly be bought in shops,* and complex sentences, such as *It is fortunate that most rivers are able to be crossed by bridges that are strong enough for cars.* Whether tested for auditory or written comprehension PV had no difficulty with the simpler sentences but she performed close to chance when trying to classify the complex sentences. The data from patient PV are therefore consistent with the data from articulatory suppression experiments on normal subjects and suggest that articulatory encoding may only be important when dealing with more complex sentences in which the memory load is high. It is also important to note that PV's comprehension difficulties were not worsened by articulatory suppression – a finding one would expect in some one without an articulatory loop.

Vallar and Baddeley's interpretation of PV's performance has, however, been questioned by Howard and Butterworth (1989). Their point is that the co-occurrence of a comprehension deficit and impaired memory span does not, of necessity, mean that the latter deficit underlies the former. Brain lesions rarely have an isolated effect on mental processes and it could be that PV's two problems have independent causes. Howard and Butterworth also claim that defective memory span cannot be the basis of comprehension deficits because of a patient known as RE (Butterworth et al., 1986). This patient had a memory span deficit similar to PV but no comprehension difficulties.

Howard and Butterworth also suggest that the arguments for the involvement of the articulatory loop in comprehension are not motivated by any independently derived theory as to what role phonological storage plays in comprehension. As a result the claim that phonological storage is essential to comprehension arises only because evidence of defective memory span is associated with comprehension difficulties. Vallar and Baddeley (1989) produce various counter-arguments including, for example, pointing out that RE had her memory span deficit from birth. Vallar and Baddeley argue that only acquired deficits shed light on the organization of mental processes because, in developmental disorders, the whole basis of mental processes may be developed atypically.

Vallar and Baddeley do not, however, provide any additional discussion as to how phonological storage might be relevant to comprehension. This issue is addressed in a study by Waters, Caplan and Hildebrandt (1991) in which the comprehension abilities of another patient with severely reduced memory span, BO, were investigated. BO was given a wide range of sentences to comprehend and generally her performance was excellent. However, some difficulties were observed. She did, for example, have more difficulty understanding a sentence such as *Patrick said that Joe kicked Eddie* than a syntactically comparable one using animal names rather than proper nouns, *The monkey that kissed the elephant scratched the frog*. On the basis of these findings Waters et al. suggest that deficit affects 'post interpretive processes' which can be defined as elements of comprehension that occur once the basic meaning of an utterance has been encoded. Thus, without the help of phonological coding, holding proper nouns in memory might be more difficult than holding real nouns because the former have a less elaborate representation in memory.

Recently the articulatory loop model has been developed to involve two components: a phonological store and an articulatory store. Thus the former might be employed when judging whether two letters rhyme or not and the latter for storing articulatory information. This distinction has been motivated by experimental work (see Baddeley, 1990; Vallar and Papagno, 1995) and has recently been supported by PET scanning studies showing that tasks addressing the two types of store give rise to different patterns of cortical activation (Perani, Bressi and Cappa, 1993).

Summary

The study of spoken language impairments has enabled some progress in understanding the modular organization of linguistic processes. Pure word deafness appears to arise from defective auditory analysis which prevents access to an auditory input lexicon. Identification of the latter is based on the phenomenon of pure word meaning deafness in which words can be written accurately to dictation but not understood and where performance on an auditory lexical decision task is normal. Auditory phonological agnosia, in which only real words can be repeated, provides evidence for a direct link between acoustic analysis and speech output. In anomia the patient appears to have lost specific entries in the speech output lexicon. The deficit may reflect disorganization of semantic memory or loss of phonological output. Anomia is determined by a number of factors including word frequency and the age at which a word is acquired. There is also evidence from anomia that proper nouns may be represented differently. Neologistic jargonaphasia appears to be a form of 'phonological derailment' in which, for some reason, the subject fails to monitor the accuracy of their speech output. Deep dysphasia involves the ability to repeat real words but not nonwords. However, these patients sometimes make semantic paraphasias. This suggests that they are responding via a semantic route rather than the proposed route going directly from the auditory input lexicon to the speech output lexicon.

Agrammatism refers to the idea that patients with Broca's aphasia can be characterized as suffering from a common problem involving the construction of syntax within speech. This is a controversial area in which some have argued that no generalization across individual cases of agrammatic speech is possible. Selective deficits in dealing with prosody have also been demonstrated. Damage to the left hemisphere appears to affect non-emotional prosody (e.g. pauses emphasizing word boundaries) whereas right hemisphere damage impairs the ability to understand emotional prosodic cues. Selective deficits in auditory verbal short-term memory have now been identified and indicate that this form of memory is implicated in certain more complex aspects of comprehension.

8

Reading and Writing Disorders

Dearest creature in creation
Studying English pronunciation,
I will teach you in my verse
Sounds like corpse, corps, horse, and worse.
I will keep you, Susy, busy,
Make your head with heat go dizzy;
Tear in eye your dress you'll tear.
So shall I! Oh hear my prayer:
Pray, console your loving poet,
Make my coat look new, dear, sew it.
Just compare heart, beard, and heard,
Dies and diet, lord and word.
Sword and sward, retain and Britain.

The above is part of a poem written by a Dutchman, G. N. Trenite, in which he expresses his frustration at the inconsistency of English spelling. Reading the poem makes you aware of the complex process underlying reading. How do we, for example, allocate three successively different sounds to 'ea', as in 'heart', 'beard', and 'heard' rather than give the same pronunciation every time. Alternatively, why might we not be tempted to pronounce horse and worse in the same way? Chapter 1 introduced us to how the study of **acquired dyslexia** can shed light on

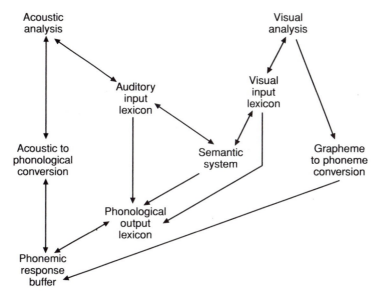

Figure 8.1 An extension of figure 7.2 to include a modular account of reading. After Ellis and Young (1988)

questions such as this and in this chapter we will examine in some detail how studies of acquired reading and writing impairments have enabled us to uncover fundamental facts about the manner in which normal reading and writing is achieved.

Extending the Modular Account of Language

Figure 8.1 shows an expansion of figure 7.2 so as to include modules concerned with reading. Within the model a written word is first subjected to **visual analysis** in order to establish its constituent graphemes – these comprise both individual letters and certain combinations of letters (e.g. 'ch'). The output of visual analysis then feeds two 'routes', one going to the **visual input lexicon** and the other into the **grapheme-to-phoneme conversion rules**. The visual input lexicon comprises individual representations of all the words we are able to read. It is important to stress that this lexicon does not represent meaning, only information about the letter patterns of known words. The grapheme-to-phoneme correspondence rules are not word-specific but constitute our internalized knowledge about the principles of English pronunciation which we can bring to bear on both words we know and those that are unfamiliar.

Once a word is processed within the **visual** input lexicon its representation can make contact with the **semantic system**. Note that, as with spoken input, the lexical semantic route involves two-way connections so as to allow higher levels to facilitate lower levels of analysis (e.g. the speeding of word recognition by the provision of semantic context). From the semantic system there is an output to the **phonological output lexicon** which allows a particular meaning to be mapped on to the specific spoken output which is then converted into phonemes and produced as speech via the **phonemic response buffer** – this is known as the lexical semantic route. Alternatively, or in parallel, a speech output for a word can be derived from a mapping of the **grapheme-to-phoneme correspondence rules** on to the speech output. A third 'direct route' is also illustrated. Evidence for this route is controversial and for the present moment our discussion will be concerned with only the lexical semantic route and that involving grapheme-to-phoneme conversion.

Peripheral Dyslexias

Acquired peripheral dyslexia is any disruption of reading due to malfunction of the early stages of word recognition. Three forms of peripheral dyslexia are typically identified: letter-by-letter reading, neglect dyslexia, attentional dyslexia. All these deficits arise in the visual analysis system, so it is clear that depiction of this as a single module in our diagram is somewhat of an oversimplification, and we shortly consider at least one attempt to expand this module into additional components.

In attentional dyslexia there is a problem in identifying the constituent elements of words. Thus a letter can be read in isolation but not when it is part of a word. At a higher level single words can be read in isolation but not when flanked by other words that have to be ignored (Shallice and Warrington, 1977). The explanation of attentional dyslexia is unclear at present. Shallice (1988) has suggested that the disorder represents damage to an attentional filter whose role is to control the output of a letter analysis system. Under normal conditions this mechanism can create an attentional 'window' which enables only the relevant component of the input to proceed to higher levels of analysis. Thus when attempting to identify the letter *i* in the word *bite*, the filter would suppress the letters *bte*. Similarly, when reading a word in a sentence the attentional mechanism would suppress other words so as to allow word recognition to proceeed more effectively.

Shallice's account thus places the locus of the deficit at the level of letter analysis. However, Warrington, Cipolotti and McNeil (1993) have challenged this view. They present patient BAL who showed the classic features of attentional dyslexia. The authors examined how various forms of flanking affected the degree of attentional dyslexia. They found, for example, that placing flanking items further from the target did not reduce the attentional deficit – a positive effect might be expected because wider spacing should make it less likely that irrelevant information could come within the defective attentional window. On this basis and other data Warrington et al. argue attentional dyslexia occurs at a later stage of processing. More recently Price and Humphreys (1993) have produced another account of attentional dyslexia in terms of the co-occurrence of two separate deficits.

In letter-by-letter reading the patient appears to read by assembling a response one letter at a time. As a result the time taken to read a word grows monotonically as the length of the word increases. Neglect dyslexia was mentioned briefly in chapter 4 and most commonly involves the inability to read the left side of words. As a result 'cowboy' might be read as 'boy'. Caramazza and Hillis (1990b) have put forward a model of visual word recognition which divides visual word recognition into a series of stages similar to those proposed by Marr (1976) for object recognition. The first stage of this model is a **retino-centric feature map** in which the various features of the letters are identified. The second stage is a 'viewer-centred' representation of the letters comprising the word which is termed a **stimulus centred letter shape map**. This representation is not determined by retinal position and will be the same regardless of whether the word was presented centrally or eccentrically. Output from here inputs to a **word centred grapheme description**. The important point about this level is that the representation is the same regardless of the nature of the input. Thus the word CHAIR written normally, in mirror writing, upside down or in different types would have the same representation (see figure 8.2).

Two patients are presented who appear to exhibit deficits at different levels in the model. HR (Rapp and Caramazza, 1991) is a letter-by-letter reader who also exhibited a number of spatial impairments which collectively suggested a deficit at the retinocentric or stimulus centred levels of processing. If normal subjects are asked to search for an X among an array of O's their performance will not be affected by how many O's there are in the array. This suggests that processing resources are usually sufficient to search the whole array in parallel and thus the X is found at the same rate whatever the number of distractors. However, when HR was given this task, time taken to find the X increased as the number of distractors increased. The authors argue that this reflects a deficit which leads to the sequential rather than parallel allocation of attention to different locations. As a result each location must be

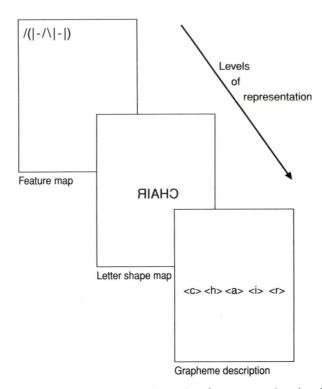

Figure 8.2 Schematic illustration of levels of representation in visual word recognition for a mirror-reversed word projected to the upper right quadrant. The first level of analysis is the retino-centric feature map (upper left panel), followed by a stimulus-centred letter shape map (middle panel), and, finally, the word-centred grapheme description (lower right panel). From Caramazza and Hillis (1990b), reproduced with permission of Lawrence Erlbaum Associates Ltd, Hove, UK.

searched individually with a consequent increase in search time as more distractors are added. Her letter-by-letter reading is seen as arising from the same deficit. Faulty processing prevents the parallel availability of letters in the stimulus centred letter map with the result that each letter has to be dealt with sequentially thus greatly slowing down the rate at which letters are presented to the higher levels of analysis.

The second patient is NG (Caramazza and Hillis, 1990b), a left-handed woman who showed the relatively unusual phenomenon of right-sided neglect. When asked to read normally presented words of differing lengths the overwhelming majority of errors involved right-sided letter positions. NG was also asked to read words presented vertically, mirror reversed and to recognize words from their oral spelling. In all cases NG made the same kinds of right-sided errors as she did with normally presented words. The fact that this common error pattern occurred irrespective of format led Caramazza and Hillis to propose that NG's deficit involved a processing impairment within the word centred grapheme description. The authors have recently reported similar findings in two additional patients (Hillis and Caramazza, 1995b).

The Caramazza and Hillis model provides a plausible account of letter-by-letter reading and neglect dyslexia and, although not attempted, it might also be possible to integrate the phenomenon of attentional dyslexia. However, their theory has its critics and alternative accounts exist (e.g. Humphreys and Riddoch, 1993). Furthermore, the whole area is made more difficult because there appears to be so much variability in peripheral dyslexias. Price and Humphreys (1993) have argued that attentional dyslexia may sometimes be the outcome of two separable deficits, and letter-by-letter reading appears to have many variants. Warrington and Shallice (1980), for example, have argued that reading in letter-by-letter reading involves a 'spelling in reverse' process. However, Hanley and Kay (1992) present evidence contrary to this view in that their patient, PD, appears to use quite different strategies in reading and spelling. PD is also contrasted with another letter-by-letter reader reported by Reuter-Lorenz and Brunn (1990). This patient showed the word superiority effect in that recognition accuracy for letters was greater when embedded in words compared with nonwords. This effect is attributed to information in the visual input lexicon facilitating lower-level visual analysis and thus suggests that access to the visual input lexicon was normal. However, PD failed to show this effect and thus his letter-by-letter reading may have a different origin (Kay and Hanley, 1991). Neglect dyslexia is also considered to be a multi-faceted disorder (Ellis, Young and Flude, 1993) and the relation between neglect dyslexia and neglect more generally has yet to be clarified. The proper explanation of peripheral dyslexias thus seems a long way off.

Surface Dyslexia

Surface dyslexia is the first form of central acquired dyslexia we will consider. Central dyslexias can be defined as reading impairments occurring at levels beyond visual analysis. Surface dyslexia was first described by Marshall and Newcombe (1973) and is an acquired reading disorder characterized by an inability to read exception words (e.g. pint, broad, gauge) correctly. Many cases of surface dyslexia have now been

Table 8.1   TOB's reading of irregular words. Actual pronunciations are shown in phonetic script

pretty	/ prɛti /	were	/ wɪə /
beret	/ bɛrɛt /	tomb	/ tɒm /
regime	/ rɛgaɪm /	deaf	/ dif /
pint	/ pɪnt /	colonel	/ cɒlonel /
sweat	/ swit /	bear	/ bɪə /
vase	/ vez /	bowl	/ boual /
deny	/ dɛni /	pear	/ pɪə /
thyme	/ θaɪmi /	steak	/ stik /

described (see the volume by Patterson, Marshall and Coltheart, 1985; and case studies such as McCarthy and Warrington, 1986b). My own experience with surface dyslexia came from my investigations of TOB (Parkin, 1993) who was first discussed back in chapter 3. TOB exhibited a very striking and 'pure' surface dyslexia; table 8.1 shows the responses TOB made when presented with a range of exception words and it can be seen that his responses are all very strong regularizations – TOB's reading thus seems entirely based on grapheme-to-phoneme correspondence rules. However, when asked to read regular words and nonwords he made very few errors even when quite complex items were presented (e.g. chitterling, huckaback). Three other things were also notable. First, TOB's problem with exception words was much more apparent for lower-frequency words. Second, he was never able to explain the meaning of any word he could not pronounce correctly. Third, he could reliably distinguish exception words from nonwords even though he could not pronounce them.

If we refer back to figure 8.2 a plausible explanation of surface dyslexia is immediately apparent. Within the model pronunciation can be achieved via the lexical route or via grapheme-to-phoneme correspondence rules. To account for TOB's problems we need only specify a deficit at some point between the visual lexicon and semantic system. A deficit of this kind would explain why he pronounces solely on the basis of rules even though he is able to distinguish words, including those he cannot pronounce correctly, from nonwords. In addition, because he can only generate a phonological input to the semantic system it explains why he cannot comprehend any word that he cannot pronounce correctly.

The dual route theory thus provides a seemingly clear account of surface dyslexia but it has not been without criticism. Primarily this has stemmed from those who propose that there is essentially one rather than two processes involved in the derivation of sound from the printed word. An early piece of evidence favouring the two-route model was the demonstration that irregular words took longer to pronounce and were prone to the generation of regularization errors. To account for this it was suggested that delays and regularization errors arose because of the conflict arising between the correct lexically-derived pronunciation and the incorrect pronunciation based on grapheme-to-phoneme conversion rules. In contrast the pronunciation of regular words was unimpeded by the two-route arrangement because both routes yielded the same output.

Evidence against the two-route model emerged from the study of so-called 'inconsistent' words. These were defined as words having regular grapheme-to-phoneme correspondence but with one or more 'orthographic neighbours' in which a shared graphemic pattern was pronounced in an irregular manner. Thus HINT and ROAD are inconsistent because of their respective neighbours PINT and BROAD. Inconsistent words were thus contrasted with 'consistent' words in which the graphemic patterns always shared the same pronunciation (e.g. TAKE, HOPE).

In an experiment by Glushko (1979) it was shown that inconsistent words gave rise to pronunciation times comparable to those found with exception words and were significantly slower than pronunciation times of consistent regular words. In addition it was also shown that nonwords based on inconsistent letter patterns (e.g. RINT and TROAD) took longer to pronounce than nonwords based on consistent letter patterns. From these experiments (see also Kay and Marcel, 1981) it was concluded that a single process, known as **analogy**, underlies the pronunciation of both words and nonwords. Briefly, it was proposed that the pronunciation of any letter string, word or nonword, was derived by seeking an analogy with our knowledge about the pronunciation of known words. This process would clearly be most efficient when the available analogies were consistent compared with the inconsistent case in which a resolution and response choice would have to occur.

Connectionist Modelling and Surface Dyslexia

The idea of a **single route model** of pronunciation was further advanced in the connectionist model of reading developed initially by Seidenberg and McClelland, 1989 (see figure 8.3). They trained a network to associate graphemic and phonemic knowledge using a back propagation method (see chapter 1). Essentially the network operated by mapping the relation between triples of letters and their corresponding phonemic descriptions: GAVE, for example, would be represented as GA, GAV,

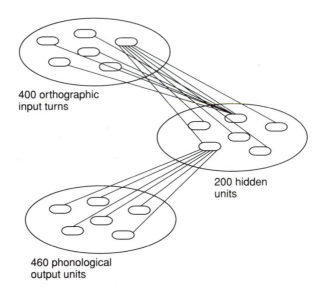

400 orthographic
input turns

200 hidden
units

460 phonological
output units

Figure 8.3 Outline of the implemented part of the Seidenberg–McClelland model of reading aloud. (Only some of the connections are shown. All units in any layer are connected to all units in the next layer, and all the hidden units have backward-operating connections to all input units.) From Coltheart et al. (1993). Copyright © 1993 by the American Psychological Association. Reproduced with permission.

AVE. The model was trained on 2897 monosyllabic words of at least three letters and the number of times a word was presented for learning was varied to take account of its frequency within the language.

Training was extensive involving 150,000 trials but it was shown that, eventually, the model performed very much like humans. In particular it showed a 'regularity effect' taking longer to pronounce irregular words compared with regular words. The next step was to give the model a 'lesion' and examine how it performed when presented with words it previously was able to pronounce correctly. The first attempt was not a great success (Patterson, Seidenberg and McClelland 1989), a large number of reading errors were produced but the pattern did not resemble that of surface dyslexia.

A second attempt by Patterson (1990) was more successful. She compared the reading of the lesioned model with two surface dyslexic patients, KT (McCarthy and Warrington, 1986b) and MP (Bub, Canceliere and Kertesz, 1985). The model provided a good match for MP's reading errors but did not simulate the extent of KT's deficit. Patients vary in severity so an obvious explanation of the discrepancy was that the lesion was not severe enough to account for impairments such as KT's. One step, therefore, might be to 'lesion' the network further but a problem here was that 'lesions' of this type produced a severe disruption of regular word reading – something that was not apparent in KT or any other clear cases of surface dyslexia.

Damage to the Seidenberg and McClelland model does not, therefore, provide a pattern of real word reading comparable to more severe cases of surface dyslexia. Another problem arises when we consider nonwords. Surface dyslexics typically perform well on nonwords (MP was 96% accurate reading a list of 44 nonwords and KT achieved 97% accuracy on a list of 86 nonwords) but Seidenberg and McClelland's undamaged model has only mild success at reading nonwords achieving accuracies of between 51 per cent and 65 per cent. Thus on both the reading of words and nonwords the behaviour of the network does not approximate surface dyslexia to any significant degree.

Phonological Dyslexia

Another problem for the Seidenberg and McClelland model, along with any other that specifies only a single route pronunciation system, is the phenomenon of **phonological dyslexia** – something we encountered briefly in chapter 1. This condition, originally reported by Beauvois and Dérousené (1979) involves an impairment in reading nonwords relative to real words. A particularly clear case is WB described by Funnell (1983). WB scored approximately 90 per cent correct when reading real words (these included uncommon abstract words such as satirical) despite an almost complete inability to read simple monosyllabic nonwords. When confronted with letters he could give their names but not their sounds even though he could repeat the latter when spoken to him.

Seidenberg and McClelland (1989) did not address phonological dyslexia in their model but indicated that a future modification might address reading comprehension and thus provide a basis within which phonological dyslexia could arise. Essentially they were suggesting that phonology might be derived by two routes: the grapheme-to-phoneme route already implemented and a second route involving graphemes-to-semantics – semantics-to-phonology. On this basis, damage to only the first route would mean that just real words could be read because only these could allow access to phonology via the semantic system.

Discussing this idea Coltheart, Curtis, Atkins and Haller (1993) drew attention to Funnell's (1983) observation that WB did not appear 'dependent on semantic mediation for the pronunciation of words'. This conclusion derived from a series of experiments showing in various ways that he had a notable semantic impairment. Thus, he failed considerably on tasks requiring the matching of a correctly read word with its picture and was often unable to decide which of two words was closer to another in meaning (e.g. bough or twig/branch).

Surface Dyslexia and the Dual Route Model

The above account shows that single route models of reading fail to give a satisfactory account of both surface and phonological dyslexia. This is the conclusion reached by Coltheart et al. (1993) who also note that single route models cannot explain a number of other fundamental facts about normal reading. Coltheart et al. propose that a dual route model, i.e. one where a word's pronunciation can be derived lexically or via grapheme-to-phoneme rules, still offers the best account of normal skilled reading. However, they acknowledge that dual route models, as they stand, tend to be static representations of the mature reading system. In contrast, models such as the Seidenberg and McClelland model embody an essential feature of real reading systems – the ability to learn. Coltheart et al. have started to develop a **dual route cascaded model** embodying both a lexical and a grapheme-to-phoneme correspondence (GPC) route to pronunciation. At present most of the research has been concerned with the GPC route.

The GPC component attempts to derive grapheme-to-phoneme correspondence rules from words that it is presented with. With each word the model first attempts a mapping of each grapheme on to a separate phoneme. This is successful for many words (e.g. MINT) but does not deal with those in which two or more graphemes correspond to a single phoneme (e.g. EEL, BLIGHT). Here the model uses a more complicated procedure in order to derive a multi-letter rule. Context sensitivity is also acquired by the model in that it learns, for example, that an initial 'c' is pronounced differently depending on the vowel that follows it.[1]

The model was trained on the same words used by Seidenberg and McClelland and was found to read 78 per cent accurately. This is not surprising because 22 per cent of the word sample are exception words

---

[1] There may also be a case for including position-specific information within the grapheme-to-phoneme rules. Consider the grapheme 'g'. On a single grapheme-to-phoneme rule 'g' would be considered irregularly pronounced in SIGN because the typical pronunciation of 'g' is that found in GOOD, GUY etc. However, if we consider a bigger unit, e.g. IGN, then G is being pronounced regularly in SIGN. However, this rule in turn depends on a positional constraint in that, at the beginning of the word, G is pronounced in the normal manner, e.g. IGNORE.

so one would not expect a rule-based procedure to be correct. In contrast to exception words the model performed well on both inconsistent and consistent words. On nonwords the GPC model read 98 per cent accurately whereas the best performance from any other model was 71 per cent.

The GPC component of the Coltheart et al. model thus appears to provide a good simulation of human ability to read both regular words and nonwords. It is, of course, necessary to combine this with a lexical route to account for our reading of irregular words and thus provide a comprehensive model of English pronunciation. Work on how the lexical route operates is less developed but progress should be quite rapid as the authors feel able to make use of existing models of visual word recognition (e.g. McClelland, 1991) to aid them in this enterprise. At present, therefore, the dual route approach to reading appears the most promising.

The Direct Route to Pronunciation

So far we have discussed two routes by which we might read a word aloud, one via the grapheme-to-phoneme route and the other via the lexical-semantic route. We have also seen that impairment to the lexical-semantic route will result in surface dyslexia – the regularization of irregular words. If this is correct it should be impossible to read an irregular word correctly but fail to understand what it means. However, people with just such a deficit have been reported.

Bub et al. (1985) describe a patient, MP, who performed extremely poorly on word comprehension tests. In a task where she had to select which of four words (chair, apple, boy, hat) was meaningfully related to 'chair' she performed at chance. Similarly when asked to match one of four written words to a picture she also performed at chance. When given regular and irregular words to read aloud she did much better on regular words and produced large numbers of regularization errors or irregular words. As with TOB, her errors were much more frequent for lower-frequency words. The demonstration that she could read some irregular words has led to the suggestion that there is a non-semantic lexical route to pronunciation, i.e. a direct link from the visual input lexicon to the speech output lexicon (e.g. Funnell, 1983; Shallice, 1988). Coslett (1991) describes WT, a patient who could read aloud words of low imagery even though she could neither comprehend them, write or repeat them. She was also unable to read nonwords. This suggests that the option of grapheme-to-phoneme rules was not available and that her reading must therefore have been achieved via a direct lexical route (as illustrated in Figure 8.1).

This 'three route' approach to reading has been attacked by Hillis and Caramazza (1991b). Their patient JJ read out regular words correctly and also some irregular words. However, from further analysis they concluded that JJ only read correctly those irregular words for which he had some indication of comprehension. Hillis and Caramazza propose a **summation hypothesis** in which words are read both via a lexical-semantic route and by grapheme-to-phoneme correspondence rules. To account for the correct reading of some irregular words in surface dyslexia they suggest that partial semantic information combines with information from the grapheme-to-phoneme route so as to specify the correct word.

A similar type of theory has been put forward to explain the consistent association between surface dyslexia and semantic dementia – this is a newly identified progressive disorder in which the primary symptom appears to be a dissolution of semantic memory (e.g. Patterson, Graham and Hodges, 1994; Patterson and Hodges, 1992). Patterson et al. have proposed that comprehension plays a crucial role in binding together phonological segments in the speech output lexicon. When semantic memory deteriorates the 'semantic glue' binding together the phonological elements breaks down and lexically-based pronounciation becomes impaired. As a critical test of their theory they suggest that semantic glue is essential for normal performance on a word repetition task in which subjects have to repeat back a sequence of unrelated words. In support of this they showed that three patients with semantic dementia could only perform the word span task normally when it involved words that they could still comprehend – thus suggesting that comprehension is crucial for the maintenance of word phonology.

The debate over the direct route continues. Hillis and Caramazza (1995a) describe three patients whose reading ability is considered consistent with a two-route model. GLT, for example, correctly read 92 per cent of words for which he was able to choose the correct picture instead of a semantically-related picture, 72 per cent of words where he rejected an unrelated picture but matched the word to a semantically related picture, and only 44 per cent of words where he was unable to match the word with its synonym. These data thus suggest that the availability of some semantic information does seem crucial for reading words aloud. However, in the same issue of the journal, Goodall and Phillips (1995) report a woman known as AN who was able to read words better than nonwords. Following training, however, she did learn to read nonwords despite being unable to name the constituent elements or read the nonwords when the elements were recombined to form new nonwords. Because nonwords have no meaning the authors argue that this result could only have been achieved by learning to pronounce the nonwords via the direct lexical route.

Most recently Funnell (in press) reports the case of EP, a woman who developed a very distinct surface dyslexia due to a dementing illness. She examined EP's abilities to repeat sequences of known and unknown words but, unlike Patterson et al., she found no difference. However, it is perhaps important that Funnell's task may have been less taxing. In addition, careful investigation of EP's oral reading and comprehension of the same words revealed a consistent relationship between knowledge of word meaning and oral reading. The only irregular words she could read correctly were those which she could also respond accurately to in a word picture matching task so long as the alternative distractor picture came from a different semantic domain. In contrast, irregular words that she could not read were matched at chance even when the target picture was accompanied by a distractor from a different semantic domain.

Funnell's result thus suggest that surface dyslexia is linked to comprehension ability, although it would appear that the degree of comprehension required is rather vague. A recent study by Cipolotti and Warrington (1995) appears to challenge this. DRN read aloud irregular words extremely well but defined them very poorly. However, as Funnell notes, requiring definitions is a particularly strong test of semantic knowledge, and it is possible that DRN might have shown better indications of knowledge with a less demanding test.

On balance, it would seem that the ability to pronounce irregular words correctly depends on the availability of some limited comprehension of those words also being possible. This seems to cast doubt on the idea of a direct lexical route in which correct pronounciation can be achieved wholly independent of meaning. Two theories, 'semantic glue' and the summation hypothesis have been put forward to account for this. However, there are still doubts as to how this interaction between oral reading and semantics should be explained (Funnell, in press).

Deep Dyslexia

This disorder was formally identified by Marshall and Newcombe (1973). They described two patients, GR and KU, who made a variety of interesting word substitutions, or paralexias, when attempting to read words aloud. Most striking of these paralexias were **semantic errors** in which the word produced was meaningfully related to the word shown (e.g. DUEL read as SWORD). In addition, the reading ability of the patients was also strikingly affected by **imageability** – the readiness with which a word can evoke an internal visual image. Shown words high in imagery (e.g. GUITAR, BOTTLE) the patients read well but on less imageable words (e.g. JUSTICE, HOPE) they make lots of errors. This is

Table 8.2   The features of deep dyslexia as identified by Coltheart (1980).

---

1 Semantic errors (e.g. BLOWING → 'wind,' VIEW → 'scene,' NIGHT → 'sleep,' GONE → 'lost').

2 Visual errors (e.g. WHILE → 'white,' SCANDAL → 'sandals,' 'POLITE → 'politics,' BADGE → 'bandage').

3 Function-word substitutions (e.g. WAS → 'and,' ME → 'my,' OFF → 'from,' THEY → 'the').

4 Derivational errors (e.g., CLASSIFY → 'class,' FACT → 'facts,' MARRIAGE → 'married,' BUY → 'bought').

5 Nonlexical derivation of phonology from print is impossible (e.g. pronouncing nonwords, judging if two nonwords rhyme).

6 Lexical derivation of phonology from print is impaired (e.g. judging if two words rhyme).

7 Words with low imageability/concreteness (e.g. JUSTICE) are harder to read than words with high imageability/concreteness (e.g. TABLE).

8 Verbs are harder than adjectives, which are harder than nouns, in reading aloud;

9 Functions words are more difficult than content words in reading aloud.

10 Writing is impaired (spontaneous or to dictation).

11 Auditory-verbal short-term memory is impaired.

12 Whether a word can be read at all depends on its sentence context (e.g. FLY as a noun is easier than FLY as a verb).

---

most notable on **function words** (e.g. THE, IT) in which they will often fail to make a response or, if coaxed, substitute another function word. A final and consistent impairment involves a profound inability to pronounce nonwords. Coltheart (1980) reviewed various cases of deep dyslexia and concluded that, in all, there were 12 types of deficit that were regularly observed in patients with the disorder (see table 8.2; see also Coltheart, Patterson and Marshall, 1987).

Deep Dyslexia and the Modular Account

Deep dyslexia arises from lesions to the temporal lobe region of the left hemisphere and there have been a number of attempts to explain the disorder in terms of damage to the left hemisphere reading system. These approaches all assume some version of the modular account described in figure 8.2. The essential problem of deep dyslexia is that it is a consistent re-occurring cluster of symptoms. One possible account (e.g. Morton and Patterson, 1987) might be to argue that, for some reason, a number of different components in the system become damaged in parallel with a resulting range of impairments. Thus, among other things, the deep dyslexic would have deficits in grapheme-to-phoneme conversion to explain their inability to read nonwords, some form of lexical deficit to explain why function words cannot be read, a semantic memory impairment to account for semantic paralexias and imagery effects, and visual analysis problems to explain visual errors.

Critics of the multiple co-occurring deficit theory have argued that it is implausible on the grounds that brain lesions do not respect functional boundaries and, as such, would not be expected to produce consistent clusters of symptoms. This may not be wholly correct. It is known for example, that particular arteries supply specific brain regions so a disruption of that artery might lead to consistent patterns of brain damage and associated deficits reflecting the functions of those brain regions. Thus if the region of the left temporal lobe concerned with grapheme-to-phoneme correspondence and access from the visual input lexicon to semantics were adjacent anatomically, co-occurring deficits might be less surprising.

While the multiple deficit theory might be preserved in this way some theorists have viewed it as inelegant and tried to account for deep dyslexia in terms of a single deficit within the left hemisphere reading system. Foremost among these accounts is that deep dyslexia is a consequence of impaired grapheme-to-phoneme conversion as demonstrated in the inability to read nonwords.

The **phonological recoding hypothesis** proposes that reading aloud can only be performed efficiently if a phonological code is generated via GPC rules at the same time as a pronunciation is specified via the lexical-semantic route. If the phonological reading route is damaged then reading errors will occur in the absence of the confirmatory phonological information. In assessing an idea of this kind we must first consider whether there is any prima facie case that phonological recoding is implicated in normal reading. Coltheart (1987) reviews various types of experiment which have attempted to show an obligatory phonological recording stage in reading. The results of these experiments are not clear-cut but there is little basis for proposing that phonological recoding underlies word recognition and comprehension under most circumstances.

As we saw earlier English is plagued by the problem of irregularity in grapheme-to-phoneme correspondence. Thus no set of rules can be devised which will enable the correct pronunciation of all English words. Indeed there is no grapheme in English which is pronounced the same way in all words. This causes enormous difficulties for proposing a phonological recoding stage prior to accessing the visual input lexicon. On the assumption that it would have to apply pronunciation rules that work for most words, a great number of words would be unreadable because the phonological code derived would not match a lexical entry at all (e.g. BROAD, GAUGE). One way around the irregularity problem is to propose that, for irregular words, we have word-specific rules (e.g. a rule that BROAD is not 'BRODE' but 'BRAWD'). A difficulty is that normal people take considerably longer to pronounce irregular words (see chapter 1) – a finding that we would not expect if there were word-specific pronunciation rules for irregular words.

A more fundamental argument is that, on logical grounds, phonological recoding is not an optimal basis for lexical access. First, there is the problem of homophony in that differently spelled words often have the same pronunciation (e.g. SAIL, SALE). In contrast English has few examples of **heterophony** where one spelling shares two pronunciations (e.g. LEAD, LEAD). Thus, in terms of information-specificity, analysis by letter pattern is more likely to produce an unambiguous response than via phonemes. Finally it is difficult to see how the phonological recoding hypothesis could explain our easy ability to detect **pseudohomophones** like BRANE and PHOCKS so easily.

In this section we have seen that an explanation of deep dyslexia based on deficient phonological recoding seems unlikely given difficulties in demonstrating that this form of encoding could be implicated in normal reading processes. This leads us to consider an alternative and more radical single deficit account of deep dyslexia.

Deep Dyslexia as Right Hemisphere Reading

In the absence of any compelling explanation of deep dyslexia in terms of impaired left hemisphere reading, Coltheart (1987) along with Saffran, Bogyo, Schwartz and Marin (1987) have argued that the pattern of symptoms in deep dyslexia can arise because these patients are reading with their right hemisphere. In order to understand this theory, and subsequent debates that have arisen, it is important to start with an overview of the theory itself.

The basic proposal is that deep dyslexia is due to a lesion which disrupts visual access to the reading system in the left hemisphere. However, other aspects of the system are left intact so that, for example, the spoken responses of patients arise from the speech output system. Reading is thought to occur via an intact right hemisphere reading system which is able to both identify a word and assign semantics to it. This semantic code is then transferred inter-hemispherically and mapped on to the left hemisphere speech output system. Within this theory the features of deep dyslexia arise entirely from inadequacies in the nature of semantic information generated from the right hemisphere and the manner in which it contacts the left hemisphere speech output system.

Within this account shared feature semantic paralexias arise because the semantic information from the right hemisphere does not specify the correct response sufficiently and, as a result, a word with similar features to the actual word is selected for pronunciation. Associative semantic errors arise because the right hemisphere generates a range of associates to the presented word and one of these semantic representations is transmitted instead of the correct semantics. The poorer reading of abstract words is attributed to the poorer semantic representation of those words in the right hemisphere – the argument being that the representation of meaning may be primarily image-based. In the case of function words, these have largely a syntactic function so little semantic information can be derived and thus transmitted to the left hemisphere. Nonwords represent an even more extreme case because, by definition, they have no meaning and hence no basis by which the hypothetical right hemisphere system could transmit any information about them.

To explain visual errors it was first noted that these errors were most commonly made to abstract words and that the subsequent error tended to be a more concrete word. On this basis it was suggested that a visual error could arise following the presentation of a word which, because of its abstract status, was unable to produce a semantic code of sufficient richness. However, in parallel the presented word would also partially activate other lexical entries and if one of these had a strong semantic, highly imageable representation this would be transmitted and result in a response. To give an example: presentation of HOPE could produce some activation of the highly-imageable word ROPE whose semantic code would then be transmitted.

Evidence for Right Hemisphere Reading

The right hemisphere hypothesis appears to give a reasonably neat account of deep dyslexia but it is based on one crucial assumption: that the right hemisphere posssesses the ability to identify visually, and comprehend the meaning of words. Twenty years ago a statement of this kind would have been viewed as heretical because prevailing opinion held that the right hemisphere was 'word blind' and 'word deaf' (Geschwind, 1965). However, Coltheart pointed out that claims about the non-linguistic nature of the right hemisphere rested largely on demonstrations that the right hemisphere could not speak. There was not, he argued, sufficient proof that the right hemisphere could not visually identify and comprehend words.

Various lines of evidence were produced in order to argue that the right hemisphere had reading capabilities sufficient to underpin the right hemisphere hypothesis of deep dyslexia. Central to the original argument were the data from split-brain patients (see chapter 6) from which it could be argued that the right hemisphere did have a degree of linguistic ability. However, as we saw in the account of split-brain patients, there is considerable debate about the status of right hemisphere language in these patients. First, only a small proportion of the patients had evidence of language ability in the right hemisphere. Second, some of these deficits may be the consequence of abnormal development.

A similar argument applies to data derived from patients who have suffered left hemispherectomy in that they too may have abnormal lateralization as a consequence of their illness. Patterson, Vargha-Khadem and Polkey (1989), for example, described a teenage girl who suffered a complete left hemispherectomy at the age of 13. Of most interest to our present concern is that she retained an ability to speak:

Q: 'What do you particularly like to eat?'
A: I like . . . er . . . you know . . . the . . . I can't say it now . . . well I like . . . I don't like chips a lot but . . . I like Bolognaise.'
Q: 'Do you cook?'
A: 'Yes' [I cook] 'different things. I made . . . er . . . I made . . . these (points to apple). But not that . . . these.'

From this it is evident that she has considerable speaking ability and thus evidence from her performance would not square very well with a theory founded on the absence of speech production in the right hemisphere. It is also noticeable that she tends to omit concrete words such as 'apple' while retaining the ability to utter various function words. This seems at odds with a view that the right hemisphere is specialized for concrete words.

Even if we put aside our concern that right hemisphere language, as demonstrated by split-brain patients, could be unrepresentative there are further problems. Patterson and Besner (1984) argued that if deep dyslexia were *entirely* due to reading via a right hemisphere word comprehension system then the word comprehension ability of split-brain patients and deep dyslexics ought to be largely indistinguishable. To test this they compared the word comprehension skills of two deep dyslexics with that of the two split-brain patients showing the greatest evidence of right hemisphere language function.

The results showed unequivocally that the deep dyslexics performed much better. One could, of course, argue that deep dyslexics retain some left hemisphere function and that this enables them to perform more effectively. This view has been stated explicitly by Zaidel and Schweiger (1984) who conclude that 'deep dyslexics may read more words than the disconnected right hemisphere because they sometimes use their intact left hemisphere for reading' (p. 361). The problem with this explanation is that the theory would then become untestable in that it could account for any degree of similarity between the performance of deep dyslexics and split-brain patients reading with their right hemispheres.

Normal Right Hemisphere Reading

Comparisons between the reading abilities of deep dyslexics and those of the right hemispheres of split-brain patients may, therefore, be of limited value because the latter may not give an accurate reflection of right hemisphere reading ability in normal brains. A different approach is to examine the reading abilities of the normal right hemisphere to see whether its linguistic properties are consistent with the symptoms of deep dyslexia. This can be done by examining normal subjects or the reading abilities of patients whose right hemispheres can be assumed to have been normal until they suffered brain injury.

Investigations of normal subjects involve split-field studies. In chapter 2 we saw that the human visual system is arranged so that the left visual field (LVF) projects initially to the right hemisphere and the right visual field (RVF) projects directly to the left hemisphere (see figure 2.2). If a subject is asked to fixate on a central point it can be assumed that a stimulus presented to the LVF is initially processed by the right hemisphere and vice versa for RVF presentation. However, the duration of this presentation must be brief (no more than 200 msec) otherwise the subject can make an eye movement, fixate centrally on the stimulus and thus allow processing in both hemispheres in parallel.

If the above conditions are met it is possible to get some indication of the processing capabilities of both hemispheres. Thus if a variable is found to affect the ease with which stimuli are reported from the LVF but not the RVF then that manipulation is telling us something about differences in the way the two hemispheres operate. Using this logic a number of investigators examined how imagery affected reporting words from the two visual fields. A number of studies purported to show that words high in imagery were reported better but that this effect was only significant with LVF presentation (Coltheart 1987). These studies were, however, flawed in many cases and, as Patterson and Besner (1984) note, there is no clear evidence that imagery has a greater influence with LVF presentation.

Right Hemisphere Damage and Reading

An alternative source of evidence is to study the language abilities of patients whose reading can be assumed to have developed normally until it became disrupted by lesions restricted to the right hemisphere. One study used a new technique known as **transcranial magnetic stimulation** (TMS) which can be used to temporarily disrupt specific regions of the brain. Coslett and Monsul (1994) studied JG, a man who had a severe acquired dyslexia following a stroke. He partly recovered his reading ability being able to read high-imagery words better than low-imagery words. This pattern suggested that JG might be more reliant on his right hemisphere for reading. To test this they required JG to read words when either his left or right hemisphere was subject to TMS. Without TMS he read about 65 per cent of words correctly. When the left was stimulated he continued to read 61 per cent correctly, but stimulation of the right reduced his performance to 21 per cent. These data suggest, for JG at least, that his reading is supported, at least in part, by the right hemisphere.

A more traditional approach has been to examine how patients with right hemisphere lesions deal with various types of linguistic material and, from their errors, infer the nature of right hemisphere reading (see Beeman et al. 1994; Chiarello, 1988; Joanette, Goulet and Hannequin, 1990 for reviews). The principal deficits revealed from this research are:

An inability to use relevant context to disambiguate a sentence with the literal meaning preferred even though it is inappropriate. Speech acts, such as 'Can you pass the salt' cause particular difficulty (e.g. Kaplan, Brownell, Jacobs and Gardner, 1990; Stemmer, Giroux and Joanette, 1994).

Problems drawing inferences that connect two sentences thus failing to maintain coherence within text. (Beeman, 1993)

Difficulty understanding jokes in that they fail to connect the premise of the joke with the punch line. (Brownell, Potter, Bihrle and Gardner, 1986)

Poor use of thematic sentences as a basis for organising text into a coherent sequence. (Schneiderman, Murasugi and Saddy, 1992)

On the basis of these findings Beeman et al., (1994) have put forward a **coarse semantic coding** explanation of right hemisphere reading ability. The basis of this idea is that presentation of a word to the right hemisphere results in the weak activation of large semantic fields resulting in concepts only distantly related to the presented word becoming activated. In contrast, presentation to the left hemisphere results in the strong activation of small semantic fields with only concepts closely related to the word becoming activated. The major consequence of this is that presentation of words to the right hemisphere gives rise to a somewhat vague semantic representation compared with a specific unambiguous representation when the same word is presented to the left hemisphere.

To test this theory Beeman et al. conducted a split-field experiment in which either three 'summation' primes (words weakly related to a target, e.g. FOOT, CRY, GLASS) or three unrelated primes were presented centrally prior to brief presentation of a target word (e.g. CUT) in either the LVF or RVF. It was found that summation priming, the better report of words following primes as opposed to unrelated words, was more effective in promoting word identification in the LVF, therefore, suggesting a right hemisphere advantage for coarse semantic coding. This was followed by a second experiment showing that, for LVF presentation, there was no difference in the degree of priming when the target word was preceded by a direct prime flanked by two unrelated words compared with three summation primes. In contrast RVF presentation showed greater priming with the direct prime. This experiment shows that the right hemisphere activates information closely related to the target word only slightly more than concepts more distantly related whereas the left hemisphere is able to make more specific semantic information available.

Beeman et al.'s theory is directed to the explanation of right hemisphere reading deficits of the type outlined above but it is clear that the notion of coarse semantic coding bears considerable similarity to the type of right hemisphere semantic coding thought to be responsible for the reading problems of deep dyslexics. It will thus be interesting to see whether development of this idea will shed further light on the nature of deep dyslexia.

A Connectionist Account of Deep Dyslexia

While the right hemisphere theory of reading may have its obvious attractions it is disappointing in one important respect. A major benefit of cognitive neuropsychology is that the examination of impaired performance can provide some insights into how normal mental processes operate. If what deep dyslexia represents is reading by an abnormal mechanism, the study of deep dyslexia becomes of only marginal importance.

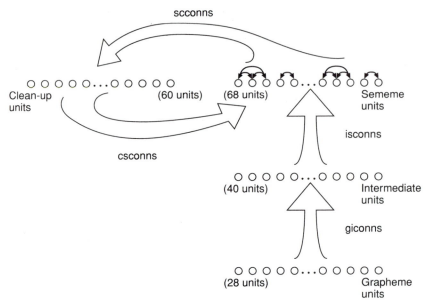

Figure 8.4   Schematic outline of Hinton and Shallice's connectionist network for learning the meaning of written words. The connections between layers are indicated using the initial letter of the two layers being connected (e.g. grapheme – intermediate = giconns, etc.). Copyright © 1991 by the American Psychological Association. Reproduced with permission.

One possibility is that attempts to explain deep dyslexia in terms of impaired left hemisphere reading processes do not work because models such as the modular account depicted in figure 8.2 are not accurate. It is possible that new models of reading might arise which could handle the phenomenon of deep dyslexia. Just such a possibility has arisen with the arrival of connectionist accounts of language function (see Harley, 1993, for an overview).

As we have seen the advantage of connectionist networks is that they can acquire particular types of knowledge and then be disrupted or 'lesioned' in some way so as to simulate the effects of brain damage itself. Hinton and Shallice (1991) devised a network in which relationships were established between graphemic, lexical and semantic units using the back propagation procedure (see figure 8.4). The semantic representation of a word was specified by units called **sememes**. These corresponded to basic semantic features such as 'main shape 2D', 'has legs', 'brown' and so on. The model was trained on 40 simple monosyllabic words (e.g. HAWK, ROCK) and was required to produce a semantic representation as an output.

An important feature of the model was that the semantic layer units were interconnected in various ways. Units denoting size, for example, were mutually inhibitory in that activation of the unit 'less than one foot high' inhibited units representing greater heights. Another important feature of the semantic layer was the presence of 'clean up' units which enabled more precise semantic descriptions to be organized in response to specific words. Once set up the network was 'lesioned' in various ways and the resulting reading errors noted.

All lesions had an effect but the closer the lesion was to the semantic component of the network the more dramatic the error pattern. In all, four types of error were noted, semantic paralexias, visual errors, visual and semantic, and other. These resemble the errors made by deep dyslexics and so it would appear that the mechanisms by which the network operates have some functional similarity to the human system which, when damaged, produces semantic- and visually-related reading errors.

In a development of this model Plaut and Shallice (1993) have attempted to model the effect of imageability on deep dyslexic reading performance. We have now encountered a number of instances where patients perform better in dealing with words that are high in visual imagery, so some account of this would seem essential to any full explanation of language deficits. They have demonstrated that increased imageability corresponds to a richer semantic representation (i.e. association with more features) within the semantic layer of the network. By lesioning the network Plaut and Shallice showed that concrete words were read more successfully than abstract words. An interesting additional finding was that a very severe lesion of the semantic system resulted in the model being better at reading abstract words. This was unexpected but could have a neuropsychological parallel in case CAV (Warrington, 1981) who is a rare example of a patient being better at reading abstract compared with concrete words. An important point, however, is that Plaut and Shallice's model simulates this double dissociation without specifying separate modules for imageable and non-imageable words. This contrasts with the modular account of deep dyslexia in which a distinction has to be drawn between the representations of these two types of word (see also Plaut, McClelland, Seidenberg and Patterson, in press).

The networks of Hinton and Shallice (1991) and Plaut and Shallice (1993) are appealing because they show that certain aspects of deep dyslexia can be simulated by lesioning network models devised to explain normal reading. A drawback, however, is that the models are not yet developed sufficiently to handle all features of the disorder. Thus the problem with function words has yet to be dealt with and the models also take no account of nonword reading. Nonetheless the success achieved so far suggests that development of these networks could lead to a genuine advance in our understanding of both normal and impaired reading processes (Hinton, Plaut and Shallice, 1993).

Spelling and Writing

Agraphia – an impairment of spelling or writing – has been identified for well over 100 years. It is also well known that agraphia is very frequently associated with aphasia. This led to the view that writing and spelling were crucially dependent on speech. Luria (1970), for example, suggested that the first stage of spelling involved breaking a word into phonemes and attaching those phonemes to the appropriate graphemes. Within this type of framework it becomes clear that preserved spelling in the absence of effective speech would not be possible.

More recent studies of agraphia have been synthesized by Ellis and Young (1988) with an initial aim of establishing that writing can exist when speech is either absent, more defective than writing, or defective in a different way to writing. An important patient in their argument is EB (Levine et al. 1982) who we encountered in chapter 1. Briefly, EB could write fluently despite lacking any ability to speak, and failed on tasks such as judging whether two visually dissimilar words rhyme (e.g. CHAIR, BEAR). This latter task suggests that EB could not even generate internal phonological codes. While EB's data are impressive in one sense we must note our previous concern: EB had 30 years experience as a speed reader and claimed to have learned to read in a way that avoided sounding out words. His unreliance on phonology is thus not surprising but whether his performance should be taken as indicative of normal cognitive organisation is another matter entirely.

A second patient is MH (Bub and Kertesz, 1982a) who was severely anomic but, despite this, she could often write the names of pictures she failed to name. In addition her spelling errors did not suggest a phonological origin. Instead her errors were morphological, for example, 'acquire' for 'acquisition' and often showed knowledge of more unusual letter configurations, for example, 'orchatria' for 'orchestra'. It was also notable that she failed to spell nonwords when they were dictated to her. As Ellis and Young point out, this is a task particularly suited to phonological mediation so her inability suggests that MH's spelling must be generated in some other way.

A third source of evidence comes from two patients JS (Caramazza et al., 1983) and RD (Ellis et al. 1983) both of whom we encountered in chapter 7. Both these patients were neologistic jargonaphasics and thus produced large number of mispronunciations. On the Boston Naming

Test, JS scored 11 out of 35 correct with written responding but 6 out of 35 with spoken naming. Given that these were the same items, there are reasonable grounds for supposing a greater impairment of spoken naming but the difference is not great. Also, although some of JS's neologisms had indications of a phonological influence (e.g. 'harb' for 'harp') others seemed to have no phonological resemblance (e.g. 'arrtal' for 'antler'). Turning to RD, Ellis and Young note the presence of bizzare spoken neologisms (e.g. 'kenelton' for 'elephant'; 'kistro' for 'screw-driver') even though they could write the names perfectly. Examples like this, they argued, were inconsistent with a spelling system reliant on a speech output system.

A final instance of preserved spelling without naming is given by Kremin (1987). Describing her patient she notes that 'ah-oh-oh' accompanied every attempt to speak and that during 'the many hours I spent with him the patient uttered [only] a few isolated words' such as the name of his therapist and the city where he lives. When asked to name 20 objects he got two correct but with written naming he got 18 out of 20 correct.

Phonological Dysgraphia

Perhaps the most compelling neuropsychological evidence against a compulsory phonemic mediation stage in assembling spellings come from a disorder known as **phonological dysgraphia**. It was first described by Shallice (1981) in a patient known as PR. When asked to write to dictation he could write most words accurately although abstract words, function words and words of very low frequency did cause problems. When he made errors they tended to be morphological, 'navigation' written as 'navigator', or similar sounding, 'custom' spelled as 'custard'. His most striking impairment was an inability to spell even simple nonwords. In addition he could not write the identity of individual letters when given their names or their sounds. When spelling of nonwords was achieved it was done by thinking of a real word that the nonword sounded like.

Other cases of phonological dysgraphia have been reported (e.g. Baxter and Warrington, 1986; Nolan and Caramazza, 1982; Roeltgen, Rothi and Heilman, 1986) and thus there seems no doubt that the cognitive system can produce correct spellings in the absence of any ability to break up a spoken word into his constituent phonemes – the assumed basis of phonemic mediation theory. For this reason it has been proposed that there must be a separate **graphemic output lexicon** which contains within it information required to output the specific written form of words. In addition, to account for failure to spell spoken nonwords we must also specify a phoneme-to-grapheme route.

At this point you may well have noticed a similarity between the characteristics of phonological dysgraphia and the reading problems experienced by deep dyslexics. Both disorders are sensitive to imageability, grammatical class, and also have great difficulty with nonwords. It is thus no surprise that a disorder known as **deep dysgraphia** has been identified where, in addition to the symptoms of phonological dysgraphia, the patients also make **semantic paragraphias** when spelling words (Bub and Kertesz, 1982b; Hatfield, 1985).

Earlier we discussed the right hemisphere theory of deep dyslexia and it is possible to make a similar case for the origin of deep dysgraphia. Support for this view comes from a study of GK, a man who suffered a massive stroke which destroyed most of his left hemisphere (Rapcsak, Beeson and Rubens, 1991). Examination of his writing performance showed the characteristics of phonological dysgraphia (see above) but, in addition, he made many semantic paragraphias (e.g. 'lawn' for 'grass'), morphological substitutions ('shipping' for 'ships') and substitution of function words ('without' for 'however'). Given the association of deep dysgraphia with large left hemisphere lesions it is tempting to entertain a right hemisphere interpretation of GK's dysgraphia – the argument being that imprecise semantic codes lead to incorrect but related word paragraphias. However, caution is required here because, in the case of GK, he appeared to have an unusually high degree of right hemisphere language and there was not a very strong parallel between his reading and spelling disorders although he did produce some semantic paralexias in single word reading.

Surface Dysgraphia

The evidence we have considered so far leads us to conclude that spellings can be generated correctly when there is obviously a defective speech output (e.g. poorer naming than spelling, spoken neologisms) and where there is no ability to spell nonwords (phonological dysgraphia). These observations lead to the conclusion that there is both a **graphemic output lexicon**, in which is stored the spellings of individual words, and a **phoneme-to-grapheme** system which allows the spelling of nonwords. These observations provide the basis for our model of spelling which is an expansion of that presented in figure 8.2 (see figure 8.5). In the model the output of both the graphemic output lexicon and the phoneme-to-grapheme conversion system feed down to the **graphemic output buffer** (see below) and to additional stages that allow both the written and oral

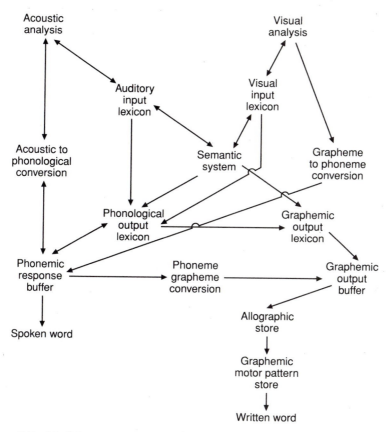

Figure 8.5 Modification of figure 8.1 to incorporate a modular account of spelling (after Ellis and Young, 1988).

spelling of words (the mechanism of the latter is still unclear so it has not been illustrated in figure 8.5).

If the model is correct then we should also expect to observe the spelling equivalent of surface dyslexia, i.e. a specific inability to spell irregular words due to disruption of the lexical graphemic route and reliance on phoneme to grapheme conversion. Surface dysgraphia has now been observed a considerable number of times. Beauvois and Dérousné (1981) described a patient who wrote nonwords well but tended to regularize the spellings of real words (e.g. 'abile' for habile'). Hatfield and Patterson (1983) reported TG who, following a stroke, produced a marked pattern of surface dysgraphia with spelling errors such as 'flud' for 'flood' and 'neffue' for 'nephew'. However, not all irregular words were mispelled with many higher-frequency irregular

Table 8.3   Examples of TOB's spelling errors

'aeroplane'	*errowplane*
'ghost'	*goast*
'squirrel'	*squiral*
'island'	*iland*
'parachute'	*parashoot*
'pigeon'	*piggin*
'soldiers'	*solgers*
'colonel'	*curnal*
'pyjamas'	*pajarmers*
'jewellery'	*jualry*
'carpet'	*carpit*
'holiday'	*hollyday*
'bananas'	*bunarners*

words spelled accurately. Case TOB (Parkin, 1993b) provided particularly striking regularizations in his spellings including acknowledgements of the author's London accent! (see table 8.3) and again there was a frequency dependent effect. For low-frequency words he spelled only 20 per cent correctly whereas he spelled 70 per cent of high-frequency irregular words correctly.

The Graphemic Output Buffer

Caramazza, Miceli, Villa and Romani (1987) reported the case of LB. They made a detailed analysis of his spelling errors and came to the following conclusions:

He produced a similar pattern of spelling errors for words and nonwords with both written, typed and oral spelling.

Spelling accuracy was unaffected by lexical factors such as word frequency, grammatical class or imageability.

Spelling was no better for common as opposed to unusual patterns of letters.

Errors in spelling were more likely as the length of the word being spelled increased.

In order to account for this case and a similar earlier one Miceli, Silveri and Caramazza (1985) and Caramazza et al. proposed that a graphemic output buffer exists which can hold the graphemic representation of a word or nonword while it is being produced. Spelling a word takes time and involves a serial process in which each grapheme is specified and then outputted in whatever way is required. For this reason the buffer acts as a form of memory. It is failure of this memory function which is assumed to lead to the spelling errors such as deletions and substitutions. Moreover, the fact that errors increase with word length is consistent with a poor memory function because, for longer words, the buffer must hold letters longer.

The absence of any lexical influence on spelling is taken to indicate that the buffer holds only graphemic information. As a result the graphemic buffer can offer no advantage in the spelling of real words over nonwords. The nature of this graphemic representation is assumed to be abstract to account for our ability to produce spellings both in written form, orally and in more unusual ways such as tracing letters on someone's back!

Recent studies have provided additional instances of patients with impairments to the graphemic output buffer (e.g. Katz, 1991; Badecker, Hillis and Caramazza, 1990). Hillis and Caramazza (1989) describe two patients showing the same basic pattern as LB. However, they note that the two patients have contrasting asymmetrical error patterns with one tending to make errors in early letter positions and the other making them more frequently at the end – this contrasted with the more typical pattern of most errors in the middle of words. While acknowledging that this asymmetry might be a chance finding, its association with right versus left brain damage in the two cases, led the authors to suggest that the graphemic output might be spatially arranged and that lateralized lesions could selectively damage the buffer on one side of the spatial array.

Peripheral Dysgraphia

The model shown in figure 8.5 contains additional modules beyond the graphemic output buffer. The first module is the **allographic store** – this is a store of letter forms or **allographs** which specify different forms of the same letter (e.g. upper versus lower case). This code is still considered abstract in that the precise size of the letter is not specified. From here the allographic code passes to a **graphemic motor pattern store** which specifies the sequence, direction and relative size of the writing strokes needed to write the allograph. Finally these motor patterns are executed by a neuromuscular module.

This model was initially developed by Ellis (1982) as a means of interpreting writing errors in normal people. However, case studies involving **peripheral dysgraphia** – which can be defined as dysgraphia arising after a response has been specified in the graphemic output buffer – have added considerable weight to the argument. De Bastiani and Barry (1991) report an instance of what they term 'allographia'. The patient showed considerable problems spelling words and nonwords but there was no evidence that lexical variables were influencing perform-ance. This would suggest, at the very least, some impairment at the level of the graphemic output buffer or further on. The most striking aspect of the patient's errors were case change errors in which he would frequently mix upper and lower case letters when writing and, in addition, he would sometimes superimpose upper and lower case ver-sions of the same letter. The effects were dependent on word length with the appearance of these allographic errors increasing in frequency with word length. This led the authors to suggest that the deficit involved the disturbed selection of allographic forms in response to graphemic information outputted from the graphemic response buffer. In this connection it is important to note Patterson and Wing's (1989) study of a patient who had specific problems producing lower case letters. This suggests a selective deficit in retrieving a specific allographic form.

Spatial or 'afferent' dysgraphia (e.g. Ellis, Young and Flude, 1987) is a form of disturbed writing in which the patients either omit or repeat strokes within letters and may also repeat letters illegally (e.g. 'upper' as 'uppper'). Deficits of this kind suggest problems in the execution of motor patterns rather than the specification of allographs. A similar type of deficit is described by Lambert, Viader, Eustache and Morin (1994). Their patient could spell normally both orally and when allowed to use letter blocks. However when asked to write she made lots of errors which were not plausible phonologically but did bear some 'grapho-motor' similarity (e.g. the substitution of a V for U). A similar case is reported by Goodman and Caramazza (1986) in which written spelling errors often included grapho-motor mistakes (e.g. 'clue' as 'clve'). In these instances there appears to be disruption between the allograph level and the specification of motor patterns. In both cases the incorrect letters were well written suggesting that the neuromuscular execution aspect of writing was intact (for an additional case of this kind see Papagno, 1992).

Phonological Output Lexicon and Spelling

The model we have been considering has one additional link: a pathway between the phonological output lexicon and the graphemic output lexicon. Some accounts of spelling do not specify this pathway (e.g. Caramazza et al., 1987) but Ellis and Young believe that it is necessary to account for certain observations. In particular they note that normal subjects often make word substitutions of homophones when writing. Thus they might write 'there' instead of 'their' and 'scene' instead of 'seen'. It is argued that these errors represent the selection of an incorrect but similar-sounding spoken output which then maps via one-to-one connections, on to the wrong entry in the graphemic output lexicon. The idea that this phonological output arises at a lexical level is based on the observation that these types of errors are invariably real words and very often involve the production of irregular spellings (e.g. 'scene'). If these spellings were being generated by phoneme-to-grapheme correspondence rules we would not expect the appearance of errors based on irregular spellings. However, given the extensive presence of homophones in English (e.g. SAIL, SALE) and the relative scarcity of homophonic errors in spelling, it seems unlikely that the phonological output buffer is regularly involved in the generation of spellings.

There are also claims that the phonological output lexicon can influence spelling when it is activated via the proposed third, non-semantic, route. We saw, for example, that GE (Patterson, 1986, see p. 142) could write both regular and irregular words to dictation even though comprehension of those words was very poor. We also considered AN (Goodall and Phillips, 1995, see pp. 166–7) who was able to learn to read nonwords but in a way that indicated she was using whole word 'lexical' representations rather than grapheme-to-phoneme rules. Phillips and Goodall subsequently (1995) demonstrated that she was also able to write accurately to dictation those nonwords she had learned to read. In the absence of any ability to spell novel nonwords to dictation the authors argued that AN's nonword spelling must be using the same 'lexical' output as that responsible for nonword pronunciation. The idea that this third route to spelling exists has been challenged by Hillis and Caramazza (1991b) who claim that a development of their summation hypothesis can be extended to deal with lexical and non-lexical spelling. However, it is not easy to see how it could account for AN's preserved spelling of nonwords.

Oral Spelling

The conventional view is that oral and written spelling are both derived from the representation stored in the graphemic output buffer (Margolin, 1984; Hillis and Caramazza, 1989). Thus in the case of oral spelling it is assumed that a grapheme-to-letter name routine is employed which in turn maps on to speech output. There are now plenty of demonstrations that oral spelling can be impaired relative to written spelling (e.g. Bub and Kertesz, 1982b) and vice versa (e.g. Lesser, 1989). If this double

Table 8.4   Comparison of oral and written spelling errors produced by JJH (Hodges and Marshall, 1992). Reproduced with permission.

Stimulus	Oral spelling	Written spelling
base	BACE	Pose
strewn	STROON	STRAWM
sure	SHURE	* * * *
cape	KAPE	CABE
wheel	WHELE	VHEL
phrase	FRAYSE	PPAC
shoe	SHU	* * * * *
fern	FIRN	FIRN
snail	SNALE	* * * *
intense	INTENCE	ENTENCE
purple	PERPUL	PURDLE
rough	RUF	RONGH

dissociation represents different patterns of damage to peripheral production systems then it follows that lexical status (e.g. word vs. nonword) could not have any effect on these patterns of impairment because these factors exert an influence prior to the arrival of a word's specification in the graphemic output buffer (see above).

This view has been challenged by Lesser (1990) who describes a patient, CS, in which it is claimed that oral and written spelling were differently affected. When CS undertook written spelling he was far more able to spell words than nonwords – something we would term phonological dysgraphia. With oral spelling, the most influential factor was spelling to sound regularity thus resulting in a surface dysgraphia. However, there are problems with the data in that oral spelling is much better overall and this may have made it difficult to detect differences with written output.

In their study of JJH, Hodges and Marshall (1992) also present evidence showing qualitative differences in oral and written spelling. Table 8.4 shows JJH's oral and written spelling of 12 words. Oral spelling provides another clear example of surface dysgraphia. The written equivalents show only one regularization error but large numbers of orthographic substitution errors. Discussing these results Hodges and Marshall dismiss the idea that these differences could arise due to diffential peripheral damage and, instead, they take up Lesser's suggestion that oral and written spelling may involve separate output buffers.

These two cases thus suggest that oral and written spelling may differ more fundamentally than currently proposed. However, both studies urge caution until further data are presented. Moreoever, in the only other study to present qualitative differences between oral and written spelling (Goodman and Caramazza, 1986), it is notable that the authors felt able to account for their findings in terms of different impairments to peripheral mechanisms.

Summary

Acquired dyslexia can take a number of forms. A primary distinction is made between peripheral acquired dyslexias, in which there is some impairment in the earlier stages of word recognition (e.g. attentional dyslexia), and central dyslexias in which there is an impairment at higher levels of processing (e.g. gaining access to semantics or spelling-to-sound correspondence). The patterns of impairment observed in the acquired dyslexias can be used to construct a modular account of the reading process. Two forms of central dyslexia were emphasized: surface dyslexia and deep dyslexia. Surface dyslexia seems best accounted for in terms of preserved access to a grapheme-to-phoneme conversion process and an impairment in lexically-based pronunciation. Deep dyslexia is character-ized by semantic errors in reading and an inability to read nonwords. An explanation in terms of impaired grapheme-to-phoneme conversion seems implausible and a multiple deficit theory lacks parsimony. An alternative account is the right hemisphere hypothesis and this gains support from laboratory studies suggesting that a semantic code for words can be generated in the right hemisphere. It is also of interest that a connectionist model of reading for meaning, when 'lesioned' produces some of the symptoms of deep dyslexia.

   There is now abundant evidence that agraphia – impairment of writing and spelling – is not dependent on spoken language. In particular phono-logical dysgraphia emphasizes that spelling can occur in the absence of phonemic mediation. It has thus been proposed that a graphemic output lexicon exists to store the spellings of all known words. In addition there is a phoneme-to-grapheme system which allows us to spell unknown words. Existence of the latter is supported by surface dysgraphia. Several lines of evidence suggest that the spelling of a word or nonword is stored in a graphemic output buffer. Information in the graphemic output buffer is held to be abstract and converted into a written response by more peripheral modules concerned with specifying the size and shape of letters. It has also been claimed that oral spelling derives from the graphemic output buffer but this idea has recently been challenged.

9

Amnesia

NA was a young soldier who suffered a bizarre accident in his early twenties. He tells his own story:

> I was working at my desk. . . . My room mate had come in [and] he had taken one of my small fencing foils off the wall and I guess he was making like Cerano de Bergerac behind me. . . . I just felt a tap on the back. . . . I swung around. . . . at the same time he was making the lunge. I took it right in the left nostril, went up and punctured the cribiform area of my brain.

NA became of great interest because of the memory problem he developed as a result (e.g. Squire and Moore, 1979). This is illustrated by his conversation with the psychologist Wayne Wickelgren.

> I was introduced to NA in a small coffee room in the Psychology Department at MIT. . . . NA heard my name and he said,
> 'Wickelgren, that's a German name isn't it?'
> I said, 'No.'
> 'Irish?'
> 'No.'
> 'Scandinavian?'
> 'Yes, it's Scandinavian.'

[*Five minutes of further conversation then Wickelgren leaves the room. Five minutes later he returns. NA looks at him as if he had never seen him before and he is reintroduced*]

'Wickelgren, that's a German name isn't it?'
I said, 'No.'
'Irish?'
'No.'
'Scandinavian?'
'Yes, it's Scandinavian.'

(Lindsay and Norman, 1972, p. 310)

There are a number of important points to note about this incident. First, memory is not completely abolished; NA retains his knowledge of language; thus he understands what is said to him and produces sensible utterances. Also he possesses sufficient memory to keep track of what is being said within the conversation. What he appears to lack is the specific ability to retain new information over any appreciable amount of time. In short, NA has **amnesia**.

Neuroanatomy of the Amnesia

As you might suspect the brain lesion leading to NA's amnesia is unusual (although, see Dusoir, Kapur, Byrnes, 1990) and there are far more common causes of the disorder. Neuropathological studies show that the amnesia is caused by disruption to either of two specific brain regions: the midline diencephalon or the medial temporal lobe. Diencephalic damage is most commonly found in Korsakoff's Syndrome – a condition principally associated with, but not exclusive to, Wernicke's Encephalopathy arising from chronic alcoholism (see Kopelman, 1995a, for a recent overview). Diencephalic damage can also emerge following strokes and tumours, and there are several reports of diencephalic damage following other unusual intra-nasal penetrating head injuries. Amnesia following medial temporal lobe damage has more widespread origins including herpes simplex encephalitis, certain forms of stroke, carbon monoxide poisoning, anoxia and insulin overdose. In the case of NA it was originally thought that the fencing foil had selectively damaged the diencephalon, but it is now clear that areas of both the diencephalon and the medial temporal lobe were damaged (Squire, Amaral, Zola-Morgan, et al. 1989).

Behavioural features of Amnesia

In a later section we will consider whether the nature of a patient's lesion is important for understanding the nature of their amnesia. For the moment, however, we will treat all amnesic patients as if they were the same and examine in more detail their unifying behavioural features. As we saw NA seems to have no difficulty in keeping track of sentences and short conversations. In chapter 1 we considered the modal model of memory in which a fundamental distinction was drawn between short-term and long-term store (STS and LTS). STS is assumed to be the memory system underlying consciousness and will be involved in tasks such as keeping in mind the early parts of this sentence while you try to comprehend the rest.

Typically neuropsychologists measure STS function using a task known as digit span. This involves the presentation of a series of single digits (e.g. 6, 9, 2, 5, 7) and requiring the subject to repeat them back in the right order. Gradually the number of digits in the sequence is increased until the subject no longer performs accurately. As we have already noted, performance on this task is remarkably consistent, with adults having a digit span of 7 plus or minus 2. Figure 9.1 shows the performance of amnesic patients and controls on digit span and various others measures of memory span. In all cases you can see that amnesic performance is comparable to that of controls thus indicating that STS function appears intact in amnesia. Indeed, it has been argued that amnesics' normal performance on tasks such as digit span represents perhaps the most compelling reason for accepting the separable existence of STS (Parkin, 1993a).

Another form of memory ability that appears preserved in amnesics is procedural memory. This term is rather imprecise but can be used to describe the memory processes underlying the acquisition of skills and certain other forms of knowledge that are not directly accessible to consciousness and whose presence can only be demonstrated by action. Typing is a good example of procedural memory. If you are an experienced typist try describing where your fingers must be positioned to type the word 'thermometer'. A description will only be possible by performing the typing action and consequently describing your finger positions.

One of the most extensively investigated amnesic patients is HM who became densely amnesic following a brain operation that removed parts of his left and right temporal lobe (see Corkin, 1984; Parkin, 1996b) for an overview of this case). His operation took place in the mid-fifties and since then he has remembered little of the day-to-day events surrounding

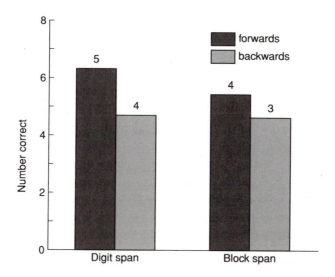

Figure 9.1 Performance of amnesic patients on digit span and block span tests. Block span is a non-verbal equivalent of digit span. Forward span requires the subject to reproduce items in the same order as the experimenter. Backward span requires the subject to reproduce them in reverse order. The numbers indicate the minimum score within the normal range.

him. However, it has been shown that he can learn new procedural memories. In one case HM was presented with the pursuit rotor task. This is essentially a test of hand–eye co-ordination in which a light beam emitted by a stylus must be focused on a spot which traces an erratic circular path. HM showed learning both within and across sessions but, on every occasion he was confronted with the test, he denied having done it before – this occurred even though he eventually learned how to turn the equipment on and begin testing. HM, and many other amnesic patients, have also shown retention of closure pictures (see figure 9.2). These are incomplete pictures which you can suddenly see are depicting something obvious like a face or an object. Once you have solved one of these pictures you are very quickly able to identify it if shown it again even though you have no conscious access to the perceptual information you acquired in order to do that. Successful learning by amnesics can again be attributed to preserved procedural memory.

Patients with amnesia have two major deficits: a severe anterograde amnesia which prevents them from acquiring any new knowledge, and retrograde amnesia where the patient is unable to remember events and knowledge learned prior to the amnesia-inducing brain damage (this is known as the pre-morbid period and contrasts with the post-morbid

Figure 9.2 Examples of closure pictures.

period which refers to events subsequent to the occurrence of brain damage). Anterograde amnesia is always present but retrograde amnesia can be extremely variable with some patients showing extensive deficits and others virtually no retrograde loss at all.

Anterograde amnesia can be demonstrated in many ways. On a test involving the free recall of a 12-word list an amnesic patient would typically recall one or two words after a one minute delay but nothing after a longer period. On a test of paired-associate learning involving unrelated pairs of words (e.g. 'obey–inch'), learning, if achieved at all, would be painfully slow. On a forced choice recognition test in which the patient had to choose between previously exposed stimulus and a novel stimulus, performance would typically be at chance (Parkin and Leng, 1993).

Retrograde amnesia is more difficult to investigate because each person's pre-morbid experience is different. Psychologists try to solve this problem by devising retrograde memory tests, which test memories one can assume that most people should have acquired through normal experience. Typically, these tests involve identifying people and events from different decades. The aim is to evaluate memories formed at a particular time but they are complicated because people and events continue to be talked about long after the decade in which they initially occurred. As an alternative one can use autobiographical cueing in which a patient has to date memories retrieved in response to specific cue words. A problem here is that memories will vary in their specificity and it will be difficult to authenticate much of what the person remembers.

Despite these methodological problems it is clear that retrograde amnesia commonly shows a temporal gradient: memories formed early in life are more likely to survive than those formed during a later period (this statement excludes the period of so-called infantile amnesia in which memories formed in the first few years of life subsequently become unavailable). This is true both for personal memories and memories of public events (see figure 9.3). In some patients temporal gradients are absent but the reverse, greater impairment of memories formed earlier in life, has never been reported. The existence of temporal gradients has been acknowledged for a long time and is often described as reflecting Ribot's Law (Ribot, 1882) which states that the vulnerability of a memory to brain injury is inversely related to its age. We will consider why this Law exists in a subsequent section (see Kopelman, 1993, for a recent review). For an overview of amnesia see Parkin (1996b).

Episodic and Semantic Memory

In our example of NA's behaviour we noted that his language appeared normal and that his difficulty arose from remembering what he had said at a particular time. A number of psychologists, most notably Tulving (1989) have argued that a dissociation of this kind indicates a functional division between episodic memory and semantic memory. Episodic memory can be defined as the 'autobiographical record' of our lives – that part of our memory that gives us personal continuity with the past and is used to retrieve information about specific personal events. It provides answers to questions such as 'what did you do yesterday?' Semantic memory corresponds to our store of knowledge about language, rules and concepts and, although derived from specific events, it resides independent of any record of those events. Thus in order to retrieve a specific piece of knowledge, such as what is the capital of Peru?, you do not have to retrieve the original episode in which you acquired that knowledge.

Clinical presentation of amnesic patients seems consistent with a selective impairment of episodic memory but a finer-grained analysis does not produce such a clear picture. Amnesic patients do not, for example, acquire new vocabulary at all easily – HM is thought to have learned only six new words since his operation in 1953. Findings like these might be countered on the grounds that episodic memory is needed for the initial retention of new language until assimilation into semantic memory has occurred.

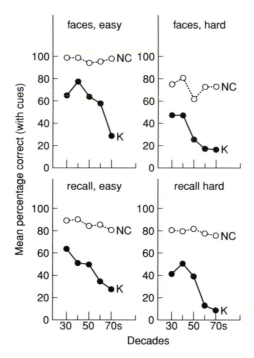

Figure 9.3 Performance of a group of Korsakoff patients and Normal Controls (NC) on test of remote memory involving the identification of famous faces and events. Note the temporal gradient showing better memory for earlier events. Data from Albert et al. (1974).

More difficult is the actual nature of retrograde memory loss. Superficially, it seems that episodic memory is the predominant impairment but this conclusion could be misleading. First, the various tests used to measure retrograde amnesia are primarily tests of general knowledge (e.g. recognizing a face, describing a world event) and failure on them cannot be construed as a specific inability to remember distinct episodes. Also the claim that amnesic patients have preserved language derives from normal performance on standardized language tests such as the vocabulary component of *Wechsler Adult Intelligence Scale*. The problem here is that these tests concentrate on the nature of language skills assumed to have been acquired in early adult life. Normal language might therefore reflect the lesser vulnerability of memories acquired early in life. Indeed a study in my laboratory by Banks and Cooper (unpublished) showed that when Korsakoff patients were asked to define vocabulary introduced during the later stages of the pre-morbid period (e.g. filofax, xerox) they were unable to do so (see also Verfaellie and Roth, in press).

The general picture thus suggests that both episodic and semantic memory are lost and, for this reason, some workers (e.g. Squire, 1987) have suggested a single term, declarative memory, should be used to describe the long-term deficit of amnesic patients. Declarative memory can be defined as any memory that can be accessed consciously, and it provides a neat contrast to procedural memory. However, as we shall see in a later section the notion of unitary declarative memory no longer seems tenable.

Explicit and Implicit Memory

In our discussion of procedural memory we noted two examples, pursuit rotor learning and perceptual closure. These are not the only tasks on which amnesics show preserved learning. Patients can, for example, show learning on a task which asks them to arrange a meaningless string of words into a sentence or to complete a jigsaw. In both instances performance improves when the task is repeated, but the patients have no recollection of having done the tasks before. If we call all this learning 'procedural memory' it is as if we are saying there is a single memory system underlying the performance of all the tasks. However, this seems very unlikely given how different the tasks are from one another, so instead we might argue that there are lots of different procedural memories each responsible for a particular form of preserved learning.

While the above conclusion might satisfy some, others have taken the view that it is confusing and, instead, have suggested that the performance on any memory task should be defined in terms of the demands the task makes on the subject. While various terms have been used the most common example of this approach involves the distinction between explicit and implicit memory (Schacter, 1987). Explicit memory corresponds to what we have already described as episodic memory: any memory task which requires the subject to recollect a previous learning experience (e.g. a word list, a personal event). Implicit memory, in contrast, is any memory test which does not, of necessity, require recollection of a previous event. If we consider our examples of preserved learning, pursuit rotor and perceptual closure, we can see that both of these meet this implicit memory criterion. In the case of pursuit rotor this is a motor skill and the knowledge acquired to enhance skill cannot be consciously accessed, so there is nothing to recollect from one session to the next. Similarly the information stored about closure pictures is not consciously accessible and learning is again independent of recollection.

Within the laboratory, implicit memory in amnesia is most commonly demonstrated using repetition priming. In a prototypical experiment the patient is presented with a list of words (e.g. WATCH) and, after a short interval two forms of test are given, cued recall and stem completion priming. In the former the patient is given the initial letters WAT——? and is asked to remember the list-word that corresponded to those three letters. Performance by amnesic patients on this test will be very poor but if asked to say the first word that 'pops' into mind beginning with those three letters the patients will say WATCH at a level well above chance. This latter effect is known as priming and it shows that the prior learning episode (presenting the word list) can influence performance even though the patient cannot consciously recollect that episode.

The performance of amnesic patients on variants of the repetition priming task has been used to investigate the nature of the memory systems responsible for implicit memory. Schacter (1990) and Tulving and Schacter (1990) have proposed that implicit memory effects are mediated by a perceptual representation system (PRS) which corresponds to a series of subsystems each dealing with a particular 'domain' of information. Each of these subsystems represents information about the form and structure of a particular type of stimulus but does not represent any information about meaning, it is held to be pre-semantic. The theory is very much tied to the modular accounts of object and language processing we identified in chapters, 3, 7 and 8. Thus PRS systems have been identified for objects at the level of structural descriptions and for words at both the auditory and verbal lexical levels.

Evidence for a structural description PRS being involved in implicit memory comes from studies by Schacter and his colleagues (e.g. Schacter, Cooper and Delaney, 1990; Schacter, 1992). In one experiment normal subjects were presented with a series of line drawings half of which depicted possible objects and the other half impossible objects (see figure 9.4). As each object appeared subjects had to decide either the main direction the object was pointing in (left vs. right) or, in the elaborative condition, to think of a real world object that the line drawing reminded them of. Two tests were then given. In the implicit memory test subjects had to decide as quickly as possible whether a line drawing was or was not a real object. A priming effect was demonstrated in that subjects made quicker decisions about real objects that had been presented in the first phase of the experiment. However, there was no effect of the type of processing undertaken and also no priming effect for impossible objects. In contrast recognition was significantly better for line drawings subjected to the elaborative task.

Schacter el al. interpret these findings as priming at the level of the stuctural description PRS. Real objects show priming because possible relations between the elements of the stimulus allow the system to derive a structural description. Setting up of this description subsequently

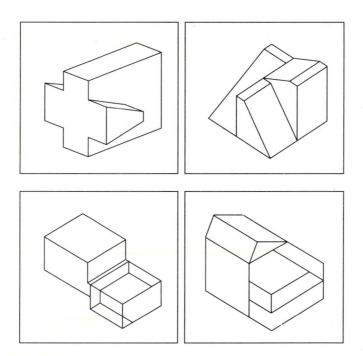

Figure 9.4 Possible and impossible stimuli used in Schacter et al.'s experiment. The upper stimuli are possible objects, the lower ones impossible objects. From Schacter et al. (1990), p. 7. Copyright © 1990 by the American Psychological Association. Reproduced with the permission.

provides a basis for recognizing this object on a subsequent occasion and thus facilitates object decision relative to a novel possible object. The view that this priming occurs at a pre-semantic levels comes from the demonstration that a manipulation which enhances recognition (elaboration) does not have any effect on priming.

Evidence for priming at the auditory level comes from an investigation of JP – a patient with word meaning deafness who we first encountered in chapter 7 (Schacter et al., 1992). As you may recall she was able to write well to dictation and repeat words she could not understand. This indicated intact lexical knowledge of heard words without comprehension. JP was exposed to a list of auditorially presented words and her implicit memory tested by presenting studied and non-studied words in white noise and requiring her to identify them. JP exhibited a priming effect, as shown by enhanced identification of studied words, of similar magnitude to controls despite no ability to recognize which words she had heard in the first phase of the experiment.

Arguments that visual word priming occurs at a pre-semantic level comes from several sources. A variety of studies have examined whether amnesic subjects can show priming for nonwords as well as words – this would be analogous with the priming effect observed for possible but not real objects. Early studies failed to demonstrate priming of nonwords but more recent evidence indicates that nonword priming is a reliable phenomenon in most amnesic subjects (e.g. Cermak, Verfaellie, Milberg et al., 1991). This finding suggests that priming is uninfluenced by semantics – a conclusion also reached from many studies showing that semantic orienting tasks have no influence on the extent of priming despite having large effects on explicit memory (for further discussion of priming and the PRS system see Schacter and Tulving, 1994).

Implicit Memory, Amnesia and Semantics

The view of implicit memory put forward above suggests that all implicit memory effects are mediated at pre-semantic level. A logical consequence of this conclusion, therefore, is that memory for meaning could not be demonstrated using implicit testing. However, there are a number of findings which suggest that implicit memory does exist for semantic information as well. Earlier, for example, we noted that amnesic subjects showed implicit memory on a sentence rearrangement task and this is not easy to explain without arguing that some sort of priming at the semantic level occurs. McAndrews, Glisky and Schacter (1987) showed amnesic subjects puzzle sentences such as 'The haystack was important because the cloth ripped' and asked them to think of the concept that made sense of it ('parachute'). This task was then again represented at intervals of up to a week and solution ability compared with novel sentences of a similar kind. At all intervals a conceptual priming effect was obtained in that solutions to previously exposed sentences were more readily available than those for novel sentences. The study compared severely amnesic subjects with moderately amnesic subjects and showed that despite far better recognition memory for the sentences in the moderately impaired group, the extent of conceptual priming for the two patient groups was indistinguishable.

Even greater retention of implicit memory comes from the study of KC, a man who became densely amnesic following a closed head injury (Tulving, Hayman and MacDonald, 1991). He was shown pictures accompanied by a sentence which was vaguely related to the picture (e.g. a man in a hospital setting with the sentence MEDICINE and cured HICCUP). Even after intervals of one year KC could still reliably produce the final word of many of the sentences he had been shown despite having no explicit recollection of having been shown the sentences.

A particular issue has been whether amnesic patients can show novel association priming. Graf and Schacter (1985) initially exposed amnesics to pairs of unrelated words (e.g. WINDOW–REASON) and then gave stem completion tests for the second member of each pair. When completion was attempted the second pair was either paired with its original partner (e.g. WINDOW–REA——?) or a different word (OFFICER–REA——?). In this way priming could be compared as a function of same or different semantic context.

The logic of this experiment is that higher levels of priming in the same versus different condition indicates that a semantic association between the previously unrelated word pairs has been established and that this contributes, in part, to the priming effect. Graf and Schacter (1985) obtained an ambiguous result in that better priming was observed in the same context condition but only for less memory-impaired patients. This suggested that explicit memory for the associations might have something to do with the observed effects. This seemed to be confirmed by a study of severely amnesic subjects which failed to show any influence of context on priming (for a related finding see Mutter, Howard, Howard and Wiggs, 1990).

Shimamura and Squire (1989) followed up the Graf and Schacter study by presenting amnesic subjects with sentences in which two words were highlighted (e.g. A BELL was hanging over the baby's CRADLE). The same manipulation of context was then undertaken but no evidence of enhanced priming with same context was found. Mayes and Gooding (1989) used a similar type of task and found that only a proportion of their amnesic subjects showed context effects in priming.

Other studies, however, suggest that implicit memory for novel associations does occur. Musen and Squire (1993) presented pairs of unrelated words for study and then tested implicit memory by measuring the speed at which these words could be read. In order to test for the influence of novel association learning, reading speed for 'old' word pairs (i.e. pairs presented during learning) were contrasted with new re-pairings of words. In this task novel association learning is demonstrated by faster reading of old word pairs. Two experiments using a single trial did not show any evidence of novel association learning but, when multiple learning trials were used, evidence for novel association learning was obtained. Paller and Mayes (1994) reported a similar finding using the 'club sandwich' paradigm in which two unrelated words (e.g. PUPPY, CACTUS) are presented briefly in quick succession. A retention test then follows in which pairs of words are presented in the same way and the subject is required to identify them. It was found that identification was most accurate when both words had been presented as a pair in the learning phase thus suggesting that some association between them had been made.

A key factor determining the novel association learning in amnesics is the nature of the initial learning phase. Graf and Schacter (1985) showed that novel associations were acquired quite readily by amnesic subjects providing the pairs were presented in an elaborative context. This involved presenting each word pair and asking subjects to decide how easily the two words could be related to each other and then requiring subjects to form a sentence using the two words.

Recently we have also been investigating novel association learning in amnesic patients (Jenkins and Parkin, in preparation). Patients with Korsakoff's Syndrome and Closed Head Injury were shown sentences in which one word was highlighted and the last word was reduced to a fragment, their task was to complete it (the answer was supplied if they failed to solve the fragment). Implicit memory was then tested by presenting the test fragment either in the context of the highlighted word presented during the study (same context) or a different word (different context). Across three experiments it was found that completion of the test fragments was significantly higher in the same context condition. Subsequent analyses indicated that this novel association priming was unrelated to measures of explicit memory.

The above studies thus show that implicit memory for semantic information can be demonstrated under a wide variety of conditions. With respect to novel associations these can be acquired under implicit conditions providing that the initial learning conditions allow elaborative processing to occur and thus unite the two items. A further factor is undoubtedly severity of amnesia with milder patients more likely to show effects – perhaps because explicit memory for the material is also partly available.

Complex Learning in Amnesia

Recently there has been interest in the possibility that amnesic subjects might be capable of more complex learning than that typically exhibited in implicit memory experiments. One set of investigations has involved the ability of amnesic subjects to learn artificial grammars (Reber, 1967). In the first phase of these experiments subjects attend to a series of letter strings which adhere to a finite grammatical system which specifies legal and illegal sequences of letters. Then they are given further strings of letters and are asked to decide whether or not each string of letters is grammatical. Typically subjects perform well above chance at this test indicating that the grammar has been learned. However, there has been debate as to whether this learning occurs via implicit learning processes or involves partial explicit recollection of the exemplars used in the learning phase. Knowlton, Ramus and Squire (1992) showed that amnesic subjects could acquire artificial grammar even though their ability to recognize the exemplars they had been trained on was extremely poor (see also Knowlton and Squire, 1994). This suggests that artificial grammar learning does not depend on partial recollection of exemplars.

Squire and Frambach (1990) explored the ability of amnesic subjects to learn on the 'sugar production task' (Berry and Broadbent, 1984). This was a computer simulation in which subjects had to maintain a desired level of output (a quantity of sugar) by manipulating a variable input (number of workers hired). Production level was determined by an equation and optimum performance could only be obtained by learning the principles embodied in this equation. Both amnesic subjects and normal subjects learned the task effectively but only normal subjects were able to state what the rules governing optimum performance were. This suggests that the critical learning occurs at an implicit level.

Recently Knowlton, Squire and Gluck (1994) examined probabilistic learning in normal and amnesic subjects. In one experiment subjects attempted to learn which of two fictitious diseases ('nermitis' or 'caldosis') was most reliably predicted by combinations of between one and four different symptoms (headache, fatigue, rash, sneezing). For any given combination of symptoms the probabilities associated with each disease could vary. Thus headache and fatigue predicted nermitis with a 90 per cent probability, whereas rash and sneezing predicted the illness with only a 43 per cent probability. On each trial subjects were presented with between one and four symptoms and were required to indicate which disease they thought the hypothetical patient was suffering from. Feedback about accuracy was given on each trial. In this and other similar tasks the amnesics learned the probability of different outcomes at rate similar to controls. However, when learning was extended control performance exceeded that of the amnesics – a finding attributed to additional explicit recollection of particular outcomes on earlier trials.

Explaining Anterograde Amnesia

Attempts to provide an explanatory theory of amnesia have concentrated on the amnesic patients' profound impairments on tests measuring the explicit recollection of new information. Perhaps the first modern theory of amnesia was the **consolidation** theory (Milner, 1966), which proposed that amnesics lack the fundamental ability to form new permanent memory traces. Soon after its proposal this theory was discounted on the grounds that the amnesic deficit was not total because amnesic patients were very clearly able to learn under certain conditions.

One of the conditions was demonstrated in a classic study by Warrington and Weiskrantz (1970) in which amnesic patients were first shown individual words. When memory was tested using conventional methods the amnesics performed poorly. However, when asked to identify degraded word forms the amnesic patients did as well as controls when the degraded words corresponded to target words they had studied. From what we have considered earlier we can see that this is just one more example of preserved procedural memory in amnesia and, as such, it is irrelevant to understanding the amnesic deficit. However, at the time a different interpretation was placed on the results. It was argued that amnesic patients suffered from high levels of proactive interference in that recall was contaminated by large numbers of additional relevant responses. However, the degraded words acted as 'surrogate' retrieval cues in that they restricted recall to only those words that would map onto the degraded form.

Warrington and Weiskrantz thus proposed a **retrieval deficit** theory of amnesia in which the deficit was localized entirely at the output stage. However, the theory failed to provide an adequate account of amnesia. It was difficult, for example, to explain why amnesic patients were able to retrieve variable amounts of their pre-morbid memories if amnesia was due to a generalized retrieval impairment. One could, rather awkwardly, restrict the theory to explaining anterograde amnesia but here the authors themselves produced additional data dismissing the retrieval deficit theory.

The Context Deficit Theory of Amnesia

One theory gaining reasonable support argues that amnesia represents a deficit in the use of **contextual information** (Mayes, 1988). Context can be defined as information associated with a specific memory that allows differentiation of that memory from other memories. In modern research it is usual to distinguish between two forms of context, **intrinsic** and **extrinsic**. Intrinsic context refers to features that are an integral part of the stimulus itself. In a face, for example, intrinsic contextual features would be eye colour, hair length, size of nose and so on. For words, intrinsic context would relate to the particular meaning extracted from the word at the time of learning. Extrinsic context corresponds to those features that are merely incidentally associated with the stimulus itself.

These extrinsic features include time of encounter and surroundings, (often referred to as temporo-spatial attributes). Studies of amnesia have concentrated on memory for extrinsic context but, more recently, possible deficits in memory for intrinsic context have also been explored.

Before going any further with the contextual deficit theory it is first necessary to consider the nature of recognition memory in a little more detail. In a seminal paper Mandler (1980) emphasized that recognition memory is not a single entity but that it comprises two separable components, **familiarity and recollection**. Familiarity corresponds to an experience such as meeting someone in the street and realizing that you know them but being unable to place them in a specific context. Recollection refers to the additional ability of retrieving the specific context within which a familiar person has been encountered.

Recently Jacoby (e.g. Jacoby, 1991; Jacoby, Toth and Yonelinas, 1993) has proposed the **process dissociation framework** as a means of measuring the extent to which a subject's recognition response is determined by familiarity or contextual retrieval. In a typical experiment subjects are presented with two successive lists of words, one spoken and the other visually presented. Two types of recognition test follow: In the **exclusion** condition subjects were required to make a contextual recollection in that they were required to identify only words from list 2. In the **inclusion** condition no contextual demands were imposed, subjects were just told to recognize words from either list. The assumption of this methodology is that recognition of a list 1 word in the exclusion condition indicates that the subject has forgotten the context of that word's presentation and that the recognition response is based on familiarity. The extent to which familiarity-based responding is occurring is based on comparing incorrect recognition of list 1 words in the exclusion condition with the recognition rate for those words in the inclusion condition.

Using Jacoby's technique Verfaellie and Treadwell (1993) demonstrated that amnesic recognition memory was largely based on estimates of familiarity – thus suggesting that the amnesic deficit rests primarily on failing to remember context. However, in a critique of this study, Roediger and McDermott (1994) have argued that the Jacoby procedure is difficult to interpret with amnesics because their recognition memory is generally so defective. In a subsequent reply, Verfaellie (1994) addresses these concerns and remains confident in her original conclusions concerning amnesic recognition memory.

Earlier studies using different methods also point toward poor contextual memory in amnesics. Winocur and Kinsbourne (1978) examined how Korsakoff amnesics performed on the A→B, A→C paired associate paradigm. Here patients are first asked to learn one response to a stimulus (e.g. elephant→cigar) and then, on a second list, associate the original stimulus with a new response (elephant→telephone). Typically amnesics show many 'intrusions' on this test in that on the A→C phase they tend to recall many of the A→B associations. However, when the A→C phase took place in an environment that was very distinct from that used in the A→B phase the number of A→B intrusions was significantly lower. It was presumed that the distinctive context provided in the A→C phase enabled the associations to become linked with sufficient contextual information to discriminate them more effectively from those learned in the A→B phase. Amnesics may, therefore, be poor at encoding extrinsic context under normal conditions but be able to utilize it providing it is sufficiently distinctive.

Huppert and Piercy (1978a) investigated the performance of Korsakoff amnesics and normal people on a task involving temporal discrimination. The subjects saw 80 pictures on one day followed by a different set of 80 pictures on the following day. Within each set half the pictures were shown once and the remainder shown three times. Ten minutes after the day 2 presentation ended, subjects were shown a sample of pictures from days 1 and 2. Subjects were asked to decide whether or not each picture had been seen 'today' (i.e. on day 2 as opposed to day 1). As one would expect both groups most often placed pictures seen three times on day 2 in the 'today' category and pictures shown once on day 1 least often. However, the groups differed in that amnesics were just as likely to categorize as 'today' pictures seen three times on day 1 as compared with those seen once on day 2. In contrast, control subjects placed very few of the repeated day 1 pictures in the 'today' category but correctly categorized over two-thirds of the pictures seen only once on day 2.

On the assumption that familiarity fades with time, the performance of amnesics indicates that their decisions about context were determined by the overall familiarity of each picture. Thus pictures presented three times on day 1 seemed as recent to amnesics as those presented once on day 2 because both were associated with similar amounts of familiarity. In contrast, the performance of normal subjects seems determined by both factors. The more accurate identification of pictures presented three times on day 2 compared with those presented once suggests that familiarity plays a role. However, the fact that normals accurately distinguished pictures presented once on day 2 from those presented three times on day 1 indicates that their responses involved an additional search stage in which each picture was linked to a specific temporal context, i.e. 'day 1' or 'day 2'. The fact that the amnesics could not do this implies they have no record of temporal context.

One problem with Huppert and Piercy's study was that amnesic and normal subjects were tested over the same retention interval. Thus not only were amnesics poorer on temporal discrimination they also performed worse overall. This allows for the possibility that the temporal discrimination deficit might characterize poor memory in general and not reflect a specific impairment in amnesia. To test for this Meudell, Mayes, Ostergaard and Pickering (1985) replicated Huppert and Piercy's finding but also repeated the experiment on normal subjects using much longer retention intervals. The effect of this was to make the normal people's memory as poor as the Korsakoffs' in the study. Despite this, the normal subjects were far more able to discriminate events in time thus suggesting that Korsakoff amnesia is qualitatively different to poor normal memory.

More than One Form of Amnesia?

As we have seen amnesia can arise from damage to two very distinct regions of the brain – the midline diencephalon and the medial temporal lobe region. Some theorists (e.g. Warringtron and Weiskrantz, 1982) have argued that this is not problematic because, although distinct, these two brain regions are linked together as parts of the limbic system. As a result it is not surprising that similar deficits arise when each of the regions is damaged independently.

A problem with this unitary view of amnesia is that it presupposes that the limbic system comprises a memory circuit in which all the structures play the same role in memory formation. Unfortunately it is not easy to take this further and explain exactly what this circuit is achieving. The only formal proposal was that of Warrington and Weiskrantz (1982) in which they suggested that normal memory depends on the moderation of semantic memory in the temporal lobes by cognitive mediational mechanisms located in the frontal cortex. Cognitive mediation was defined as those processes which enable the use of imagery, elaboration and other means of embellishment known to enhance memory. In experimental terms the existence of cognitive mediation might be manifest in experiments where instructions to use imagery exert a beneficial effect on performance.

Warrington and Weiskrantz argued on the basis of their own work and others that imagery instructions did not enhance the memory performance of amnesics. However, Leng and Parkin (1988a) pointed out that some of these studies involved very poor levels of performance which would make any effects difficult to detect. They went on to show, in line with several other studies, that imagery does improve amnesics' memory quite considerably. Thus using the only operational definition of cognitive mediation, there was no evidence of a deficit in amnesics.

An alternative to the 'circuit' view of amnesia is that different components of the limbic system undertake different functions within memory. The major corollary of this view is that damage to different limbic sites should produce qualitatively different impairments of memory. Work in this area is in its infancy but, as we shall see, there is emerging evidence of important differences between patients whose amnesia arises from damage centred on the temporal lobes and that due to damage in the midline diencephalon.

LHermitte and Signoret (1972) carried out the first study purporting to show a difference between temporal lobe and diencephalic amnesia. They compared patients with Korsakoff's Syndrome with three patients suffering extensive temporal lobe damage following herpes simplex encephalitis. A number of tasks were used but the basic finding was that the TL patients learned less effectively and forgot more rapidly than the Korsakoffs.

There are, however, problems with studies comparing forgetting rates in different groups of patients. Amnesic patients vary in the severity of their deficit in ways similar to patients with other neuropsychological disorders. As a result any difference in forgetting rate might be spurious because the groups being compared differed in the severity of their amnesia. To get around this a number of authors have advocated a 'titration procedure' to equate initial learning and thus try and circumvent differences in severity. A good example is a study by Huppert and Piercy (1978b) in which they compared the fogetting rate of controls, a group of Korsakoffs and the temporal lobe amnesic HM. They presented 120 pictures, memory for which was tested after ten minutes, one day and seven days. Acquisition was equated at ten minutes by using variable exposure during learning. Controls saw each picture once for only one second, Korsakoffs each picture for eight seconds and HM saw each picture for ten seconds.

At ten minutes HM's score fell just within the Korsakoff range therefore allowing, it was claimed, a rate given similar levels of acquisition. HM appeared to forget more rapidly but this result has been challenged. Weiskrantz (1985) points out that if HM's performance is replotted as in terms of retention as a proportion of initial acquisition (rather than just his raw recognition rate) his forgetting curve is similar to the Korsakoffs. Another problem is that although matched at ten minutes after the end of the learning sequence there are big differences in the amount of time elapsed since the start of learning. For controls the retention interval starts only two minutes after the learning sequence started whereas for HM, retention starts twenty minutes after learning commenced (for an overview of case HM, see Parkin 1996c).

Context Memory in Diencephalic and Temporal Lobe Amnesia

Most work in this area has been carried out in my own laboratory in conjunction with Nick Leng and, most recently, Nikki Hunkin. Our starting point was that the various experiments described earlier in which amnesic patients had shown very poor memory for context relied almost exclusively on Korsakoff patients. As a result these experiments were more appropriately described as demonstrations that diencephalic amnesia could be attributed to a contextual memory deficit.

We set out to discover whether a contextual impairment might also explain the memory impairment experienced in survivors of herpes simplex encephalitis and other patient groups in which amnesia arose as a consequence of primary temporal lobe damage (Parkin, Leng and Hunkin, 1990). To do this a recency judgement task was devised. On Trial 1 a 2×2 array of pictures was presented and the subject was instructed to try and remember them. Following a 60-second interval involving distracting activity the patient was required to pick the four target pictures from an array of 16 pictures. This procedure was then repeated three times except that pictures that had been targets became distractors and vice versa. Three more trials were given and the subject's task was to indicate which four pictures they had been asked to identify *most recently*. By the fourth trial each picture had been a target once and a distractor three times. The effect of this was that, after Trial 1, all items were familiar and some record of temporal context was required for correct recognition.

Korsakoff patients showed a marked drop in performance from Trial 1 whereas the TL group did not show a reliable drop in performance until Trial 4 (see figure 9.5a). A possible problem with these findings is that Korsakoff patients are known to be very sensitive to proactive interference. To check that this was not the explanation the experiment was repeated using completely different items on each trial and, as figure 9.5b shows, both groups performed similarly under these conditions (Hunkin and Parkin, 1993).

As we saw earlier, it has been suggested that temporal lobe amnesics forget more rapidly. It was therefore possible that the good performance of the temporal lobe patients on the recency judgement task arose because they simply forgot the pictures used on each trial very quickly. To test this possibility we repeated the original recency experiment varying the retention interval from 30 to 120 seconds (Hunkin and Parkin, 1993). If rapid forgetting were contributing to the good perform-ance of the temporal lobe group one would have expected poorer

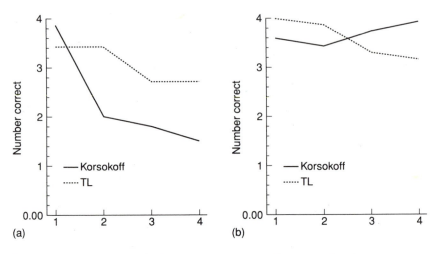

Figure 9.5 Performance of Korsakoff patients and Temporal Lobe (TL) amnesics on two versions of the recency judgement task.

performance with 30 second intervals compared with 120. However, the results showed no difference in performance across retention intervals, thus suggesting that rate of forgetting was not important.

In a further study (Hunkin, Parkin and Longmore, 1994) we have compared diencephalic and temporal lobe amnesics on the list discrimination task. In this task subjects are presented with two lists of sentences separated by 3 minutes of conversation. Subjects are then presented with a single list of sentences containing both targets and distractors, and are asked to identify the sentences they saw in the learning sequence. Further, contingent on identifying a target they are required to say whether it occurred in the first or second list.

The list discrimination task provides measures of both recognition and memory for temporal order. The two groups did not differ in terms of recognition. However, there was a marked difference in memory of temporal order. In line with an earlier study by Squire (1982), the diencephalic group were at chance on discrimination but the temporal lobe group performed significantly above chance. Moreover, the latter group also showed a strong correlation between recognition and correct list discrimination.

Incidental Frontal Lobe Dysfunction and Forms of Amnesia

The experiments reported so far appear to show that diencephalic amnesics differ from temporal lobe amnesics on two tasks – recency judgement and memory for temporal order. A problem, however, is that most of the amnesic patients used in these studies were either Korsakoff patients or survivors of herpes simplex encephalitis. Both these patient groups create a complication because, along with their respective diencephalic and temporal lobe lesions they also have damage to the frontal cortex. This difference tends to vary systematically between the groups with Korsakoffs suffering primarily dorso-lateral lesions and the herpes simplex patients orbito-frontal damage. This difference is also reflected in behavioural performance on different tests of frontal lobe function (see Leng and Parkin, 1988b).

The presence of frontal lobe damage in the amnesic patients is important because, as we shall see in the next chapter, the frontal lobes play a significant role in memory performance. For now we note only that impaired recency judgements and loss of memory for temporal order have both been found in patients with circumscribed frontal lesions (see next chapter). It was therefore possible that the apparent group differences on the recency task stemmed from the different patterns of frontal lobe damage present within the groups rather than any qualitative difference in their underlying amnesia.

To investigate this possibility we examined the relationship between performance on the recency task and measures of frontal lobe dysfunction. No correlations were found and there were also no correlations between frontal function and our measure of temporal order memory in either patient group. A problem, however, was that the diencephalic amnesics performed at chance on the list discrimination measure thus making any conclusions about a lack of correlation between this measure and frontal function impermissible. However, we have recently been gathering evidence from single case studies of patients who have suffered discrete lesions to the diencephalon and by examining how these patients perform on the same memory tasks as those used to evaluate Korsakoff patients it has been possible to discover whether impairments shown these patients reflect their basic diencephalic pathology or are due to the more widespread cortical damage that is usually present as well. Thus if we observe exactly the same type of memory impairment in a patient with a discrete lesion of the diencephalon as that shown by a Korsakoff we can assume, on the grounds of parsimony, that the latter's memory failure is of diencephalic origin.

JR was in his early 40s when he suffered a small haemorrhage which produced a relatively small lesion in a region of the thalamus known as the dorsomedial nucleus. The effect, however, was quite devastating in that he developed a severe verbal memory impairment. We gave JR the list discrimination task using both words and abstract designs and his performance on discrimination was at chance even though his recognition memory for abstract designs was much better than that for words (Parkin, Rees, Hunkin and Rose, 1994). JR's impairment on list discrimination, which we have also shown in another patient, MK, also with diencephalic damage but no frontal involvement (Parkin and Hunkin, 1993), suggests that the contextual memory deficit shown by Korsakoffs may be a feature of their diencephalic pathology rather than additional frontal damage they have suffered. In addition it is of interest that this deficit in temporal context memory is not found for remote memory in either JR or MK (see also Bowers, Verfaellie, Valenstein and Heilman, 1988). In contrast Korsakoff patients are markedly unable to make judgements about the temporal characteristics of remote memories. This provides a strong indication that the mechanisms underlying the temporal dimension of remote memory are unrelated to the processes that allow the acquisition of new temporal memory

Present evidence thus suggests that the context deficit theory only appears to work well for patients with diencephalic amnesia, although we must acknowledge that some studies showing disproportionately impaired context memory in amnesia have used mixed groups of patients (e.g. Verfaellie and Treadwell, 1993). The deficit responsible for temporal lobe amnesia is less obvious at present. However, in a series of articles I have suggested that a plausible explanation is that these patients have a consolidation deficit which affects both the storage of contextual and target information, and for this reason there is no disproportionate impairment of one relative to the other (e.g. Parkin, 1992).

The Fractionation of Retrograde Amnesia

From an earlier section it would appear that retrograde amnesia tends to affect both semantic and episodic distinction thus undermining the underlying reality of these two forms of memory. However, more recent studies of retrograde memory impairment have argued against the simple loss of declarative memory argument by demonstrating that remote memory can fractionate in a number of different ways.

A good case in point is RFR who became globally amnesic as a consequence of herpes simplex encephalitis (Warrington and McCarthy, 1988). This patient's RA was severe in that he could not given an accurate description of any public or personal event from his past. He could not identify friends, nor even his close family. Given this, it was surprising to discover that he could define words and abbreviations introduced during the pre-morbid period. This contrasts directly with cases like HM and suggests that new vocabulary can be acquired in an otherwise dense retrograde amnesia.

A further observation was that RFR, although unable to name people, could discriminate a famous face from an unknown face. He was also able to give the surname of a famous person when cued with first name plus the initial letter of the surname. This suggested that RFR might know more about people than revealed by his basic naming ability. Subsequent observations indicated that RFR often possessed considerable information about people, but this never extended to any events that these people had featured in (McCarthy and Warrington, 1992). These conversations describing his accurate account of two friends illustrate the point:

'He's a colleague I've known for many years. I think we are both in the
    . . . unit.'
'Can you describe him?'
'He is a rather chunky individual. Everything is large except for his
    height which is about 5'10". I'm not sure if he has ginger hair . . . He
    is an outgoing character of Scottish descent. I vaguely remember
    joking references towards his Scottish ancestry and his love of whisky.
    He does have a very attractive wife with the very apt first name of
    Eve.'

A second friend:

'He is a fellow committee member of my church. There is something
    special about him. I think he is called doctor but he is not an MD type
    doctor . . . He is an angular individual who is quite thin although he
    doesn't look frail. He is balding and has light coloured hair.'

In both instances RFR's descriptions were confirmed as highly accurate. Further experiments led Warrington and McCarthy to propose that RFR had a memory for people but not events ('Actors without Scripts'). The authors suggest that these findings suggest that our remote memory for people is more complex than initially thought in that personal identity information appears separate from events involving those persons. Interpreting this dissociation is, however, problematic. One possible explanation is that RFR may know more about names and personal characteristics because this information has been presented more frequently. However, the authors counter this view by noting that RFR often had detailed knowledge about people associated with specific events but no knowledge of the events themselves. An interpretation in terms of salience was also ruled out. RFR could, for example, give a clear biography of his father but could not recollect anything about events surroundings his death.

McCarthy and Warrington argue that remote memory is configured in a way so as to allow the separate representation of people and events, although the exact manner in which this occurs is not specified in any detail. Other studies indicate that memory for public events may be distinct from personal events. DeRenzi, Liotti and Nichelli (1987) present a woman with a dense amnesia for public events but an intact ability to remember personal events – a pattern also reported by Kapur, Young, Bateman and Kennedy (1989). In contrast O'Connor, Butters, Miliotis, Eslinger and Cermak (1992) report the converse with greater impairment on autobiographical tests.

A study by Hodges and McCarthy (1993) also indicates a degree of fractionation in remote memory. Their patient PS suffered a small stroke which damaged the thalamus. We will consider other aspects of this case later but the critical point here concerns the pattern of his remote memory deficit. PS had a profound loss of personal memory: he only has accurate recall for his early life up until his service in the Navy during the Second World War. He still insists that he is on active Navy duty, complains about rationing and annoys his wife by asking for a blackout each night.

This poor autobiographical memory contrasts markedly with his relatively good knowledge about famous people which includes a striking ability to remember temporal information. Thus when shown three famous faces (e.g. three Prime Ministers) he was very efficient at specifying which had been famous either most or least recently. At this point PS's deficit might seem consistent with a distinction between episodic and semantic memory. However, on a subsequent test concerning famous events he performed poorly and, not surprisingly, was not able to arrange them in their correct temporal order (see also Kapur, 1994, for a further instance of fractionated remote memory).

These studies suggest, minimally, that it is unwise to assume a single system governing the recall of both autobiographical information and general knowledge. However, acceptance of the episodic/semantic account remains controversial in the light of data presented in several of the above studies. However, as Hodges and McCarthy note, there is no consistency in the types of test being used to assess remote memory. Until this occurs there is a danger that apparently 'innocuous' differences between testing procedures may be suggesting differences across patient groups or within patients that may not be reliable. Providing these constraints are dealt with, the study of retrograde amnesia will prove very interesting in the future.

The Relationship between Anterograde and Retrograde Amnesia

In an earlier section we saw that lesion site may be critical in determining the deficit responsible for amnesia. It is a natural step to consider whether a similar approach will shed light on the nature of retrograde impairments and, in so doing, also provide us with evidence concerning any possible relation between anterograde and retrograde deficits. If we first consider patients with temporal lobe amnesia it is evident that a single deficit could not explain both types of deficit. Earlier we saw that HM despite a severe anterograde impairment, had only a relatively mild retrograde impairment. In addition there is case RB (Zola-Morgan, Squire and Amaral, 1986) who presented dense anterograde amnesia with only a minimal retrograde deficit following an ischemic lesion which affected only the CA1 field of the hippocampus. In contrast to these we can also observe patients with extremely extensive retrograde amnesias. One particular group are survivors of herpes simplex encephalitis who will often have lost most of their pre-morbid memory.

Another feature of the temporal lobe amnesias, especially the more severe ones, is that recall often appears to have an 'empty feel' to it. SS (Cermak and O'Connor, 1983), a post-encephalitic amnesic, had no recall of specific events. Rather his recall comprised a limited repertoire of stories about his past which resembled a kind of folklore. Indeed the authors concluded that, for all intents and purposes, SS could not recollect any episodes at all. Wilson and Wearing (1995) report a similar pattern for the post-encephalitic amnesic CW.

The variable nature of retrograde amnesia found in temporal lobe amnesics alongside consistent and severe impairments on anterograde tests moves us to conclude that the two deficits do not have the same underlying cause. One plausible argument, for example, is that these patients have a consolidation deficit, plus a variable disruption of the sites involved in the storage of memories. This is consistent with observations that it is only those temporal lobe patients with large lesions extending outside the hippocampal region that also show extensive retrograde loss.

An additional problem, however, is to explain why the temporal gradient exists in patients with temporal lobe amnesia. The selective preservation of early memories suggests that they are stored in a way that makes them less vulnerable to disruption but the nature of this difference remains a mystery. One idea put forward by Squire, Cohen and Nadel (1984) was that the process of memory consolidation was a long-term process and that, following an initial fixation, new memories were further modified as they became integrated with other memories. From this perspective, retrograde amnesia is not so much due to disrupted storage but a consequence of interference with the final phase of consolidation.

A difficulty with the consolidation theory is its implausibility from an evolutionary perspective. Why should a system evolve in which memories remain in a non-consolidated state for so long? A consolidation period of months might be feasible but not the 20–30 years exhibited in many patients. An alternative is to suggest that each time we use an existing memory we create a new record of that memory, i.e. retrieval of a memory replicates it within the system. On the assumption that older memories will, on average, have been retrieved more often than newer memories they will have more representations. From this it follows that any damage to the storage sites will tend to disrupt more recent memories because these have less storage sites available. However, at the time of writing no convincing theory of temporal gradients in temporal lobe amnesia has been put forward.

The majority of diencephalic amnesics studied have been patients diagnosed with Korsakoff's Syndrome following a prolonged period of alcoholism. As figure 9.2 showed, these patients regularly demonstrate a severe retrograde amnesia characterized by a marked temporal gradient in which memories for the early part of the pre-morbid period are retrieved more easily.

The link between alcoholism and Korsakoff's Syndrome has led some to suggest that the temporal gradient is due to the cumulative effects of alcoholism on learning during the pre-morbid period – the argument being that the alcoholism causes increasing difficulties in learning new information, particularly in the years immediately preceding the onset of amnesia proper. In terms of this continuity hypothesis the temporal gradient reflects a form of anterograde rather than retrograde impairment.

There can be little doubt that chronic alcoholism does impair learning ability but this cannot be the principal explanation of temporal gradients in Korsakoff patients (Parkin, 1991b). Although most frequently observed as a consequence of alcoholism, Korsakoff's Syndrome is actually due to a thiamine deficiency that usually arises as a consequence of excess alcohol consumption. For this reason it has been possible to observe rare instances of Korsakoff's Syndrome not associated with alcoholism. We observed one case known as CM (Parkin, Blunden, Rees and Hunkin, 1991) who developed Korsakoff's Syndrome following intravenous feeding. She showed a profound retrograde amnesia indistinguishable from that found in alcoholic patients.

Another convincing argument against the continuity hypothesis is the case of PZ (Butters, 1984). He was a university professor who drank very heavily throughout his academic career. Finally he developed Korsakoff's Syndrome with a typical dense retrograde amnesia. However, in the period just preceding this he wrote an accurate autobiography. If the continuity hypothesis were correct this would simply not have been possible. Most convincing, however, are cases involving diencephalic lesions not associated with Wernicke's Disease at all. In particular, the thalamic amnesic PS we considered earlier provides compelling evidence that extensive remote memory loss in diencephalic amnesia can occur without association with alcoholism (for another instance see Graff-Radford, Tranel, Van Hoesen and Brandt, 1990).

An alternative unitary view of diencephalic anterograde and retrograde amnesia is that it reflects a common processing deficit. In the previous sections we have seen that the contextual deficit theory provides a reasonable explanation of anterograde amnesia in diencephalic amnesia. Can it also explain retrograde amnesia? This possibility was explored by Parkin, Montaldi, Leng and Hunkin (1990) in a study of 20 Korsakoff patients. They employed a prototype famous faces test for UK populations in which each face is tested in two versions: 'no-context' where there are minimal cues to facial identity (e.g. Mrs Thatcher in a flak jacket) and a 'context' version involving obvious contextual cues (e.g. Mrs Thatcher outside 10 Downing St). Parkin et al. reasoned that if a contextual deficit were responsible for the retrograde impairment, contextual cues should be most effective for the most poorly retrieved memories – those representing the more recent pre-morbid periods. However, the opposite result occurred in that contextual cues enhanced recall most for earlier pre-morbid memories.

On the basis of their results Parkin et al. suggested that, in line with temporal lobe amnesia, the retrograde deficit in diencephalic amnesia also appeared to be a storage deficit. There is, however, a problem. Korsakoff patients do suffer extensive lesions so, on this basis alone, they have sufficient damage to make an explanation based on impaired storage plausible. However, as Hodges and McCarthy (1993) point out, this is inconsistent with other evidence. The authors' first point is that the lesions suffered by their patient, PS, are very small when compared with the cortical lesions suffered by temporal lobe amnesics showing severe retrograde loss. On this basis they argue that the deficit cannot be due to any damage to a hypothetical storage site because this would simply not be big enough.

Instead the authors couch their explanation of diencephalic amnesia in terms of contemporary theories of autobiographical memory which propose that the repesentation of individual events is organized thematically around major life events and time periods (Conway, 1990).

Retrieval of an event is then seen as a strategic problem solving exercise in which, in the first instance, the relevant theme must be accessed before any specific event can be located and retrieved.

From what we have considered so far it has been argued that these storage sites reside in the temporal lobes. From evidence we consider in the next chapter it is reasonable to suppose that these strategic components of memory are located in the frontal cortex. If this model is correct, a failure to retrieve autobiographical memory could be due to disruption of the storage sites, the strategic components or the interconnection between the two. Hodges and McCarthy propose that diencephalic amnesia arises because there is a vital disconnection between the storage sites and those processes responsible for access. In the case of temporal lobe amnesia the general life themes may be there (e.g. the ability of SS to relate general characteristics about himself) but storage of events is gone. In contrast, diencephalic amnesics may be impaired because the retrieval mechanisms cannot interact effectively with the store of memories.

Hodges and McCarthy's idea is an interesting one but can it explain one other important feature of diencephalic amnesia? – the pervasive temporal gradient. The authors are forced to conclude that, for some reason, early adult life themes have a more robust representation that enables them to influence retrieval when later life themes fail. This is certainly consistent with the autobiographical memory literature which also shows that early adulthood has some special status (Conway, 1990). However, the reasons for this, and any subsequent implications for explaining temporal gradients are as yet unclear (Jansari and Parkin, 1996).

A final point concerning this disconnection theory is whether it could also be invoked to explain the anterograde impairment in diencephalic amnesia. In principle it could be that new learning is ineffective because memories cannot be organized in a context relevant to the underlying organization of autobiographical memory. If correct, then one prediction might be that the severity of the anterograde and retrograde deficits should be correlated since both were due to the same impairment. Several studies using Korsakoff patients have failed to find this overall correlation but three have reported a correlation between anterograde impairment and retrograde amnesia for the decade immediately preceding the onset of amnesia (see Parkin, 1991). This suggests a link between the deficits but it is difficult to interpret on the grounds that Korsakoff's Syndrome often has an insidious onset over months or even years, so that specifying the exact point at which anterograde impairment started is difficult.

At present the origin of temporal gradients remains a mystery. It is possible, however, that further theoretical developments might shed light on how it arises. One possibility is that the temporal gradient, at least in instances where defective storage can be assumed, reflects some degree of redundancy in memory representation. This idea proposes that individual memories will vary in their extent of representation. Thus memories that are extremely important to us, such as our name and where we live, are represented in many different ways. In contrast, single events have only one representation. Now, if one makes one further assumption that redundancy will tend to be greater, on average, for older memories (this seems reasonable given that the older an event is the more opportunity there has been to discuss it, and thus form an additional representation), then it is more likely that memories of older events will survive brain injury because they are represented in many different places.

Focal Retrograde Amnesia

In the previous section it became clear that in neither temporal lobe or diencephalic amnesia was there any evidence of a link between the deficits underlying anterograde and retrograde amnesia. We examined cases such as RB in which anterograde impairment was very extensive but retrograde impairment minimal. However, can we observe the reverse – severe retrograde amnesia in the absence of significant anterograde amnesia?

In a recent article Kapur (1992) has identified what he has termed focal retrograde amnesia (FRA). This refers to a memory impairment in which the primary deficit is a loss of remote memory with performance on anterograde tests only mildly impaired. A problem with this type of disorder is that some of the patients may be suffering from psychogenic disorders, i.e. be psychiatrically disturbed, or they may be **malingering** – in some way faking memory impairment (for a discussion on psychogenic amnesia see Kopelman, 1995b, and a recent paper by Leng and Parkin, 1995, describes the features of malingering). However, once these possibilities are discounted, a range of case histories in which focal retrograde amnesia is presented within the context of identifiable brain injury can be identified (see also Parkin, 1996d).

In order to examine at least two types of explanation that may be required to explain FRA I will describe two recent cases. The first of these is TJ (Kapur, Ellison, Parkin et al., 1994) who suffered from a radionecrotic illness which destroyed large areas of his temporal lobes. On tests of remote memory he performed extremely badly, whether this involved memory for personal information or public events. Thus on a test of autobiographical cueing he performed best when recalling his early life and showed worst recall of events in the period just prior to the start of his illness – this temporal gradient was also present in his public event memory. However, on tests of anterograde learning, such as story recall, he performed within normal limits.

TJ's drastic impairment of remote memory in the presence of relatively normal performance on tests of new learning is most readily explained in terms of defective storage. The lesions suffered by TJ are extremely large and occur in brain areas now identified as the storage sites for memory. In contrast those areas thought to be concerned with formation of memory (e.g. the hippocampus) are spared. From this anatomical evidence it is reasonable to propose that lack of remote memory occurs simply because those memories are not longer represented. New learning is still possible because not all areas have been damaged and those that remain can undertake the representation of new events. This interpretation can also be applied to two more recent cases of focal retrograde amnesia associated with temporal lobe lesions (Hokkanen, Launes and Vataja et al., 1995; Markowitsch, Calabrese and Liess et al., 1992).

The second case is DH, reported by Hunkin, Parkin and Bradley et al. (1995) and this requires an alternative explanation. DH was a young man who suffered a closed head injury at the age of 21. Assessment of memory function using tests indicated performance within the normal range. On tests of autobiographical memory, however, he was very impaired in that he cannot clearly recollect any personal experience from the time before his injury – this is an extremely unusual pattern because, as in the case of TJ, recollection from early adult life is usually spared relative to other time periods. Another interesting feature of DH's memory is that he performs normally on public events tests even for the period where his autobiographical recollection is zero.

DH's retrograde amnesia is odd and made all the more puzzling by his underlying brain lesion. One might expect that a deficit so dramatic as his would be caused by a substantial brain lesion. However, MRI scans of his brain show lesions in the two occipital lobes plus a small lesion in the right parietal lobe. Notably there are no lesions in the areas damaged in TJ. An explanation of DH's FRA is not clear, but one possibility is suggested by a recent theory of memory representation put forward by Damasio and Damasio (1993). They suggest that the knowledge retrieval involves a reconstructive process in which various features of entity (e.g. the colour and shape of an object) are retrieved from different locations in the cortex and combined to give a unified representation. Areas of the brain responsible for this combinatorial function are known as **convergence zones** (CZ) and these will vary in their scope depending on the type of information being represented. Thus, for an object, a representation might only be visual or might be enlarged to incorporate other properties such as sound and smell.

At the highest level of this hierarchy are CZs which deal with events. Here an event will be characterized as the time locked co-occurrence of various entities which together constitute a particular event. It is possible that what has happened to DH is that the relatively small area of the brain in which event related CZs are located has been damaged. As a result retrieval of events from his pre-injury past is not possible because the various entities that need to be retrieved concurrently to reproduce an event are no longer bound together by a CZ. Two pieces of evidence help to make this account more plausible. First, DH's parietal lesion lies in an area that is now known to be implicated in the retrieval of events (see next chapter) and second, DH has shown a remarkable ability to relearn his past. However, this he describes as now being able to 'read a book about myself'. It is possible to suggest that relearning occurs because the memorial elements of those memories are still there and thus learning is facilitated. True recollection cannot return, however, because the CZ required to time lock them into the original event is no longer there.

Summary

Amnesia is a global loss of memory caused by damage to either the midline of the diencephalon or the medial temporal lobe. Patients with amnesia have a distinguishing profile. STS function appears intact, procedural memory is preserved and intelligence is largely unaffected. The primary deficit is a severe anterograde amnesia along with a variable retrograde amnesia. Debate surrounds how the deficit should be described. A deficit in episodic memory is consistent with the pattern of anterograde impairment but cannot explain retrograde amnesia in which both episodic and semantic elements are impaired. An alternative account of impaired declarative memory is preferred. A different approach is to examine amnesia from the task-based perspective of explicit vs. implicit memory. Here it is clear that amnesics are impaired on explicit memory tasks but show remarkable preservation of learning on implicit tasks, which extends to the acquisition of novel information including complex learning tasks. At present the most promising explanation of anterograde amnesia is that it stems from a deficit in memory for context. However, it is possible that this theory may only properly account for diencephalic amnesia. Retrograde amnesia shows a temporal gradient and may exhibit various fractionations. The origin of the temporal gradient is not presently understood. The phenomenon of focal retrograde amnesia indicates that severe remote memory impairment can occur in the presence of less severe anterograde learning difficulties.

10

The Frontal Lobes and Executive Deficits

The two lobes of the frontal cortex comprise just under one-third of the cortex and comparisons with other species indicate that it has, in proportional terms, undergone its greatest enlargement in humans (Fuster, 1989). This suggests that the role of the frontal cortex is likely to be complex and that the functions it subserves will include many of those that are thought by some to set humans aside from other animals. Aristotle believed that there was a 'common sense' which was common to all the 'special senses'. Figure 10.1 shows Blumenbach's illustration of the human brain from 1840 and you can see that the 'communis sensus' is placed in the frontal cortex with specific abilities located in more posterior parts of the brain. The positioning of a common sense mechanism overseeing the rest of the brain's activity in the frontal lobes may well have been for completely spurious reasons, but that is now how the major role of the frontal cortex is viewed. Indeed the first neuropsychological evidence supporting this idea of frontal function arose just a few years after Blumenbach's diagram was published.

Phineas Gage

Without doubt, the most famous case history in neuropsychology is that of Phineas Gage (McMillan, 1987). On 13 September 1848 Phineas

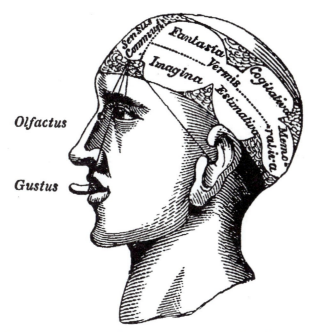

Olfactus

Gustus

Figure 10.1   Blumenbach's illustration of the brain dated 1840.

Gage was employed as a railroad engineer in New England and his job was to lay explosive and detonate it. The procedure involved boring a hole, placing the explosive, and then covering it over with sand. After this a fuse and a tamping iron were used to set off the explosive. Due to a mistake Gage placed the tamping iron directly on the explosive at which point it exploded sending the tamping iron right through his skull and then twenty or so feet into the air (see figure 10.2). Remarkably Gage did not lose consciousness and was able to walk to the cart that took him to hospital.

Gage did not die from this terrible injury, a finding that has been attributed to the hot tamping iron cauterizing the wound as it passed through his head. He lived for another 20 years and in some ways the injury seemed to have remarkably few consequences. He had little difficulty with language or memory and his physical abilities appeared unaltered. However, there were changes: Gage had previously been considered an outstanding employee with excellent prospects but now he was unreliable, disrespectful and lacked any social skills. His employer soon dismissed him, to his friends he was 'No longer Gage'.

In 1866, five years after his death, John Harlow proposed that Gage had suffered damage to the frontal lobes. Further, Harlow proposed that

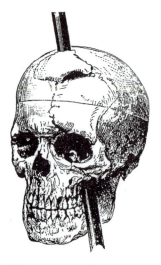

Horrible Accident. Phineas P. Gage, a foreman on the Rutland Railroad at Cavendish, Vt., was preparing for a blast on Wednesday last, when the powder exploded, carrying through his head an iron instrument, an inch and a fourth in circumference, and three feet and eight inches in length. The iron entered on the side of his face, shattering the upper jaw, and passing back of the left eye, and out the top of his head. Singularly enough, he was alive at two o'clock the next afternoon, in full possession of his reason, and free from pain.

Figure 10.2   Phineas Gage's skull showing the trajectory of the tamping iron. Text insert is a copy of the newspaper report at the time. From McMillan (1987) reprinted with permission of Academic Press.

Gage's changed behaviour indicated that the frontal lobes were the region of the brain concerned with planning and the maintenance of socially acceptable behaviour. Harlow's proposal was largely ignored at the time but recent evidence firmly indicates that he was right (Harlow, 1868, 1993).

Gage's body was exhumed in 1866 and the skull, along with the offending tamping iron, have been preserved for posterity in a Harvard museum. This enabled Damasio, Grabowski and Frank et al. (1994) to subject Gage's skull to modern neuroimaging techniques in order to establish the exact nature of his brain lesion. Using a reconstructed brain similar to that of Gage and an estimate of the tamping iron's most likely trajectory, they concluded that his lesion would have involved several aspects of the left and right frontal lobes (principally the orbito-frontal and anterior medial areas) but no other brain region.

The behavioural deficits attributed to Gage's frontal lesions are consistent with other evidence from frontal injuries. Frontal lesions are a common consequence of closed head injury and, along with memory impairment, adverse changes in personality are common in this patient group. More specifically detailed case studies of patients with similar damage to that suffered by Gage are known to suffer the same sociopathic changes. Saver and Damasio (1991) report EVR, a man who developed abnormal social conduct following an operation which removed areas of the frontal lobes similar to those damaged in Gage:

> EVR's social conduct, however, was profoundly altered following his operation. In succeeding years his personal relationships deteriorated and his financial decisions led to bankruptcy. He has not been able to hold steady employment, and now lives in a sheltered environment, unable to support himself or his family. On matters of minimal consequence, for example when deciding on clothes to wear or restaurants in which to dine, EVR may become consumed by extended deliberations, unable to reach a reasonably prompt and efficient decision. In contrast to this pattern of inappropriate social decision-making in real-life/real-time settings ... [in] ... clinical interviews EVR appears able to proffer sensible social insights, make subtle distinctions between ambiguous concepts, and comment with wit and discernment upon daily events. (p. 1242)

The Frontal Lobes as an 'Executive'

Clinical impressions from patients like EVR have motivated a view that frontal damage impairs the ability to plan and organize which has led, in turn, to the 'executive' concept of frontal function. Within modern neuropsychology this idea was first attributable to Luria (1966) who proposed that the frontal lobes were responsible for programming and regulating behaviour, and verifying whether any given activity was appropriate for a situation. Similarly Stuss and Benson (1987) have suggested that the frontal executive system comprises a number of component processes each of which can influence two basic functional systems: drive and sequencing. These processes in turn feed down and moderate a range of other systems which lie outside the frontal lobes.

The idea of an executive has been most extensively developed by Norman and Shallice (1986). In their approach they propose that an individual's responses can be controlled in two fundamentally different ways. The majority of responses are under fairly automatic control. They are triggered by environmental cues which in turn contact specific schema, each of which has many subcomponents. A familiar example is driving: all of us may have experienced arriving home having driven several miles but having no recollection of the journey. Yet to achieve this we will have changed gear many times, operated the indicators, turned left or right and so on. The fact that all this happens without recollection suggests that the various programs used to execute the different component actions are automatic.

At some point there may be a clash between two routine activities. To deal with this Norman and Shallice propose a **contention scheduling** operation in which the relative importance of different actions is assessed and routine behaviour adjusted accordingly. As we all know our behaviour is not simply a set of routine automatic operations, there are many occasions when we deliberate and consciously impose a specific action. Consider driving again: If a British person drives in France many of the routine driving actions are now inappropriate because the traffic drives on the right and not the left. Thus on encountering a roundabout our routine tendency to look right must be inhibited and a look to the left made instead.

To explain willed actions Norman and Shallice propose an additional **Supervisory Activating System** (SAS) which becomes active whenever the routine selection of operations is inappropriate. Thus the SAS will become active when an individual encounters, danger, novelty and temptation, and where response options arise that require a decision. Norman and Shallice suggest that the SAS concept provides a useful way of understanding slips of action. When I drive home from the University I always take the same route. This is useful in one sense because it has become highly routine and requires little thought. Problems arise, however, when I have to go somewhere else because I frequently set off on my homeward route. Within Norman and Shallice's model this failure can be attributed to some failure of the SAS to maintain the novel goal.

Neuropsychological Evidence for the SAS

In his 1988 account Shallice outlines two types of situation that could reveal a deficit in SAS function:

1   Because responses controlled by contention scheduling alone have arisen through habit they will only change slowly. Thus in circumstances where they are strongly triggered they will persist until inhibited by the SAS. With damage to the SAS a situation of this kind would give rise to rigid inflexible behaviour.

2   If an environment contains no particularly salient information the SAS would function so as to inhibit responding. However, a deficient SAS operating in these circumstances might allow inappropriate responses to occur.

On this basis, damage to the frontal lobes might be associated with two types of behavioural difficulty: behavioural rigidity – known as perseveration, and a tendency towards distraction. Evidence for perseveration following frontal damage is widespread. The Wisconsin Card

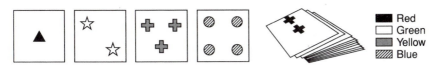

Figure 10.3 The Wisconsin Card Sorting Test. Reproduced from Lezak (1983) with permission of Oxford University Press.

Sorting Test (Grant and Berg, 1948) and its variants (e.g. Nelson, 1976) requires subjects to sort multidimensional stimuli by rule (see figure 10.3). Initially subjects choose a rule to sort by (e.g. grouping cards together by colour) and after six successful applications of that rule they are required to change the rule. In patients with frontal impairments there are often perseverations in that the patient continues to sort with the previous rule even when they are explicitly told that it is wrong (Milner, 1963).

A second type of task which frontal patients often perseverate are those measuring mental fluency. At the simplest level these tests might simply require subjects to generate as many words as possible beginning with a specified letter. Here subjects with frontal impairments often have difficulty changing direction and will perseverate with the same word or its obvious derivatives. A more complex fluency task is the Alternate Uses Test. Here the subject has to think up unusual uses for an everyday object. A newspaper, for example, cannot only be read but can also be used to light a fire or swat flies. Patients with frontal lesions find this task very difficult and are unable to switch easily from the typical use of the object – a deficit that fits nicely with the idea of a response system guided essentially by well-learned automatic responses.

Distractability is a well-known characteristic of frontal lobe patients that can be detected in many ways (for a recent discussion see Foster, Eskes and Stuss, 1994). When being tested their attention may easily wander and, when carrying out a task, they will often notice irrelevant things. One task that particularly reveals this is the Stroop Effect. If you are shown the word 'red' written in 'blue' ink you will have no difficulty saying what the word is. However, naming the colour of the ink can be difficult due to the distracting influence of the colour-word. Frontal patients are known to perform very poorly on the Stroop test, thus suggesting enhanced distractability, and this has recently been attributed to dysfunction in the right frontal lobe along with left and right parietal lobes (Bench, Frith and Grasby et al., 1993).

Shallice notes the phenomenon of utilization behaviour (LHermitte, 1983) in which frontal patients grasp at objects placed near them even though specifically told not to do so:

> While seated, the patient took a glass, gave it to the examiner and then
> picked up a jug. He poured water into the glass and, having put down
> the jug, took the glass from the hand of the examiner and drank the
> water. Taking a pack of cigarettes, he hesitated a moment, then opened
> it and drew out a cigarette. He looked puzzled at it being a non-smoker.
> A few seconds later, he held it to the mouth of the examiner who accepted
> it and taking the lighter which was in the examiner's hand, near his
> knees, the patient lit the cigarette. Questioned on this behaviour he
> simply said 'You held out objects to me; I thought I had to use them'.
> (pp. 245–6)

Here it seems that the patient's habitual responses to the objects are
being triggered even though they are not demanded by the situation.
This would be compatible with the continuing function of the contention
scheduling system in the absence of sufficient monitoring and control by
the SAS (see also Shallice, Burgess, Schon and Baxter, 1989).

There is now abundant evidence that the frontal lobes are implicated
in various aspects of planning and organizational behaviour. Patient
EVR (above) clearly had problems in organizing his life and a similar
deficit has been reported by Goldstein, Bernard and Fenwick et al.
(1993). Their patient had undergone a left frontal lobectomy which led
to increased difficulty making decisions – on one occasion he took two
weeks to decide which slides to use in a presentation. However, despite
his known pathology he performed normally on standard tests of frontal
lobe function such as WCST.

Goldstein et al. further evaluated their patient on the 'Six Elements
Task'. Devised by Shallice and Burgess (1991), this test measures higher-
order planning deficits by requiring the subject to carry out three
different tasks, each with two components, within 15 minutes. Although
showing some difficulty he still performed within normal limits. He was
then given the 'Multiple Errands Task', also devised by Shallice and
Burgess. This task is carried out in a pedestrian precinct and requires the
patient to carry out a number of tasks in situations where minor
unforeseen events might occur. There are eight tasks in total of which
six are simple requests. The seventh requires the patient to be in a
specific place 15 minutes after starting and the eighth requires the
recording of four pieces of information during the errands. Here the
patient did encounter considerable difficulties, getting some tasks wrong
and failing some altogether.

This case is very interesting because it shows that marked higher-order
deficits can arise in the absence of impairments on standard tests of
frontal function. Goldstein et al. attempt to explain this by arguing that
standard tests such as WCST do not rely so heavily on SAS functions.
However, this is a difficult argument to maintain given that the repeated ,

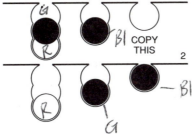

Figure 10.4 A subproblem from the computerized Tower of of London Test. Two moves (indicated) are required to make the two arrangements identical. From Owen et al. (1990) reproduced by kind permission of Elsevier Science Ltd.

failure of frontal patients on WCST is one of the principal types of evidence supporting the existence of the SAS (Shallice and Burgess, 1991). In a recent discussion of this result Burgess and Shallice suggest that it could indicate separable components of executive function underlying the multiple errands tasks compared with WCST or, seemingly more likely, that the errands task is a more sensitive measure of frontal impairment.

Group studies also provide evidence for frontally mediated impairments of planning. Owen, Downes and Sahakian et al. (1990) examined a group of frontal patients on the Tower of London task. In this task two sets of three coloured balls are presented, one set in the top half of a screen and the other in the bottom. They were described to the subjects as snooker (pool) balls because they appeared to be hanging in sockets which could each hold a maximum of three balls (see figure 10.4). Each half of the screen had three pockets, one capable of holding three balls, one able to hold two balls and one that could be filled by only one ball. On each trial three balls (one red, one blue and one green) were placed in each set of pockets and the subject asked to arrange the bottom set into the same configuration as the top set. Each problem required a minimum of two moves to reach a solution.

A series of rules governed how subjects could complete the test (e.g. a ball in a lower part of the pocket could not be moved if there was another ball above it). It was found that the patients did not differ from controls in the time they spent planning their first move, but subsequent to that the patients thought more about each additional move. In a subsequent study Morris, Ahmed, Syed and Toone (1993) confirmed frontal involvement in the Tower of London. They found that regional cerebral blood flow in control subjects attempting the task increased in the left frontal lobe overall and that subjects who spent more time planning their moves and thus taking less moves overall showed the highest increase.

The Fractionation of Frontal Function

In the Norman and Shallice model the SAS is conceived of as a single entity but evidence now exists to suggest that some heterogeneity within higher-order impairments must be accepted. Eslinger and Grattan (1993) drew a distinction between two forms of frontal lobe function reactive and spontaneous flexibility. Reactive flexibility was defined as a readiness to shift cognition and behaviour freely in response to the changing demands of a situation. As a process it is typified by the WCST in which the subject continually has to alter a response pattern in response to instruction. Spontaneous flexibility describes the ready flow of ideas and answers in response to a question. This is typically measured by fluency tasks such as the Alternate Uses Test and word fluency where subjects are required to think divergently. Applying these tests to a group of neurological patients they found that the two types of test were associated with different patterns of frontal injury.

A new sorting test devised by Delis, Squire, Bihrle and Massman (1992) provides additional evidence for the heterogeneity of frontal function. In this task subjects were presented with sets of six cards which could be sorted according to eight different rules. Three conditions were employed: spontaneous sorting in which the subjects generated their own rules; structured sorting where the examiner sorted the cards and the subject explained what the rule was; and cued sorting in which the examiner told the subject which rule to use. Analysis showed that no single deficit, such as perseveration, could be evoked to explain all the deficits and that some componential analysis of frontal function was necessary to account for the results.

Burgess and Shallice (in press) have recently reported the Hayling Test. Subjects are presented with a sentence in which the last word is omitted and they must complete the sentence. The sentences have obvious completions (e.g. He mailed the letter without a . . .?) and in the first part the subjects' task is to complete the sentence with whatever word they choose. In the second part they must complete the sentence with a word that does not make sense. Frontal patients showed two deficits, a delay in initiating a response on straightforward completion and an inhibition impairment – frontal patients found it much more difficult to complete the sentences with a word that did not make sense. Correlational analysis showed a surprising lack of relationship between the measures of initiation and inhibition, thus suggesting that the two measures reflect different components of frontal ability.

Memory Impairment following Frontal Lobe Damage

There is now abundant evidence that the frontal cortex plays an active role in certain aspects of remembering. This perhaps most strikingly seen in frontal patients who exhibit **confabulation** – the tendency to produce fabricated accounts of past events. Typically, confabulations are divided into two types. In **momentary confabulation** the patient makes up plausible but incorrect memories whereas in **fantastic confabulation** the memories relate events that could not possibly have happened. Fantastic confabulation has attracted considerable interest because here there appears to have been some breakdown in the patient's ability to verify the truth of their memory – a fact that has led to the description 'honest lying'. Another feature of this disorder is that patients will maintain the truth of their confabulations no matter how implausible. The following is a short excerpt of an interview between a confabulating patient and a psychologist:

Q. How old are you?
A. I'm 40, 42, pardon me, 62
Q. Are you married or single?
A. Married.
Q. How long have you been married?
A. About four months.
Q. What's your wife's name?
A. Martha.
Q. How many children do you have?
A. Four. (He laughs.) Not bad for four months.
Q. How old are your children?
A. The eldest is 32, his name is Bob, and the youngest is 22, his name is Joe.
Q. How did you get these children in 4 months?
A. (He laughs again.) They're adopted.
Q. Who adopted them?
A. Martha and I.
Q. Immediately after you got married you wanted to adopt these older children?
A. Before we were married we adopted one of them, two of them. The eldest girl Brenda and Bob, and Joe and Dina since we were married.

Q. Does it all sound a little strange to you, what you are saying?
A. (He laughs.) I think it is a little strange.
Q. I think when I looked at your record it said that you've been married
   for over 30 years. Does that sound more reasonable to you if I told
   you that?
A. No.
Q. Do you really believe that you have been married for 4 months?
A. Yes.

(from Moscovitch, 1989)

We will return to the nature of confabulation after we have considered other memory impairments associated with frontal damage.

Source Amnesia

Source amnesia occurs when a person remembers an event or fact correctly but fails to remember the source of their knowledge. To demonstrate this Schacter, Harbluk and McLachlan (1984) presented amnesic patients with fictitious facts (e.g. Bob Hope's father was a fireman) which were spoken by either of two experimenters. Recall tests showed that the facts could often be recalled but that the patients rarely remembered the source of the facts. A link with defective frontal function was established by showing that those subjects with greatest source amnesia performed most poorly on tests of frontal lobe function. Shimamura and Squire (1987) also found evidence of a link between frontal function and source amnesia.

Studies of ageing now indicate that the frontal lobes undergo quite a dramatic decline as we get older (see later section). This raises the possibility that typical age-related memory loss might be explained, in part at least, as a consequence of frontal dysfunction. We will consider this in more detail later but, for now, we restrict ourselves to the effects of age on source amnesia. Craik, Morris, Morris and Loewen (1990) demonstrated source amnesia effects in a group of older subjects and, furthermore, showed that the extent of this deficit was related directly to impairments on tests of frontal lobe function. A similar finding is reported in Schacter, Osowiecki, Kaszniak, et al. (1991) and recently Glisky, Polster and Routhieaux (1995) have shown that elderly subjects classed as having low frontal abilities perform worse on source memory tests than those classified as high frontal. Collectively, there seems good evidence that source memory depends on intact frontal lobe functioning (however, see the recent study of Spencer and Raz, 1994).

A related memory ability is **metamemory** – this describes our ability to know whether or not our memories contain a particular piece of information. An example of this might be failing to recall the capital of Peru (Lima) but knowing you would be able to recognize it if shown to you – an ability usually described as **feeling of knowing**. Janowsky, Shimamura and Squire (1989) presented frontal patients and controls with sentences and then asked them to recall key words. Thus shown the sentence 'At the museum we saw some ancient relics made of clay' they would subsequently be presented with 'At the museum we saw some ancient relics made of ——?' and would be asked to recall the last word. If they could not they were asked to rate their ability to recognize the word when presented. When tested over a substantial delay, frontal patients' metamemory was impaired relative to controls.

False Recognition

When evaluating recognition, memory subjects are shown target stimuli to remember and then are given a subsequent sequence of stimuli as a recognition test. This sequence will comprise a random sequence of the targets plus novel stimuli termed **distractors**. In **yes–no** recognition the subject examines each item serially and decides whether or not it was a stimulus they were asked to remember. Yes–no recognition can be tested either by presenting all the stimuli in a single array or by means of a **single probe** technique in which each stimulus appears individually and a response is required. In a **forced choice** recognition test a target stimulus is presented along with one or more alternatives and the subject has to choose which item is the target. In recognition testing a correct response is usually referred to as a **hit**, failure to identify a target is a **miss**, and incorrect identification of a distractor is termed a **false alarm**.

Studies of patients with frontal lobe damage have begun to identify a subset of patients who make abnormal numbers of false alarms in recognition memory. Delbecq-Dérousné, Beauvois and Shallice (1990) report that RW made large numbers of false alarms. RW's manner indicated that he was as sure about his false alarms as he was about hits. On recall he performed better although along with correct information he produced much more incorrect information (intrusion errors) than control subjects.

We have also encountered a patient like RW. JB (Parkin, Bind-schaedler, Harsent and Metzler, 1996; Parkin, Binschaedler and Poz, in preparation) produces large numbers of false alarms on most tests of recognition memory. On average his hit rate is 80 per cent (within normal range) but his false alarm rate, around 40 per cent, is extremely abnormal. In one experiment he was asked to judge whether he was 'sure' or 'not sure' about whether he had correctly recognized a stimulus. For both hits and false alarms he gave predominantly 'sure' responses. Like RW he produces large numbers of recall intrusions amongst correct information. Sometimes these intrusions are random but on other occasions they clearly come from other events. In one instance he was asked to recall the instructions for the experiment. The first part was correct but he then effortlessly introduced extra information involving instructions from an experiment he had done several days before.

Schacter, Curran and Galluccio (in press) describe BG who also had circumscribed damage to the frontal lobes. Across a variety of tasks BG made excessive numbers of false alarms even though, like JB, his hit rate remained normal. Like RW and JB, BG is also very confident about his false alarms. Using the recognition and conscious awareness paradigm (RCA–see below) it was shown that BG frequently associated his false alarms with specific recollections.

JB has been investigated extensively in an attempt to understand why he produces so many false alarms (Parkin, Bindschaedler and Poz, in preparation). The answer does not appear to be that he does not try. When given a financial incentive to respond as accurately as possible, something he greeted with great enthusiasm, he produced a hit rate of 95 per cent, but his false alarm rate was 48 per cent. Interestingly, JB considered that the incentive had helped him improve his memory. One possible clue about the nature of JB's faulty recognition memory comes from a series of forced choice recognition experiments. In the first phase JB was shown a series of words and was then presented with pairs of words, one of which was the target and the other a distractor. This he performed well. In the next experiment the procedure was repeated except that the distractors were the same as those used in the first experiment. At this point JB's performance was reduced to chance. However, subsequent experiments using completely new materials again allowed normal performance. What this experiment shows is that JB can recognize words quite well providing he can rely on familiarity alone (see chapter 9). However, when familiarity does not provide sufficient cue his forced choice recognition is poor. It is for this reason that he performs so badly when distractors are used across two tests because he cannot discriminate their familiarity from that of the targets.

The Montreal Studies

A different but complementary approach to the role of the frontal cortex in memory has been developed by Milner and her colleagues in Montreal.

These studies have been primarily based on patients who have undergone neurosurgery for disorders such as brain tumours. As a result it has been possible to have a clear indication of the brain lesions suffered by patients and has allowed the mapping of different functions to different parts of the frontal cortex. In addition the methods used in these studies have also been strongly influenced by lesion studies in non-human primates.

Prisko (1963; see Milner, 1964) demonstrated that frontal patients had problems deciding whether a stimulus was the same or different to one presented 60 seconds earlier. However, this effect only occurred when the same small set of stimuli were used across all trials. When different stimuli were used on each trial the frontal patients performed normally. This finding suggested that the patients might have difficulty encoding the temporal context – i.e. on trials where the stimuli are all familiar because of repeated presentation, normal performance can only be achieved by allocating a specific temporal marker when any given stimulus is presented.

In a much cited follow up Corsi (1972; cited in Milner, 1971; but see also Milner, Corsi and Leonard, 1991) devised a recency discrimination task in which subjects were presented with pairs of stimuli. At various intervals a test card appeared with a ? between the stimuli and subjects decided which of the two stimuli had been seen most recently. On some trials both stimuli would have been seen previously but at different elapsed intervals (e.g. 8 versus 16 trials ago), thus making the judgement one of relative recency. However, when one of the stimuli was novel the task was effectively one of just recognition. The key result, obtained using words, pictures and abstract designs, was that the frontal patients were impaired on recency discrimination but not recognition. However, this pattern varied as a function of lesion site with left frontal lesions impairing performance on words and right-sided lesions impairing recency judgments for pictures and abstract designs.

Smith and Milner (1984; see also Smith and Milner, 1988) presented stimuli a variable number of times and then asked subjects to estimate how often a particular stimulus had been presented. Frontal patients did not differ from controls in estimating relatively low frequencies of occurrence, but as the frequency increased to a maximum of nine, significant impairments in the frontal patients emerged. Petrides and Milner (1982) devised the self-ordered pointing task. Here subjects were presented with a stack of cards each presenting the same stimuli in a regular array but with the position of the stimuli varying. The task was to point at the stimulus, but taking care to point at the same stimulus twice. Patients with right frontal lesions exhibited only a mild impairment on pictures and abstract designs but the left frontal group were severely impaired on all versions of the task. This suggested that the left frontal cortex was specifically involved in the planning, execution and monitoring of responses.

Recently, Rocchetta and Milner (1993) have demonstrated that frontal lesions can cause problems in retrieval. A well-known phenomenon in normal memory is the part-list cueing effect: If subjects are asked to learn a word list and, at test, are presented with part of the list as cues, their recall of the other items will be poorer than if no cues are given at all. This deficit is thought to arise because the cues come to dominate the retrieval process at the expense of the uncued items. The authors found that, compared with controls and other brain damaged subjects, patients with left frontal lesions showed a much greater part-list cueing effect. This suggested that the left frontal lobe was specifically involved in strategic aspects of retrieval.

Frontal Lobe Function and Memory: A Theoretical Framework

From the above we can see that there is now extensive evidence concerning the involvement of the frontal lobes in various aspects of memory performance. Our task now is to try and produce a theoretical framework that might accommodate the findings. In developing the SAS account of frontal lobe function, Shallice (1988) has incorporated a view of memory put forward by Norman and Bobrow (1979). This model acknowledges that retrieval from memory is, in many cases, a problem-solving activity. When attempting to remember what you did at a certain time yesterday, for example, the answer will not readily spring to mind. Instead, you may need to set up some form of hypothesis, for example, 'Yesterday was Saturday and that is when I usually go shopping. So yesterday at around 4 p.m. I would have been in the high street.' Using this form of information a more precise hypothesis about what you might have been doing could be formed, until this actual event was located. In this way the SAS operates on memory by specifying a possible description of an event, matching this with the contents of memory and, if verified as accurate, producing that event as a memory.

Hanley, Davies, Downes and Mayes (1994) have presented evidence from a patient known as ROB who sustained damaged to the caudate – a structure closely associated with the frontal lobes. She was given a task which compared recall and recognition using tasks that are matched for difficulty in control subjects (Calev, 1984). On the recall task, ROB performed very poorly but on recognition she was no different to controls. Hanley et al. suggest that this is exactly the kind of deficit one might expect to see with a selective disruption to the system specifying descriptions. Thus ROB's recall is impaired but recognition occurs normally because a recognition test bypasses the need for specifying any description. Hanley et al.'s account also suggests that the pattern of high false alarm rates found in patients such as RW and JB could be attributed to the reverse deficit. Here, it is argued, descriptions are retrieved from memory but defective verification allows both the presence of intrusions in recall and the tendency to make large numbers of false alarms. Within this framework it is easy to envisage confabulation occurring if the verification process is particularly defective. In this instance it is therefore of relevance that both RW and JB had exhibited confabulation during the early course of their illness.

Other findings are also consistent with this outline theory. Rocchetta and Milner's (1993) demonstration of enhanced part-list cueing effects could be attributed to an impairment of specifying descriptions at recall. It is also widely documented that frontal patients' memory can often improve immensely if given prompts to help them. This is particularly evident in autobiographical recall (for background see chapter 9) in that frontal patients can produce vague memories and require a lot of prompting before producing something specific (Baddeley and Wilson, 1988). CB (Parkin, Yeomans and Bindschaedler, 1994), for example, was particularly poor when asked to retrieve specific memories to cue words such as 'flowers'. Thus he would spontaneously give responses such as 'I like flowers' but, when prompted, he was able to recollect a specific memory. Similarly, MP (Parkin and Barry, 1991) at first claimed that the autobiographical recall task was 'impossible' but, again in response to the word 'flowers', eventually recalled a meal with her husband in some detail.

At this point it would seem that every aspect of memory disturbance following frontal damage could be attributed to impairments in retrieval. Thus we could, for example, also extend the impaired retrieval theory to account for findings such as poor temporal discrimination and impaired frequency judgements. Here, it might be argued, presentation of the target results in a recognition response based on familiarity information. It can be argued that familiarity information corresponds to a routine automatic component of memory which provides the SAS with a trigger that there is more stored about this target in memory. Thus on finding an item familiar the SAS should enact further retrieval operations to retrieve the associated contextual information required for a full-blown recognition response. Similarly, a source memory error might arise because of failure to retrieve all the information associated with a newly acquired fact.

There is a problem, however, in that many of the memory impairments associated with frontal lobe damage could be a consequence of encoding problems rather than retrieval. In order to store information in memory effectively it is necessary to plan how it will be retrieved. This is somewhat analogous to library storage in which a book's location is specified by a catalogue entry. Given the large amount of information stored in our memories, considerable planning is required to ensure that a memory is stored away correctly. As we have seen the frontal lobes are intimately concerned with planning, so it is not unreasonable to suppose that this function relates directly to how memories are encoded. Connected with this account is Rocchetta's (1986) finding that frontal patients are poor at organizing information into categories which, in turn, impairs their recall performance. On this basis, poor memory for source, for example, might arise because the source information was never encoded. Similarly, impaired estimates of frequency and memory for temporal order could also reflect an inability to encode the relevant attributes of an event.

One way of disentangling faulty encoding and faulty retrieval involves the use of orienting tasks (see chapter 9) which are specifically known to enhance memory at the encoding stage. The logic here is that if a memory impairment is due to defective encoding then a manipulation that enhances encoding should reduce the deficit. We tried this with JB by observing the difference in his memory performance when he did and did not use orienting tasks during learning. The results were extremely clear; orienting tasks greatly reduced his level of false alarms without any appreciable change in hit rates (Parkin et al., in preparation).

The next step is to explain why encoding improves JB's memory by reducing false alarms. Earlier we saw that JB, left to his own devices, appears to recognize items on the basis of their familiarity rather than their contextual features. Overall this leads him to make numerous false responses because he responds positively to any featural overlap between a distractor and his memory for targets. A plausible assumption, therefore, is that encoding instructions have increased the contextual element of his memory and thus reduced his sensitivity to the incidental familiarity cues shared by distractors.

However, additional findings suggest that this straightforward account of JB's memory impairment will not suffice. In one experiment, for example, JB was asked to remember a list of nonwords based on unfamiliar letter patterns and then discriminate them from similar nonwords he had never seen before. In this instance one would assume that the scope for familiarity cues was severely reduced because the stimuli were meaningless and had never been encountered before, yet JB made as many false alarms on this test as he did in a conventional test (as did BG when given a similar kind of test [see Schacter et al. in press]).

Similarly when given a recognition test in which no targets appeared he produced a 'hit rate' similar to that when targets were present (Parkin et al. in prep.).

Recently Schacter (in press) has provided a theoretcial framework within which findings of this kind might be understood. It stems from Conway and Rubin's (1993) distinction between general and event specific memory. In the context of a list learning experiment general memory would be 'I saw a list of words' while event specific memory would be a record of each word on the list. In the case of their patient BG Schacter et al. argue that he has a defective retrieval process which sets up a general event representation which has poor item specific content. As a result most items are considered targets because they fit the poorly focused description of the event (e.g. words). To emphasise this point Schacter et al. report an experiment in which BG was asked to remember pictures of furniture and clothing and where the distractors were all pictures of animals. Under these conditions BG performed normally making virtually no false alarms – a finding which Schacter et al. attribute to the general event context (i.e. I saw pictures of furniture and animals) being sufficient to discriminate targets from distrators. Returning to JB it is also possible to argue that he too produces poorly focused event descriptions. However, the fact that an encoding manipulation improves his memory suggests that, unlike BG's proposed impairment, JB's deficit lies in the acquisition phase of memory.

Studies of frontal patients thus suggest that executive processes may be involved at both the encoding and retrieval stages of memory. A new approach using in vivo neuroimaging has confirmed this view. In these experiments normal subjects undertake memory experiments while being PET scanned (see chapter 1) at the same time. This procedure is able to identify those brain regions that are most active at any point during performance of a task. Shallice, Fletcher, Grasby et al. (1994) devised experiments which enabled them to distinguish between encoding and retrieval operations, and examined the pattern of brain activity resulting from each. The results showed that the left frontal lobe was associated with encoding operations and the right frontal lobe associated with retrieval. In addition retrieval was also associated with activation of a parietal lobe structure known as the precuneus – the significance of parietal lobe involvement in retrieval was mentioned earlier in our account of focal retrograde amnesia.

Findings similar to those of Shallice et al. have now been reported by Tulving, Kapur and Craik et al. (1994). Thus it seems reasonable to propose a distinction exists between right and left frontal involvement in memory in terms of encoding versus retrieval. Consistent with this is the fact that BG (Schacter et al., 1995) had a lesion to the right frontal lobe.

However, it is unlikely that this relatively simple difference will be sufficient to describe frontal involvement in memory. Petrides and his colleagues (e.g. Petrides, Alivisatos, Evans and Meyer, 1993a; Petrides, Alivisatos, Meyer and Evans, 1993b) have used in vivo neuroimaging to make finer-grained distinctions between memory tasks and and the frontal lobes. They have shown, for example, that the self-ordered pointing task and a conditional associative learning task activate different regions of the frontal cortex.

Frontal Dysfunction and the Neuropsychology of Age-related Memory Loss

As we get older it is inevitable that our memory starts to fail. In particular our ability to recall and recognize new information declines substantially. This pattern of cognitive decline is associated with loss of neurones in the brain, particularly from the frontal cortex. This has led to the idea that normal age-related memory loss (NARML) might, in part at least, be related to a loss of memory abilities specifically associated with the frontal lobes. This issue has been explored on a purely behavioural basis by examining relationships between performace on memory tasks dependent on frontal function and subjects' ability on standard frontal tasks such as WCST.

We have already noted source amnesia in the elderly and its relation to frontal dysfunction. More recently, the relationship between frontal dysfunction and NARML has been examined in other aspects of memory performance. Parkin and Walter (1992) compared the accuracy of yes–no recognition memory in three age groups and found a small but significant age effect. In addition, using a technique which we term the recognition and conscious awareness (RCA) paradigm (Gardiner, 1988), subjects also had to classify each recognized target on a subjective basis. If recognition involved specific recollection of a target's prior occurrence (e.g. an image it evoked) it was classified as a 'remember' (R) response whereas recognition based simply on familiarity was classified as a 'know' (K) response. The effects of age on the distribution of R and K responses were dramatic: with increasing age, subjects made substantially higher numbers of K responses even in subgroup comparisons where age had no effect on recognition accuracy at all. This was not due to less confidence in the older subjects but was significantly related to frontal lobe function – increased K responding being associated with greater errors on WCST. There was, however, no relationship between the K measure and spontaneous fluency.

Parkin, Walter and Hunkin (1995) compared young and elderly

subjects on the list discrimination task (LDT) which measures both recognition and the ability of subjects to recollect the temporal or context information about a target's prior presentation (e.g. which list was a target in? was the target presented to your left or right?). No age differences on recognition were found but the elderly performed much worse on memory for temporal context. The extent of the deficit in temporal context memory correlated with deficits in spontaneous but not reactive flexibility. These findings concerning frontal function and memory for temporal context in the elderly coincide with demonstrations that focal frontal lesions produce similar types of impairment (see below).

Finally, a recent study by Parkin and Lawrence (1994) gave elderly subjects three tests of spontaneous flexibility and WCST as a measure of reactive flexibility. Performance on these measures was correlated with the subject's performance on two memory tasks considered to have a component sensitive to the role of the frontal cortex in memory function. One task, release from proactive interference, correlated with measures of spontaneous flexibility but not reactive flexibility. A second task measuring recall difficulty relative to recognition (Calev, 1984) showed the reverse set of relationships. Discussing these results Parkin and Lawrence concluded that there is a relationship between certain aspects of memory function and the frontal disturbances that occur as a natural consequences of ageing. However, these changes do not reflect a single 'frontal factor'. Rather there appear to be different memory functions which are associated with different components of frontal function.

It is also of some significance that ageing tends to increase the probability of false alarms in recognition tests even though hit rates can remain at the same level as younger subjects (Kausler, 1994). There is now evidence that this increase in false alarms may, as in the case of JB (above), be related to an increased reliance on familiarity. Bartlett and Fulton (1991), for example, found that older subjects made more false alarms on a facial recognition test, and that these false alarms were made to faces that shared some featural similarities with the targets.

An Alternative to the Central Executive

In this chapter we have seen that damage to the frontal lobes results in a wide range of deficits. Attempts to characterize these deficits have centred on the idea of an executive which interacts with different subsystems controlling routine actions. There is certainly a great deal of evidence consistent with this approach and the attraction is how the same hypothetical executive could be implicated in apparently different tasks such as memory and problem solving. However, there is the problem that frontal functions dissociate from one another. Thus, as we have seen, tests of reactive flexibility appear distinct from those of spontaneous flexibility. Both types of tasks have an executive component so, on the assumption of a single executive, we should not expect to see dissociations arising.

In an alternative theory of frontal function, Goldman-Rakic (1987) has proposed that the frontal cortex is essentially a working memory system in which associations are formed between goals, environmental stimuli and stored knowledge. The initial basis for her theory is the fact that damage to the frontal lobes greatly impairs delayed response learning in non-human primates. Briefly, an animal watches food being stored in one of two locations but is prevented from responding for a few seconds. In animals with frontal lesions this delay is sufficient to cause a significant impairment in performance. This deficit, which can also be demonstrated in humans with frontal lesions (e.g. Freedman and Oscar-Berman, 1986), is attributed to an inability to keep the stimulus and response elements of the task together during the delay period. To account for the dissociation between tasks Goldman-Rakic suggests that different areas of the frontal cortex carry out the same type of function on different inputs.

Recently Kimberg and Farah (1993) have put forward a simulation of frontal function based on the Goldman-Rakic theory. Their first step was to simulate the performance of four frontal tasks using the ACT-R model of cognition (Anderson, 1993) – this model is specifically designed for modelling the association between goals, stimuli and stored knowledge. Within this simulation each task involves a number of working memory elements which are associated by activation pathways. The simplest of the tasks used was a motor sequencing task in which five actions had to be performed in succession to five different stimuli. The appropriate action for any stimulus has a major activation pathway associated with it, but there are also less active pathways linked to the other possible actions – this allows for the natural possibility that someone might forget the appropriate action and perform another action from the same set.

Observations of frontal patients performing motor sequence tasks have shown that two types of error occur. Patients may perseverate and perform the same action repeatedly or perform another action from the same set. These two forms of error have been termed 'continuous perseveration' and 'stuck-in-set' perseveration respectively (Sandson and Albert, 1984). Kimberg and Farah set about 'damaging' their simulation by weakening the associations between the working memory elements for each task. The result of this was to make the correct link between any two elements less easy to discriminate and hence provide a basis for incorrect responding. For the motor sequence task it was found that the majority of errors resulting from this damage were continuous perseverations but, in addition, non-perseverative stuck-in-set errors were also quite frequent. Damage to the representation of this task thus corresponded to the pattern of deficits found in frontal patients; a similar pattern was obtained for the other three tasks. On this basis Kimberg and Farah argue it is not necessary to specify a dysfunctional central executive to account for all patterns of frontal deficit. Rather, in line with Goldman-Rakic, they suggest that frontal functions are compartmentalized and that each of these is served by its own working memory function which can become selectively disrupted.

Kimberg and Farah's theory accounts for what is observed but seems distinctly unparsimonious in specifying the independent representation of the same function across different parts of the frontal lobes. Moreover, most neuropsychologists appear more comfortable, intuitively at least, with the existence of some single executive which, in many ways, corresponds to an acknowledgement of the self and free will. Also, the existence of dissociations between frontal tasks may not be as difficult for the central executive theory as it first seems. Frontal tasks have many components outside the role specified for the executive and it may be disruption of these components which causes dissociations between tasks. Nonetheless it is interesting to note that attempts to show that, in normal subjects, the control of various tasks shares a common executive component has so far failed to find any supporting evidence (Allport, Styles and Hsieh, 1994).

Summary

Clinical impressions from patients with frontal lobe damage suggest that this region of the brain is concerned with high-level executive functions. As a result damage to frontal lobes can impair tasks such as planning and problem solving. A widely discussed model of executive function is that put forward by Norman and Shallice. They contend that most mental operations are routine and that the priority of one set of actions over another is usually determined by contention scheduling. However, when a problem arises these routine activities are over-ridden by the supervisory activating system which ensures that a new and appropriate response is made. Two types of behavioural difficulty are predicted if the supervisory activating system becomes damaged: perseveration and distraction. Impaired performance by frontal patients on tasks such as the Wisconsin Card Sorting Test and Stroop supports this view. Frontal patients also perform poorly on planning tasks such as the Tower of London.

There is growing evidence that frontal function may be fractionated possibly into tests of reactive and spontaneous fluency. However, more fine-grained distinctions between elements of frontal function are likely to be required. Memory deficits can also occur following frontal lobe damage and it seems plausible to attribute these to impaired executive functions. Thus frontal patients have problems using appropriate retrieval strategies and may also be impaired in their ability to evaluate the truth of a memory – a finding particularly emphasized by the phenomenon of confabulation and high levels of false alarms. Source amnesia also appears related to executive dysfunction. Recently it has been argued that memory loss due to normal ageing has the same underlying cause as that found following frontal lobe damage. An alternative account of frontal function which rejects the concept of an executive has been put forward.

References

Akelaitis, A. J. (1944). A study of gnosis, praxis and language following section of the corpus callosum and anterior commissure. *Journal of Neurosurgery*, *1*, 94–102.

Albert, M. S., Butters, N. and Levin J. (1979). Temporal gradients in the retrograde amnesia of patients with alcoholic Korsakoff's Disease. *Archives of Neurology*, *36*, 211–16.

Allport, A., Styles, E. A. and Hsieh, S. (1994). Shifting intentional set: Exploring the dynamic control of tasks. In C. Umilta and M. Moscovitch (eds), *Attention and Performance XV*. Cambridge, Mass.: MIT Press.

Anderson, J. R. (1993). *Rules of the Mind*. Hillsdale, NJ: Erlbaum.

Ashcraft, M. H. (1993). A personal case history of transient anomia. *Brain and Language*, *44*, 47–57.

Atkinson, R. C. and Shiffrin, R. M. (1968). Human memory: A proposed system and its control processes. In K. W. Spence and J. T. Spence (eds), *The Psychology of Learning and Motivation* (Vol. 2,). New York: Academic Press.

Attneave, F. (1968). Triangles as ambiguous figures. *American Journal of Psychology*, *81*, 447–53.

Auerbach, S. H., Allard, T., Naeser, M., et al. (1982). Pure word deafness: analysis of a case with bilateral lesions and a defect at the prephonemic level. *Brain*, *105*, 271–300.

Baddeley, A. D. (1990). *Human Memory: Theory and Practice*. Boston: Allyn and Bacon.

Baddeley, A. D. and Hitch, G. J. (1977). Working Memory. In G. A. Bower (ed),

Recent Advances in Learning and Motivation (vol. 8, pp. 647–67). New York: Academic Press.

Baddeley, A. D., Thomson, N. and Buchanan, M. (1975). Word length and the structure of short-term memory. *Journal of Verbal Learning and Verbal Behavior, 14,* 575–89.

Baddeley, A. D. and Wilson, B. (1988). Frontal amnesia and the dysexecutive syndrome. *Brain and Cognition, 7,* 212–30.

Badecker, W. and Caramazza, A. (1985). On considerations of method and theory governing the use of clinical categories in neurolinguistics and cognitive neuropsychology: the case against agrammatism. *Cognition, 20,* 97–125.

Badecker, W., Hillis, A. E. and Caramazza, A. (1990). Lexical morphology and its role in the writing process. *Cognition, 35,* 205–44.

Badecker, W., Nathan, P. and Caramazza, A. (1991). Varieties of sentence comprehension deficits: A case study. *Cortex, 17,* 311–22.

Barbur, J. L., Forsyth, P. M and Findlay, J. M. (1988). Human saccadic eye movements in the absence of the geniculo-calcarine projection. *Brain, 111,* 63–82.

Barbur, J. L., Ruddock, K. H. and Waterfield, V. A. (1980). Human visual responses in the absence of the geniculo-calacarine projection. *Brain, 103,* 905–28.

Bartlett, J. C. and Fulton, A. (1991). Familiarity and recognition of faces in old age. *Memory and Cognition, 19,* 229–38.

Basso, A., Capitani, E. and Laiacona, M. (1988). Progressive language impairment without dementia: A case with isolated category-specific naming defect. *Journal of Neurology, Neurosurgery, and Psychiatry, 51,* 1201–7.

Bauer, R. M. (1984). Autonomic recognition of names and faces in prosopagnosia: A neuropsychological application of the guilty knowledge test. *Neuropsychologia, 22,* 457–69.

Bauer, R. M. (1993). Agnosia. In K. M. Heilman and E. Valenstein (eds), *Clinical Neuropsychology,* (pp. 215–78). New York: Oxford University Press.

Baxter, D. M. and Warrington, E. K. (1986). Ideational agraphia: A single case study. *Journal of Neurology, Neurosurgery, and Psychiatry, 49,* 369–74.

Bay, E. (1953). Disturbances of visual perception and their examination. *Brain, 76,* 515–51.

Baylis, G. C., Driver, J. and Rafal, R. D. (1993). Visual extinction and stimulus repetition. *Journal of Cognitive Neuroscience, 5,* 453–66.

Baynes, K., Tramo, M. J. and Gazzaniga, M. S. (1992). Reading with a limited lexicon in the right hemisphere of a callosotomy patient. *Neuropsychologia, 30,* 187–200.

Beaumont, J. G. and Davidoff, J. B. (1992). Assessment of visuo-perceptual dysfunction. In J. R. Crawford, D. M. Parker and W. W. McKinlay (eds), *Handbook of Neuropsychological Assessment.* Hove: Lawrence Erlbaum.

Beauvois, M. F., Dérousné, J. and Bastard, V. (1980). *Auditory parallel to phonological alexia.* Paper presented at the Third European Conference of the International Neuropsychological Society, Chianciano, Italy.

Beauvois, M. F. and Dérousené, J. (1979). Phonological alexia: Three dissociations. *Journal of Neurology, Neurosurgery and Psychiatry, 42,* 1115–24.

Beauvois, M. F. and Dérousné, J. (1981). Lexical or orthographic agraphia. *Brain*, *104*, 21–49.

Beeman, M. (1993). Semantic processing in the right hemisphere may contribute to drawing inferences from discourse. *Brain and Language*, *44*, 80–120.

Beeman, M., Frieman, R. B., Grafman, J., Perez, E., Diamond, S. and Beadle Lindsay, M. (1994). Summation priming and coarse semantic coding in the right hemisphere. *Journal of Cognitive Neuroscience*, *6*, 26–45.

Behrmann, M. and Moscovitch, M. (1994). Object-centred neglect in patients with unilateral neglect: Effects of left-right coordinates of objects. *Journal of Cognitive Neuroscience*, *6*, 1–16.

Behrmann, M., Moscovitch, M., Black, S. E. and Mozer, M. (1990). Perceptual and conceptual factors underlying neglect dyslexia: Two contrasting case studies. *Brain*, *113*, 1163–83.

Behrmann, M., Moscovitch, M. and Winocur, G. (1994). Intact visual imagery and impaired visual perception in a patient with visual agnosia. *Journal of Experimental Psychology: Human Perception and Performance*, *20*, 1068–87.

Bench, C. J., Frith, C. D., Grasby, P. M., Friston, K. J., Paulesu, E., Frackowiak, R. S. J. and Dolan, R. J. (1993). Investigations of the functional anatomy of attention using the stroop test. *Neuropsychologia*, *31*, 907–22.

Benson, D. F. (1979). Neurologic correlates of anomia. In H. Whitaker and H. A. Whitaker (eds), *Studies in Neurolinguistics* (Vol. 4). New York: Academic Press.

Benson, D. F. (1993). Aphasia. In K. M. Heilman and E. Valenstein (Eds.), *Clinical Neuropsychology*. New York: Oxford University Press.

Benson, D. F. and Greenberg, J. P. (1969). Visual form agnosia. *Archives of Neurology*, *20*, 82–9.

Benton, A. L. (1980). The neuropsychology of facial recognition. *American Psychologist*, *35*, 176–86.

Benton, A. L. (1990). Facial recognition 1990. *Cortex*, *26*, 491–9.

Benton, A. L. and Van Allen, M. W. (1972). Prosopagnosia and facial discrimination. *Journal of Neurological Science*, *15*, 167–72.

Berndt, R. S. (1987). Symptom co-occurrence and dissociation in the interpretation of agrammatism. In M. Coltheart, G. Sartori and P. Job (eds), *The Cognitive Neuropsychology of Language* (pp. 221–33). London: Erlbaum.

Berndt, R. S., Basili, A. and Caramazza, A. (1987). Dissociation of functions in a case of transcortical sensory aphasia. *Cognitive Neuropsychology*, *4*, 79–101.

Berry, D. and Broadbent, D. (1984). On the relationship between task performance and associated verbalizable knowledge. *Quarterly Journal of Experimental Psychology*, *36A* 209–31.

Berti, A. and Rizzolatti, G. (1992). Visual processing without awareness: Evidence from unilateral neglect. *Journal of Cognitive Neuroscience*, *4*, 345–51.

Biederman, I. (1987). Recognition by components: A theory of human image understanding. *Psychological Review*, *94*, 115–45.

Bisiach, E. and Luzzatti, C. (1978). Unilateral neglect of representational space. *Cortex*, *14*, 129–33.

Bisiach, E., Luzzatti, C. and Perani, D. (1979). Unilateral neglect, representational schema and consciousness. *Brain, 102,* 609–18.

Bisiach, E. and Rusconi, M. L. (1990). Break-down of perceptual awareness in unilateral neglect. *Cortex, 26,* 643–9.

Blythe, I. M., Bromley, J. M., Kennard, C. and Ruddock, K. H. (1986). Visual discrimination of target displacement remains after damage to the striate cortex in humans. *Nature, 320,* 619–21.

Blythe, I. M., Kennard, C. and Ruddock, K. H. (1987). Residual vision in patients with retinogeniculate lesions of the visual path. *Brain, 110,* 887–905.

Bodamer, J. (1947). Prosopagnosie. *Arch Psychiatr Nervenkr., 179,* 6–54.

Bogen, J. E. (1993). The Callosal Syndromes. In K. M. Heilman and E. Valenstein (eds), *Clinical Neuropsychology.* Oxford: Oxford University Press.

Bogen, J. E. and Vogel, P. J. (1965). Neurologic status in the long term following cerebral commissurotomy. In F. Michel and B. Schott (eds), *Les Syndromes de Disconnexion Calleuse chex L'Homme.* Lyon: Lyon: Hospital Neurologique.

Bornstein B., Sroka, M. and Munitz, H. (1969). Prosopagnosia with animal face agnosia. *Cortex, 5,* 164–9.

Boucart, M. and Humphreys, G. W. (1992). The computation of perceptual structure from collinearity and closure: Normality and pathology. *Neuropsychologia, 30,* 527–46.

Bowers, D., Bauer, R. M., Coslett, H. B. and Heilman, K. M. (1985). Processing of faces by patients with unilateral hemisphere lesions. 1. Dissociation between judgments of facial affect and facial identity. *Brain Cognition, 4,* 258–72.

Bowers, D., Coslett, B., Bauer, R. M., Speedie, L. and Hielman, K. M. (1987). Comprehension of emotional prosody following unilateral hemispheric lesions: Processing defect vs. distraction defect. *Neuropsychologia, 25,* 317–28.

Bowers, D., Verafaellie, M., Valenstein, E. and Heilman, K. M. (1988). Impaired acquisition of temporal information in retrosplenial amnesia. *Brain and Cognition, 8,* 47–66.

Bramwell, B. (1897). Illustrative cases of aphasia. Reprinted in 1984 as A case of word meaning deafness. *Cognitive Neuropsychology, 1,* 249–58.

Brion, S. and Jedynak, C. P. (1972). Trouble du transfer interhemispherique a propos de trois observations de temeurs du corps calleux: Le signe de la main etrangere. *Revue Neurologique (Paris), 126,* 257–66.

Brownell, H. H., Potter, H. H., Bihrle, A. M. and Gardner, H. (1986). Inference deficits in right brain-damaged patients. *Brain and Language, 27,* 310–21.

Bruce, V. and Young, A. (1986). Understanding face recognition. *British Journal of Psychology, 77,* 305–27.

Bruyer, R. (1991). Covert face recognition in Prosopagnosia: A review. *Brain and Cognition, 15,* 223–35.

Bruyer, R., LaTerre, C., Seron, X., Feyereisen, P., Strypstein, E., Pierrard, E. and Rectem, D. (1983). A case of prosopagnosia with some preserved covert remembrance of familiar faces. *Brain and Cognition, 2,* 257–84.

Bub, D., Cancelliere, A. and Kertesz, A. W. (1985). Whole-word and analytic translation of spelling to sound in a non-semantic reader. In K. E. Patterson, J. C. Marshall and M. Coltheart (eds), *Surface Dyslexia* (pp. 15–34). London: Lawrence Erlbaum.

Bub, D. and Kertesz, A. W. (1982a). Deep Agraphia. *Brain and Language*, *17*, 146–65.

Bub, D. and Kertesz, A. W. (1982b). Evidence for lexographic processing in a patient with preserved written over oral single word naming. *Brain*, *105*, 695–717.

Burgess, P. W. and Shallice, T. (in press). Fractionation of the frontal lobe syndrome. *Revue de Neuropsychologie*, *3*.

Butter, C. M. and Trobe, J. D. (1994). Integrative agnosia following progressive multifocal leukoencephalopathy. *Cortex*, *30*, 145–58.

Butters, N. (1984). Alcoholic Korsakoff's Syndrome: An update. *Seminars in Neurology*, *4*, 226–44.

Calev, A. (1984). Recall and recognition in mildly disturbed schizophrenics: The use of matched tasks. *Journal of Abnormal Psychology*, *93*, 172–7.

Campbell, R., Landis, T. and Regard, M. (1986). Face recognition and lip reading: a neurological dissociation. *Brain*, *109*, 509–21.

Campion, J., Latto, R. and Smith, Y. M. (1983). Is blindsight an effect of scattered light, spared cortex, and near-threshold vision? *Behavioural and Brain Science*, *6*, 423–48.

Capgrass, J. and Reboul-Lachaux, J. (1923). L'illusion des 'sosies' dans une delire systematise chronique. *Bulletin de la Societe Clinique de Medecine Mentale*, *2*, 6–16.

Capitani, E., Laiacona, M., Barbarotto, R. and Trivelli, C. (1994). Living and non-living categories. Is there a 'normal' asymmetry? *Neuropsychologia*, *32*, 1453–63.

Caplan, D. (1986). In defense of agrammatism. *Cognition*, *24*, 263–76.

Caplan, D. (1992). *Language, Structure, Processing Disorders*. Cambridge, MA: MIT Press.

Caramazza, A. (1984). The logic of neuropsychological research and the problem of patient classification of aphasia. *Brain and Language*, *21*, 9–20.

Caramazza, A. (1986). On drawing inferences about the structure of normal cognitive systems from the analysis of patterns of impaired performance: The case for single-patient studies. *Brain and Cognition*, *5*, 41–66.

Caramazza, A. (1988). When is enough, enough? A comment on Grodzinsky and Marek's 'Algorithmic and heuristic processes revisited'. *Brain and Language*, *33*, 390–9.

Caramazza, A. and Badecker, W. (1989). Patient classification in neuropsychological research. *Brain and Cognition*, *10*, 256–95.

Caramazza, A. and Badecker, W. (1991). Clinical syndromes are not God's gift to cognitive neuropsychology: A reply to a rebuttal to an answer to a response to the case against syndrome-based research. *Brain and Cognition*, *16*, 211–27.

Caramazza, A., Berndt, R. S. and Basili, A. G. (1983). The selective impairment of phonological processing. *Brain and Language*, *18*, 128–74.

Caramazza, A. and Hillis, A. E. (1989). The disruption of sentence production: Some dissociations. *Brain and Language*, *36*, 625–50.

Caramazza, A. and Hillis, A. (1990a). Where do semantic errors come from? *Cortex*, *26*, 95–122.

Caramazza, A. and Hillis, A. E. (1990b). Levels of representation, co-ordinate frames, and unilateral neglect. *Cognitive Neuropsychology, 5/6,* 391–445.

Caramazza, A., Hillis, A. E., Rapp, B. C. and Romani, C. (1990). The multiple semantics hypothesis: Multiple confusions? *Cognitive Neuropsychology, 7,* 161–90.

Caramazza, A., Miceli, G., Villa, G. and Romani, C. (1987). The role of the graphemic buffer in spelling: Evidence from a case of acquired dysgraphia. *Cognition, 26,* 59–85.

Caramazza, A. and Zurif, E. B. (1976). Dissociation of algorithmic and heuristic processes in language comprehension. *Brain and Language, 3,* 572–82.

Carney, R. and Temple, C. M. (1993). Prosopanomia: A possible category-specific anomia for faces. *Neuropsychologia, 10,* 185–95.

Cermak, L. S. and O'Connor, U. (1983). The anterograde and retrograde retrieval ability of a patient with encephalitis. *Neuropsychologia, 21,* 213–34.

Cermak, L. S., Verfaellie, M., Milberg, W., Letourneau, L. and Blackford, S. (1991). A further analysis of perceptual identification priming in alcoholic Korsakoff patients. *Neuropsychologia, 29,* 725–36.

Chattergee, A., Mennemeier, M. and Heilman, K. M. (1992). The psychophysical power law and unilateral spatial neglect. *Brain and Cognition, 25,* 107–30.

Chertkow, H., Bub, D. and Kaplan, D. (1992). Constraining theories of semantic memory processing: Evidence from dementia. *Cognitive Neuropsychology, 9,* 327–65.

Chiarello, C. (1988). More on words, hemifields, and hemispheres; A reply to Schwartz and Kirsner. *Brain and Cognition, 7,* 394–401.

Chomsky, N. (1959). Review of Skinner's Verbal Behavior. *Language, 35,* 26–58.

Chomsky, N. (1981). *Lectures on Government and Binding.* Dordrecht: Foris.

Cipolotti, L. and Warrington, E. K. (1995). Semantic memory and reading abilities: A case report. *Journal of the International Neuropsychological Society, 1,* 104–10.

Cohen, G. and Faulkner, D. (1986). Memory for proper names: Age differences in retrieval. *British Journal of Developmental Psychology, 4,* 187–97.

Coltheart, M. (1980). Deep dyslexia: A review of the syndrome. In M. Coltheart, K. E. Patterson and J. C. Marshall (eds), *Deep Dyslexia,* (pp. 22–47). London: Routledge and Kegan Paul.

Coltheart, M. (1987). Reading, phonological recoding, and deep dyslexia. In M. Coltheart, K. E. Patterson and J. C. Marshall (eds), *Deep Dyslexia.* London: Routledge and Kegan Paul.

Coltheart, M., Curtis, B., Atkins, P. and Haller, M. (1993). Models of reading aloud: Dual-route and parallel-distributed-processing approaches. *Psychological Review, 100,* 589–608.

Coltheart, M., Patterson, K. E. and Marshall, J. C. (1987). Deep dyslexia since 1980. In M. Coltheart, K. E. Patterson and J. C. Marshall (eds), *Deep Dyslexia.* London: Routledge and Kegan Paul.

Conway, (1990). *Autobiographical Memory.* Milton Keynes: Open University Press.

Conway, M. A. and Rubin, D. C. (1993). The structure of autobiographical memory. In A. F. Collins, S. E. Gathercole, M. A. Conway and P. E. Morris (eds), *Theories of Memory*. Hillsdale, N. J.: Lawrence Earlbaum.

Corballis, M. C. (1994). Can commissurotomized subjects compare digits between the visual fields? *Neuropsychologia, 32*, 1475–86.

Corballis, M. C. (1995). Line bisection in a man with complete forebrain commissurotomy. *Neuropsychology, 9*, 147–56.

Corballis, M. C. (in press). Visual integration in the split brain. *Neuropsychologia*.

Corballis, M. C. and Trudel, C. I. (1993). Role of the forebrain commissures in interhemispheric intergration. *Neuropsychology, 7*, 306–24.

Corkin, S. (1984). Lasting consequences of bilateral medial temporal lobectomy: Clinical course and experimental findings in HM. *Seminars in Neurology, 4*, 249–59.

Corsi, P. M. (1972). *Human memory and the medial temporal regions of the brain*. Unpublished PhD, McGill University.

Coslett, H. B. (1991). Read but not write 'idea': Evidence for a third reading mechanism. *Brain and Language, 40*, 425–43.

Coslett, H. B., Bowers, D., Fitzpatrick, E., Haws, B. and Heilman, K. M. (1990). Directional hypokinesia and hemispatial inattention in neglect. *Brain, 113*, 475–86.

Coslett, H. B. and Monsul, N. (1994). Reading with the right hemisphere: Evidence from transcranial magnetic stimulation. *Brain and Language, 46*, 198–211.

Courbon, P. and Frail, G. (1927). Syndrome d'illusion de Fregoli et schizophrenie. *Bull. Soc. Clin. Med. Ment., 15*, 121–5.

Courbon, P. and Tusques, J. (1932). Illusions d'intermetamorphose et de charme. *Annales medico-psychologiques, 90*, 401–5.

Cowey, A., Small, M. and Ellis, S. (1994). Left visuo-spatial neglect can be worse in far than in near space. *Neuropsychologia, 32*, 1059–66.

Cowey, A. and Stoerig, P. (1991). The neurobiology of blindsight. *Trends in Neuroscience, 14*, 140–5.

Craik, F. I. M., Morris, L. W., Morris, R. G. and Loewen, E. R. (1990). Relations between source amnesia and frontal functioning in older adults. *Psychology of Ageing, 5*, 148–51.

Cronin-Golomb, A. (1986). Subcortical transfer of cognitive information in subjects with complete forebrain commissurotomy. *Cortex, 22*, 499–519.

Cutting, J. (1990). *The Right Cerebral Hemisphere and Psychiatric Disorders*. Oxford: Oxford University Press.

D'Erme, P., Robertson, I., Bartolomeo, P., Daniele, A. and Gainotti, G. (1992). Early rightwards orienting of attention on simple reaction time performance in patients with left-sided neglect. *Neuropsychologia, 30*, 989–1000.

D'Esposito, M., McGlinchey-Berroth, R., Alexander, M. P., Verfaellie, M. and Milberg, W. P. (1993). Dissociable cognitive and neural mechanisms of unilateral visual neglect. *Neurology, 43*, 2638–44.

Damasio, A. R. and Damasio, H. (1993). Cortical systems for retrieval of concrete knowledge: The convergence zone framework. In C. Koch and J. L.

Davis (eds), *Large Scale Neural Theories of the Brain*. Cambridge, MA: MIT Press.

Damasio, A. R., Damasio, H. and Tranel, D. (1990). Impairments of visual recognition as clues to the process of memory. In G. M. Edelman, W. E. Gall and W. M. Cowan (eds), *Signal and Sense: Local and Global Order in Perceptual Maps*. New York: Wiley-Liss.

Damasio, A. R., Damasio, H. and Van Hoesen, G. W. (1982). Prosopagnosia: anatomic basis and behavioral mechanism. *Neurology, 32*, 331–41.

Damasio, H., Grabowski, T., Frank, R., Galaburda, A. M. and Damasio, A. R. (1994). The return of Phineas Gage: Clues about the brain from the skull of a famous patient. *Science, 264*, 1102–05.

Dandy, W. E. (1936). Operative experience in cases of pineal tumor. *Archives of Surgery, 33*, 19–46.

De Bastiani, P. and Barry, C. (1989). A cognitive analysis of an acquired dysgraphic patient with an 'Allographic' writing disorder. *Cognitive Neuropsychology, 6*, 25–41.

De Haan, E. H. F., Bauer, R. M. and Greve, K. W. (1992). Behavioral and physiological evidence for covert recognition in a prosopagnosic patient. *Cortex, 28*, 77–95.

De Haan, E. H. F., Young, A. W. and Newcombe, F. (1987). Face recognition without awareness. *Cognitive Neuropsychology, 4*, 385–415.

Delbecq-Dérousné, J., Beauvois, M. F. and Shallice, T. (1990). Preserved recall versus impaired recognition. *Brain, 113*, 1045–74.

Delis, D. C., Squire, L. R., Bihrle, A. and Massman, P. (1992). Componential analysis of problem-solving ability: Performance of patients with frontal lobe damage and amnesic patients on a new sorting test. *Neuropsychologia, 30*, 683–97.

Della Salla, S., Marchetti, C. and Spinnler, H. (1991). Right-sided anarchic (alien) hand: A longitudinal study. *Neuropsychologia, 29*, 1113–27.

Denes, G. and Semenza, C. (1975). Auditory modality-specific anomia: Evidence from a case of pure word deafness. *Cortex, 11*, 401–11.

De Renzi, E., Faglioni, P., Grossi, D. and Nichelli, P. (1991). Apperceptive and associative form of prosopagnosia. *Cortex, 27*, 213–21.

De Renzi, E., Liotti, M. and Nichelli, P. (1987). Semantic amnesia with preservation of autobiographic memory. *Cortex, 23*, 575–97.

De Renzi, E. and Lucchelli, F. (1993). The fuzzy boundaries of apperceptive agnosia. *Cortex, 29*, 187–215.

De Renzi, E., Perani, D., Carlesimo, G. A., Silveri, M. C. and Fazio, F. (1994). Prosopagnosia can be associated with damage confined to the right hemisphere – an MRI and PET study and a review of the literature. *Neuropsychologia, 32*, 893–902.

Doody, R. S. and Jankovic, J. (1992). The alien hand and related signs. *Journal of Neurology, Neurosurgery and Psychiatry, 55*, 806–10.

Driver, J., Baylis, G. C., Goodrich, S. J. and Rafal, R. D. (1994). Axis-based neglect of visual shapes. *Neuropsychologia, 32*, 1353–66.

Driver, J., Baylis, G. C. and Rafal, R. D. (1992). Preserved figure-ground segregation and symmetry perception in visual neglect. *Nature, 360*, 73–5.

Driver, J. and Halligan, P. W. (1991). Can visual neglect operate in object-centred co-ordinates? An affirmative single-case study. *Cognitive Neuropsychology*, *8*, 475–96.

Druks, J. and Marshall, J. C. (1991). Agrammatism: An analysis and critique, with new evidence from four Hebrew-speaking aphasic patients. *Cognitive Neuropsychology*, *8*, 415–33.

Dusoir, H., Kapur, N., Byrnes, D. P., McKinstry, S. and Hoare, R. D. (1990). The role of diencephalic pathology in human memory: Evidence from a penetrating paranasal brain injury. *Brain*, *113*, 1695–706.

Eccles, J. C. (1965). *The Brain and the Unity of Conscious Experience*. Cambridge: Cambridge University Press.

Efron, R. (1968). *What is Perception?* (Vol. 4). New York: Humanities Press Inc.

Ellis, A. W. (1982). Spelling and writing (and reading and speaking). In A. W. Ellis (ed.), *Normality and Pathology in Cognitive Functions*. London: Academic Press.

Ellis, A. W. (1984). Introduction to Bramwell's (1887) case of word-meaning deafness. *Cognitive Neuropsychology*, *1*, 245–8.

Ellis, A. W., Miller, D. and Sin, G. (1983). Wernicke's aphasia and normal language processing: A case study in cognitive neuropsychology. *Cognition*, *15*, 111–44.

Ellis, A. W. and Young, A. W. (1988). *Human Cognitive Neuropsychology*. London: Lawrence Erlbaum Associates.

Ellis, A. W., Young, A. W. and Flude, B. (1993). Neglect and visual language. In I. H. Robertson and J. C. Marshall (eds), *Unilateral Neglect: Clinical and Experimental Studies*. Hove: Erlbaum.

Ellis, A. W., Young, A. W. and Flude, B. M. (1987). 'Afferent dysgraphia' in a patient and in normal subjects. *Cognitive Neuropsychology*, *4*, 465–86.

Ellis, H. D. (1989). Past and recent studies of prosopagnosia. In J. R. Crawford and D. M. Parker (eds), *Developments in Clinical and Experimental Psychology*. New York: Plenum.

Ellis, H. D., dePauw, K. W., Christodoulou, G. N., Papageorgiou, L., Milne, A. B. and Joseph, A. B. (1993). Responses to facial and non-facial stimuli presented tachistoscopically in either or both visual fields by patients with the Capgras delusion and paranoid schizophrenics. *Journal of Neurology, Neurosurgery, and Psychiatry*, *56*, 215–19.

Ellis, H. D. and Florence, M. (1990). Bodamer's (1947) paper on Prosopagnosia. *Cognitive Neuropsychology*, *7*, 81–105.

Ellis, H. D., Whitley, J. and Luaute, J.-P. (1994). Delusional misidentification. *History of Psychiatry*, *V*, 117–46.

Ellis, H. D. and Young, A. W. (1990). Accounting for delusional misidentifications. *British Journal of Psychiatry*, *157*, 239–48.

Emmorey, K. (1987). The neurological substrates for prosodic aspects of speech. *Brain and Language*, *30*, 305–20.

Eslinger, P. J. and Grattan, L. M. (1993). Frontal lobe and frontal-striatal substrates for different forms of human cognitive flexibility. *Neuropsychologia*, *31*, 17–28.

Etcoff, N. L., Freeman, R. and Cave, K. R. (1991). Can we lose memories of faces? Content specificity and awareness in a prosopagnosic. *Journal of Cognitive Neuroscience, 3*, 25–41.

Evans J. J., Heggs, A. J., Antoun, N. and Hodges, J. R. (1995). Progressive prosopagnosia associated with selective right temporal atrophy. *Brain, 118*, 1–13.

Farah, M. J. (1989). Mechanisms of imagery-perception interaction. *Journal of Experimental Psychology: Human Perception and Performance, 15*, 203–11.

Farah, M. J. (1990). *Visual Agnosia*. Cambridge, Mass.: MIT Press.

Farah, M. J. (1991). Patterns of co-occurrence among the associative agnosias: Implications for visual object representation. *Cognitive Neuropsychology, 8*, 1–19.

Farah, M. J., Hammond, K. M., Mehta, Z. and Ratcliff, G. (1989). Category-specificity and modality-specificity in semantic memory. *Neuropsychologia, 27*, 193–200.

Farah, M. J., Levine, D. N. and Calvanio, R. (1988). A case study of mental imagery deficit. *Brain and Cognition, 8*, 147–64.

Farah, M. J., Levinson, K. L. and Klein, K. L. (1995). Face perception and within-category discrimination in prosopagnosia. *Neuropsychologia, 33*, 661–74.

Farah, M. J. and McClelland, J. L. (1991). A computational model of semantic-memory impairment: Modality-specificity and emergent category-specificity. *Journal of Experimental Psychology, 120*, 339–57.

Farah, M. J., O'Reilly, R. C. and Vecera, S. P. (1993). Dissociated overt and covert recognition as an emergent property of a lesioned neural network. *Psychological Review, 100*, 571–88.

Fendrich, R., Wessinger, C. M. and Gazzaniga, M. S. (1992). Residual vision in scotoma: Implications for blindsight. *Science, 258*, 1489–91.

Fleminger, S. (1992). Seeing is believing: The role of 'Preconscious' perceptual processing in delusional misidentification. *British Journal of Psychiatry, 160*, 293–303.

Fleminger, S. and Burns, A. (1993). The delusional misidentification syndromes in patients with and without evidence of organic cerebral disorder: A structured review of case reports. *Biological Psychiatry, 33*, 22–32.

Fodor, J. A. (1983). *The Modularity of Mind*. Cambridge, Mass.: MIT Press.

Forstl, H., Almeida, O. P. and Owen, A. M. et al. (1991). Psychiatric neurological and medical aspects of misidentification syndromes; a review of 260 cases. *Psychological Medicine, 21*, 905–10.

Foster, J. K., Eskes, G. A. and Stuss, D. T. (1994). The cognitive neuropsychology of attention: A frontal lobe perspective. *Cognitive Neuropsychology, 11*, 133–47.

Franklin, S., Turner, J. and Morris, J. (1994). *Word meaning deafness: Effects of word type*. Paper presented at the International Conference on Spoken Language Processing.

Freedman, M. and Oscar-Berman, M. (1986). Bilateral frontal lobe disease and selective delayed response deficits in humans. *Behavioural Neuroscience, 100*, 337–42.

Fujii, T., Rukatsu, R., Watabe, S., Ohnuma, A., Teramura, K., Kimura, I., Saso, S. and Kogure, K. (1990). Auditory sound agnosia without aphasia following a right temporal lobe lesion. *Cortex, 26*, 263–8.

Funnell, E. (1983). Phonological processes in reading: New evidence from acquired dyslexia. *British Journal of Psychology, 74*, 159–80.

Funnell, E. (in press). Response biases in oral reading: An account of the co-occurrence of surface dyslexia and semantic dementia. *Quarterly Journal of Experimental Psychology.*

Funnell, E. and Sheridan, J. (1992). Categories of knowledge? Unfamiliar aspects of living and nonliving things. *Cognitive Neuropsychology, 9*, 135–53.

Fuster, J. (1989). *The prefrontal cortex: Anatomy, physiology and neuropsychology of the frontal lobe* (2nd edn). New York: Raven Press.

Gaffan, D. and Heywood, C. A. (1993). A spurious category specific visual agnosia for living things in normal human and nonhuman primates. *Journal of Cognitive Neuroscience, 5*, 118–28.

Gardiner, J. M. (1988) Functional aspects of recollective experience. *Memory and Cognition, 16*, 309–13.

Gazzaniga, M. S. (1970). *The Bisected Brain.* New York: Appleton-Century-Crofts.

Gazzaniga, M. S. (1983a). Right Hemisphere Language Following Brain Bisection. *American Psychologist, 525*–37.

Gazzaniga, M. S. (1983b). Reply to Levy and to Zaidel. *American Psychologist,* 547–9.

Gazzaniga, M. S. (1987). Perceptual and attentional processes following callosal section in humans. *Neuropsychologia, 25*, 119–33.

Gazzaniga, M. S. (1989). Organization of the human brain. *Science, 245*, 947–52.

Gazzaniga, M. S. (1994). Blindsight reconsidered. *Current Directions in Psychological Science, 3*, 93–6.

Gazzaniga, M. S., Bogen, J. E. and Sperry, R. W. (1962). Some functional effects of sectioning the cerebral commissures in man. *Proceedings of the National Academy of Sciences USA, 48*, 1765–69.

Gazzaniga, M. S. and Smylie, C. S. (1984). Dissociation of language and cognition: A psychological profile of two disconnected right hemispheres. *Brain, 107*, 145–53.

Geschwind, N. (1965). Disconnection syndromes in animal and man. *Brain, 88*, 237–67.

Gibson, E. (1970). The ontogeny of reading. *American Psychologist, 25*, 136–43.

Glisky, E. L., Polster, M. R. and Routhieaux, B. C. (1995). Double dissociation between item and source memory. *Neuropsychology, 9*, 229–35.

Glushko, R. J. (1979). The organization and activation of orthographic knowledge in reading aloud. *Journal of Experimental Psychology: Human Perception and Performance, 5*, 674–91.

Goldberg, M. D., Mayer, N. H. and Toglia, J. U. (1981). Medial frontal cortex infarction and the alien hand sign. *Achives of Neurology, 38*, 683–6.

Goldenberg, G., Steiner, M., Podreka, I. and Deecke, L. (1992). Regional cerebral blood flow patterns related to the verification of low- and high-imagery words. *Neuropsychologia, 30,* 581–6.

Goldman-Rakic, P. S. (1987). Circuitry of primate prefrontal cortex and regulation of behavior by representational knowledge. In F. Plum and V. B. Mountcastle (eds), *Handbook of Physiology* (vol. 5, pp. 373–417): American Physiological Society.

Goldstein, L. H., Bernard, S., Fenwick, P. B. C., Burgess, P. W. and McNeil, J. (1993). Unilateral frontal lobectomy can produce strategy application disorder. *Journal of Neurology, Neurosurgery, and Psychiatry, 56,* 274–6.

Goodale, M. A., Jakobson, L. S., Milner, A. D., Perrett, D. I., Benson, P. J. and Hietanen, J. K. (1994). The nature and limits of orientation and pattern processing supporting visuomotor control in a visual form agnosic. *Journal of Cognitive Neuroscience, 6,* 46–56.

Goodale, M. A., Milner, A. D., Jakobson, L. S. and Carey, D. P. (1991). A neurological dissociation between perceiving objects and grasping them. *Nature, 349,* 154–6.

Goodall, W. C. and Phillips, W. A. (1995). Three routes from print to sound: Evidence from a case of acquired dyslexia. *Cognitive Neuropsychology, 12,* 113–47.

Goodglass, H. (1993). *Understanding Aphasia.* San Diego: Academic Press.

Goodglass, H. and Kaplan, E. (1972). *The Assessment of Aphasia and Related Disorders*: Philadelphia: Lea and Febiger.

Goodglass, H. and Kaplan, E. (1983). *The Boston Diagnostic Aphasia Examination.* Philadelphia: Lea and Febiger.

Goodman, R. A. and Caramazza, A. (1986). Dissociation of spelling errors in written and oral spelling: The role of allographic conversion in writing. *Cognitive Neuropsychology, 3,* 179–206.

Graf, P. and Schacter, D. L. (1985). Implicit and explicit memory for novel associations in normal and amnesic subjects. *Journal of Experimental Psychology: Learning, Memory and Cognition, 11,* 501–18.

Graff-Radford, N. R., Tranel, D., Van Hoesen, G. W. and Brandt, J. P. (1990). Diencephalic amnesia. *Brain, 113,* 1–25.

Grailet, J. M., Seron, X., Bruyer, R., Coyette, F. and Frederix, M. (1990). Case report of a visual integrative agnosia. *Cognitive Neuropsychology, 7,* 275–309.

Grant, D. A. and Berg, E. A. (1948). A behavioral analysis of degree of reinforcement and ease of shifting to new responses in a Weigl-type card-sorting problem. *Journal of Experimental Psychology, 38,* 404–11.

Graves, R. E. and Jones, B. S. (1992). Conscious visual perceptual awareness vs. non-conscious visual spatial localisation examined with normal subjects using possible analogues of blindsight and neglect. *Cognitive Neuropsychology, 9,* 487–508.

Greve, K. W. and Bauer, R. M. (1990). Implicit learning of new faces in prosopagnosia: An application of the mere exposure paradigm. *Neuropsycho-lgoia, 28,* 1035–41.

Grodzinsky, Y. (1984). The syntactic characterization of agrammatism. *Cognition, 16,* 99–120.

Grodzinsky, Y. (1990). *Theoretical Perspectives on Language Deficits*. Cambridge, Mass.: MIT Press.

Grodzinsky, Y. (1991). There is an entity called agrammatic aphasia. *Brain and Language, 41*, 555–64.

Halligan, P. W. and Marshall, J. C. (1991). Left neglect for near but not far space in man. *Nature, 350*, 498–500.

Halligan, P. W. and Marshall, J. C. (1993). Homing in on neglect: A case study of visual search. *Cortex, 29*, 167–74.

Hallligan, P. W. and Marshall, J. C. (1994a). Focal and global attention modulate the expression of visuo-spatial neglect: A case study. *Neuropsychologia, 31*, 13–21.

Halligan, P. W. and Marshall, J. C. (1994b). Toward a principled explanation of unilateral neglect. *Cognitive Neuropsychology, 11*, 167–206.

Hanley, J. R., Davies, A. D. M., Downes, J. J. and Mayes, A. R. (1994). Impaired recall of verbal material following rupture and repair of an anterior communicating artery aneurysm. *Cognitive Neuropsychology, 11*, 543–78.

Hanley, J. R. and Kay, J. (1992). Does letter-by-letter reading involve the spelling system? *Neuropsychologia, 30*, 237–56.

Harley, T. A. (1993). Connectionist approaches to language disorders. *Aphasiology, 7*, 221–49.

Harlow, J. (1868). Recovery after severe injury to the head. *Publications of the Massachusetts Medical Society, 2*, 327–46.

Harlow, J. M. (1993). Recovery from the passage of an iron bar through the head. *History of Psychiatry, 4*, 271–81.

Hart, J. and Gordon, B. (1992). Neural subsystems for object knowledge. *Nature, 359*, 60–4.

Hatfield, F. M. (1985). Visual and phonological factors in acquired dysgraphia. *Neuropsychologia, 23*, 13–29.

Hatfield, F. M. and Patterson, K. E. (1983). Phonological spelling. *Quarterly Journal of Experimental Psychology, 35A*, 451–68.

Hecaen, H. and Angelerques, R. (1962). Agnosia for faces (prosopagnosia). *Archives of Neurology, 7*, 92–100.

Heilman, K. M., Bowers, D., Speedie, L. and Coslett, B. (1984). Comprehension of affective and nonaffective speech. *Neurology, 34*, 917–21.

Heilman, K. M., Scholes, R. and Watson, R. T. (1975). Auditory affective agnosia: Disturbed comprehension of affective speech. *Journal of Neurology, Neurosurgery and Psychiatry, 38*, 69–72.

Heilman, K. M. and Valenstein E. (1993). *Clinical Neuropsychology*. (2nd edn). New York: Oxford University Press.

Hickok, G., Zurif, E. and Canesco-Gonzalez, E. (1993). Structural description of agrammatic comprehension. *Brain and Language, 45*, 371–95.

Hillis, A. E. and Caramazza, A. (1989). The graphemic buffer and attentional mechanisms. *Brain and Language, 36*, 208–35.

Hillis, A. E. and Caramazza, A. (1991). Mechanisms for accessing lexical representations for output: Evidence from a category-specific semantic deficit. *Brain and Language, 40*, 106–44.

Hillis, A.E. and Caramazza, A. (1995a). Converging evidence for the interaction of semantic and sublexical phonological information in accessing lexical representations for spoken output. *Cognitive Neuropsychology, 12,* 187–227.

Hillis, A. E. and Caramazza, A. (1995b). Spatially specific deficits in processing graphemic representations in reading and writing. *Brain and Language, 48,* 263–308.

Hillis A. E., Rapp, B. and Caramazza, A. (1995). Constraining claims about theories of semantic memory: More on unitary versus multiple semantics. *Cognitive Neuropsychology, 12,* 176–85.

Hillis, A. E., Rapp, B. C., Romani, C. and Caramazza, A. (1990). Selective impairment of semantics of lexical processing. *Cognitive Neuropsychology, 7,* 191–243.

Hinton, G. E., Plaut, D. C. and Shallice, T. (1993). Simulating Brain Damage. *Scientific American, 269,* 76–82.

Hinton, G. E. and Shallice, T. (1991). Lesioning an attractor network: Investigations of acquired dyslexia. *Psychological Review, 98,* 74–95.

Hird, K. and Kirsner, K. (1993). Dysprosody following acquired neurogenic impairment. *Brain and Language, 45,* 46–60.

Hirsh, K. W. and Funnell, E. (in press). Those old, familiar things: Age of acquisition, familiarity and lexical access in progressive aphasia. *Journal of Neurolinguistics.*

Hirsh, K. W. and Ellis, A. W. (1994). Age of acquisition and lexical processing in aphasia: A case study. *Cognitive Neuropsychology, 11,* 435–58.

Hittmair-Delazer, M., Denes, G., Semenza, C. and Mantovan, M. C. (1994). Anomia for people's names. *Neuropsychologia, 32,* 465–76.

Hodges, J. and McCarthy, R. A. (1993). Autobiographical amnesia resulting from bilateral paramedian thalamic infarction. *Brain, 116,* 921–40.

Hodges, J. R. and Marshall, J. C. (1992). Discrepant oral and written spelling after left hemisphere tumour. *Cortex, 28,* 643–56.

Hokkanen, L., Launes, R. and Vataja, L. et al. (1995). Isolated retrograde amnesia for autobiographical memory associated with acute left temporal lobe encephalitis. *Psychological Medicine, 25,* 203–8.

Holtzman, J. D. (1984). Interactions between cortical and subcortical visual areas: Evidence from human commissurotomy patients. *Vision Research, 24,* 801–13.

Holtzman, J. D., Sidtis, J. J., Volpe, B. T., Wilson, D. H., & Gazzaniga, M. S. (1981) Dissociation of spatial information for stimulus localization and the control of attention. *Brain, 104,* 861–72.

Hood, B. M. (1994). Disengaging visual attention in 6-month-old infants. *Infant Behaviour and Development, 16,* 405–22.

Howard, D. (1985). Agrammatism. In S. Newman and R. Epstein (eds), *Current Perspectives in Aphasia.* Edinburgh: Churchill Livingstone.

Howard, D. and Butterworth, B. (1989). Developmental disorders of verbal short-term memory and their relation to sentence comprehension: A reply to Vallar and Baddeley. *Cognitive Neuropsychology, 6,* 455–63.

Howard, D. and Orchard-Lisle, V. M. (1984). On the origin of semantic errors in naming: Evidence from the case of a global dysphasic. *Cognitive Neuropsychology, 1,* 163–90.

Humphrey, N. K. (1970). What the frogs eye tells the monkey's brain. *Brain, Behavior and Evolution, 3*, 324–37.

Humphrey, N. K. (1972). Seeing and nothingness. *New Scientist, 53*, 682–4.

Humphreys, G. W. and Quinlan, P. T. (1987). Normal and pathological processes in visual object constancy. In G. W. Humphreys and M. J. Riddoch (eds), *Visual Object Processing: A Cognitive Neuropsychological Approach* (pp. 43–105). London: Lawrence Erlbaum.

Humphreys, G. W. and Riddoch, M. J. (1984). Routes to object constancy: Implications from neurological impairments of object constancy. *Quarterly Journal of Experimental Psychology, 36A*, 385–415.

Humphreys, G. W. and Riddoch, M. J. (1987a). *To see but not to see: A Case of Visual Agnosia*. London: Lawrence Erlbaum.

Humphreys, G. W. and Riddoch, M. J. (1987b). The fractionation of visual agnosia. In G. W. Humphreys and M. J. Riddoch (eds), *Visual Object Processing: A Cognitive Neuropsychological Approach*, London: Lawrence Erlbaum.

Humphreys, G. W. and Riddoch, M. J. (1993). Interactive attentional systems and unilateral visual neglect. In I. H. Robertson and J. C. Marshall (eds), *Unilateral Neglect: Clinical and Experimental Studies*. Hove: Lawrence Erlbaum.

Humphreys, G. W. and Riddoch, M. J. (1993a). Object agnosias. *Balliere's Clinical Neurology, 2*, 339–359.

Humphreys, G. W., Riddoch, M. J. and Quinlan, P. T. et al. (1992). Parallel pattern processing in visual agnosia. *Canadian Journal of Psychology.*

Humphreys, G. W. and Riddoch, M. J. (1993b). Interactions between object and space systems revealed through neuropsychology. In D. Meyer and S. Kornblum (eds), *Attention and performance* (vol. 14, pp. 143–63). New York: Academic Press.

Hunkin, N. M. and Parkin, A. J. (1993). Recency judgments in Wernicke-Korsakoff and post-encephalitic amnesia: Influences of proactive interference and retention interval. *Cortex, 29*, 485–500.

Hunkin, N. M., Parkin, A. J. and Bradley, V. A. et al. (1995). Focal retrograde amnesia following closed head injury: A case study and theoretical account. *Neuropsychologia, 33*, 509–23.

Hunkin, N. M., Parkin, A. J. and Longmore, B. E. (1994). Aetiological variation in the amnesic syndrome. *Neuropsychologia, 32*, 819–25.

Huppert, F. A. and Piercy, M. (1978a). The role of trace strength in recency and frequency judgements by amnesic and control subjects. *Quarterly Journal of Experimental Psychology, 30*, 346–54.

Huppert, F. A. and Piercy, M. (1978b). Recognition memory in amnesic patients: A defect of acquisition? *Neuropsychologia, 15*, 643–52.

Iorio, L., Falanga, A., Fragassi, N. A. and Grossi, D. (1992). Visual associative agnosia and optic aphasia. A single case study and a review of the syndromes. *Cortex, 28*, 23–37.

Jacoby, L. L. (1991). A process dissociation framework: Separating automatic from intentional uses of memory. *Journal of Memory and Language, 30*, 513–41.

Jacoby, L. L., Toth, J. P. and Yonelinas, A. P. (1993). Separating conscious and unconscious influences of memory: Measuring recollection. *Journal of Experimental Psychology: General, 122*, 139–54.

Jankowiak, J., Kinsbourne, M., Shalev, R. S. and Bachman, D. L. (1992). Preserved visual imagery and categorization in a case of associative visual agnosia. *Journal of Cognitive Neuroscience, 4*, 119–31.

Janowsky, J. S., Shimamura, A. P. and Squire, L. R. (1989). Memory and metamemory: Comparisons between patients with frontal lobe lesions and amnesic patients. *Psychobiology, 17*, 3–11.

Jansari, A. & Parkin, A. J. (1996) Things that go bump in your life: Explaining reminiscence effects in autobiographical memory. *Psychology and Aging.*

Jenkins, V. and Parkin, A. J. *Implicit memory for novel associations in human amnesia.* Manuscript in preparation.

Joanette, Y., Goulet, P. and Hannequin, D. (1990). *Right Hemisphere and Verbal Communication.* New York: Springer Verlag.

Jocic, Z. and Staton, R. D. (1993). Reduplication after right middle cerebral artery infarction. *Brain and Cognition, 23*, 222–30.

Joseph, A. B. (1986). Focal CNS abnormalities in delusional misidentification syndromes. *Bibliotheca Psychiatrica, 164*, 68–79.

Kaplan, J. A., Brownell, H. H., Jacobs, J. R. and Gardner, H. (1990). The effects of right hemisphere damage on the pragmatic interpretation of conversational remarks. *Brain and Language, 38*, 315–33.

Kapur, N. (1992). Focal retrograde amnesia in neurological disease: A critical review. *Cortex, 29*, 217–34.

Kapur, N. (1994). Remembering Norman Schwarzkopf: Evidence for two distinct fact learning mechanisms. *Cognitive Neuropsychology, 11*, 661–70.

Kapur, N., Ellison, D., Parkin, A. J. and Hunkin, N. M. et al. (1994). Bilateral temporal lobe pathology with sparing of medial temporal lobe structures: Lesion profile and pattern of memory disorder. *Neuropsychologia, 132*, 23–38.

Kapur, N., Young, A. W., Bateman, D. and Kennedy, P. (1989). A long-term clinical and neuropsychological follow-up of focal retrograde amnesia. *Cortex, 25*, 387–402.

Kartsounis, L. D. and Warrington, E. K. (1991). Failure of object recognition due to a breakdown of figure-ground discrimination in a patient with normal acuity. *Neuropsychologia, 29*, 969–80.

Katz, R. and Goodglass, H. (1990). Deep dysphasia: An analysis of a rare form of repetition disorder. *Brain and Language, 39*, 153–85.

Katz, R. B. (1991). Limited retention of information in the graphemic buffer. *Cortex, 27*, 111–19.

Kausler, D. H. (1994). *Learning and Memory in Normal Aging.* San Diego: Academic Press.

Kay, J. and Hanley, J. R. (1991). Simultaneous form perception and serial letter recognition in a case of letter-by-letter reading. *Cognitive Neuropsychology, 8*, 249–73.

Kay, J. and Marcel, A. J. (1981). One process not two in reading aloud. *Quarterly Journal of Experimental Psychology, 33A*, 397–413.

Kean, M. L., (1985). *Agrammatism*. New York: Academic Press.

Kimberg, D. Y. and Farah. M. J. (1993). A unified account of cognitive impairments following frontal lobe damage: The role of working memory in complex, organized behavior. *Journal of Experimental Psychology: General*, 122, 411–28.

Kinsbourne. (1993). Integrated cortical field theory of consciousness. In G. R. Bock and J. Marsh (eds), *Experimental and Theoretical Studies of Consciousness*. Chichester: Wiley.

Kinsbourne, M. (ed). (1987). *Mechanisms of Unilateral Neglect*. Amsterdam: Elsevier.

Kinsbourne, M. and Warrington, E. K. (1963a). Jargon aphasia. *Neuropsychologia*, 1, 27–37.

Kinsbourne, M. and Warrington, E. K. (1963b). A study of visual perseveration. *Journal of Neurology, Neurosurgery and Psychiatry*, 26, 468.

Klein, R. and Harper, J. (1956). The problem of agnosia in the light of a case of pure word deafness. *Journal of Mental Science*, 102, 112–20.

Knowlton, B. J. and Squire, L. R. (1994). The information acquired during artificial grammar learning. *Journal of Experimental Psychology: Learning, Memory and Cognition*, 20, 79–91.

Knowlton, B. J., Ramus, S. J. and Squire, L. S. (1992). Intact artificial grammar learning in amnesia: Dissociation of classification learning and explicit memory for specific instances. *Psychological Science*, 3, 172–9.

Knowlton, B. J., Squire, L. R. and Gluck, M. A. (1994). Probabilistic classification learning in amnesia. *Learning and Memory*, 1, 106–20.

Kolb, B. and Whishaw, I. Q. (1996). *Fundamentals of Human Neuropsychology*, (4th edn). New York: Freeman.

Kolk, H. H. J., Van Grunsven, M. J. F. and Keyser, A. (1985). On parallelism between production and comprehension in agrammatism. In M. L. Kean (ed.), *Agrammatism* (pp. 165–206). New York: Academic Press.

Kopelman, M. D. (1993). Neuropsychology of remote memory. In F. Boller and J. Grafman (eds), *Handbook of Neuropsychology* (vol. 8). Amsterdam, Elsevier.

Kopelman, M. D. (1995a). The assessment of psychogenic amnesia. In A. D. Baddeley, B. A. Wilson and F. N. Watts (eds), *Handbook of Memory Disorders*. Chichester: Wiley.

Kopelman, M. D. (1995b). The Korsakoff Syndrome. *British Journal of Psychiatry*, 166, 154–73.

Kosslyn, S. M. (1994). *Image and Brain: The Resolution of the Imagery Debate*. Cambridge, MIT Press.

Kosslyn, S. M., Alpert, N. M. and Thompson, W. L. (1993). Visual mental imagery activates the primary visual cortex. *Journal of Cognitive Neuroscience*, 5, 263–87.

Kremin, H. (1987). Is there more than ah-oh-oh? Alternative strategies for writing and repeating lexically. In M. Coltheart, G. Sartori and R. Job (eds), *The Cognitive Neuropsychology of Language*. London: Erlbaum.

Kripke, S. (1980). *Naming and necessity*. Oxford: Blackwell.

Kurucz, J. and Feldmar, G. (1979). Proso-affective agnosia as a symptom of cerebral organic disease. *Journal of the American Geriatrics Society*, 27, 225–30.

Ladavas, E., Paladini, R. and Cubelli, R. (1993). Implicit associative priming in a patient with left visual neglect. *Neuropsychologia*, 31, 1307–20.

Ladd, D. and Cutler, A. (1983). Introduction: Models and measurements in the study of prosody. In A. Cutler and D. Ladd (eds), *Prosody: Models and measurements*. New York: Springer-Verlag.

Laiacona, M., Barbarotto, R. and Capitani, E. (1993). Perceptual and associative knowledge in category specific impairment of semantic memory: A study of two cases. *Cortex*, 29, 727–40.

Lambert, A. J. (1991). Interhemispheric interaction in the split-brain. *Neuropsychologia*, 29, 941–8.

Lambert, J., Viader, F., Eustache, F. and Morin, P. (1994). Contribution to peripheral agraphia: A case of post-allographic impairment? *Cognitive Neuropsychology*, 11, 35–55.

Lashley, K. S. (1929). *Brain Mechanisms and Intelligence*. Chicago: University of Chicago Press.

Leiguardia, R., Starkstein, S., Nogues, M., Berthier, M. and Arbelaiz, R. (1993). Paroxysmal alien hand syndrome. *Journal of Neurology, Neurosurgery and Psychiatry*, 56, 778–92

Leng, N. R. C. and Parkin, A. J. (1988a). Amnesic patients can benefit from instructions to use imagery: Evidence against the cognitive mediation hypothesis. *Cortex*, 24, 33–9.

Leng, N. R. C. and Parkin, A. J. (1988b). Double dissociation of frontal dysfunction in organic amnesia. *British Journal of Clinical Psychology*, 27, 359–62.

Leng, N. R. C. and Parkin, A. J. (1995). The detection of exaggerated or simulated memory disorder by neuropsychological methods. *Journal of Psychosomatic Research*, 39, 767–76.

Lesser, R. (1989). Selective preservation of oral spelling without semantics in a case of multi-infarct dementia. *Cortex*, 25, 239–50.

Lesser, R. (1990). Superior oral to written spelling: Evidence for separate buffers? *Cognitive Neuropsychology*, 7, 347–66.

Levelt, W. J. M. (1993). *Speaking: From Intention to Articulation*. Cambridge, Mass.: MIT Press.

Levine, D. N. and Calvanio, R. (1989). Prosopagnosia: A deficit in visual configural processing. *Brain and Cognition*, 10, 149–70.

Levine, D. N., Calvanio, R. and Popovics, A. (1982). Language in the absence of inner speech. *Neuropsychologia*, 20, 391–409.

Levy, J. (1983). Language, cognition, and the right hemisphere. *American Psychologist*, 538–41.

Levy, J., Trevarthen, C. and Sperry, R. W. (1972). Perception of bilateral chimeric figures following hemispheric disconnection. *Brain*, 95, 61–78.

Lezak, M. D. (1983). *Neuropsychological Assessment*, (2nd edn). Oxford: Oxford University Press.

LHermitte, F. (1983). 'Utilization behaviour' and its relation to lesions of the frontal lobes. *Brain*, 106, 237–55.

LHermitte, F. and Signoret, J. L. (1972). Analyse neuropsychologique et differenciation des syndromes amnesiques. *Revue Neurologique, 126,* 86–94.

Liepmann, H. (1908). *Drei Aufsatz aus dem Apraxiegebeit.* (vol. 1). Berlin: Karger.

Lindsay, P. H. and Norman D. A. (1972). *Human Information Processing.* San Diego: Academic Press.

Lissauer, H. (1890). A case of visual agnosia with a contribution to theory. First published as 'Ein fall von seelenblindheit nebst einem beitrage zur theorie derselben'. *Archiv fur Psychiatrie und Nervenrankheiten, 21,* 222–70.

Luchelli, F. and DeRenzi, E. (1992). Proper name anomia. *Cortex, 28,* 221–30.

Luck, S. J., Hillyard, S. A., Mangun, G. R. and Gazzaniga, M. S. (1994). Independent attentional scanning in the separated hemispheres of split-brain patients. *Journal of Cognitive Neuroscience, 6,* 84–91.

Luria, A. R. (1966). *The Higher Cortical Functions in Man.* New York: Basic.

Luria, A. R. (1968). *The Mind of a Mnemonist.* New York: Basic Books.

Luria, A. R. (1970). *Traumatic Aphasia.* The Hague: Mouton.

Luria, A. R. (1980). *Higher Cortical Functions in Man. Second Edition.* New York: Basic Books.

McAndrews, M. P., Glisky, E. L. and Schacter, D. L. (1987). When priming persists: Long-lasting implicit memory for a single episode in amnesic patients. *Neuropsychologia, 25,* 497–506.

McCarthy, R. and Warrington, E. K. (1986a). Phonological reading: Phenomena and paradoxes. *Cortex, 22,* 359–80.

McCarthy, R. A. and Warrington, E. K. (1986b). Visual associative agnosia: a clinico-anatomical study of a single case. *Journal of Neurology, Neurosurgery, and Psychiatry, 49,* 1233–40.

McCarthy, R. A. and Warrington, E. K. (1988). Evidence for modality-specific meaning systems in the brain. *Nature, 334,* 428–9.

McCarthy, R. A. and Warringron, E. K. (1990). *Cognitive Neuropsychology. A Clinical Introduction.* San Diego: Academic Press.

McCarthy, R. A. and Warrington, E. K. (1992). Actors but not scripts: The dissociation of people and events in retrograde amnesia. *Neuropsychologia, 30,* 633–44.

McClelland, J. L. (1991) Stochastic interactive processes and the effect of context on perception. *Cognitive Psychology, 23,* 1–44.

McClelland, J. L. and Rumelhart, D. E. (1986). *Parallel Distributed Processing: Explorations in the Microstructure of Cognition* (vols 1 and 2). Cambridge, MIT Press/Bradford Books.

McCloskey, M. (1993). Theory and evidence in cognitive neuropsychology: A 'radical' response to Robertson, Knight, Rafal, and Shimamura (1993). *Journal of Experimental Psychology: Learning, Memory and Cognition, 19,* 718–34.

McCloskey, M. and Caramazza, A. (1988). Theory and methodology in cognitive neuropsychology: A response to our critics. *Cognitive Neuropsychology, 5,* 583–623.

McGlinchey-Berroth, R., Milberg, W. P., Verfaellie, M., Alezander, M. and Kilduff, P. T. (1993). Semantic processing in the neglected field: Evidence from a lexical decision task. *Cognitive Neuropsychology, 10,* 79–108.

McKenna, P. and Warrington, E. K. (1980). Testing for nominal dysphasia. *Journal of Neurology, Neurosurgery and Psychiatry*, *43*, 781–8.

McMillan, M. B. (1987). A wonderful journey through the skull and brains: The travels of Mr Gage's tamping iron. *Brain and Cognition*, *5*, 67–107.

McNabb, A. W., Carroll, W. M. and Mastaglia, F. (1988). 'Alien hand' and loss of bimanual coordination after dominant anterior cerebral artery territory infarction. *Journal of Neurology, Neurosurgery and Psychiatry*, *51*, 218–22.

McNeil, J. E., Cipolotti, L. and Warrington, E. K. (1994). The accessibility of proper names. *Neuropsychologia*, *32*, 193–208.

McNeil, J. E. and Warrington, E. K. (1993). Prosopagnosia: A face-specific disorder. *Quarterly Journal of Experimental Psychology*, *46A*, 1–10.

Maher, L. M., Rothi, L. J. G. and Heilman, K. M. (1994). Lack of error awareness in an aphasic patient with relatively preserved auditory comprehension. *Brain and Language*, *46*, 402–18.

Malone, D.R., Morris, H. H., Kay, M. C. and Levin, H. S. (1982). Prosopagnosia: a double dissociation between the recognition of familiar and unfamiliar faces. *Journal of Neurology, Neurosurgery, and Psychiatry*, *45*, 820–22.

Mandler, G. (1980). Recognising: The judgement of a previous occurrence. *Psychological Review*, *27*, 252–71.

Mangun, G. R., Hillyard, S. A., Luck, S. J., Handy, T., Plager, R., Clark, V. P., Loftus, W. and Gazzaniga, M. S. (1994). Monitoring the visual world: Hemispheric asymmetries and subcortical processes in attention. *Journal of Cognitive Neuroscience*, *6*, 267–75.

Margolin, D. I. (1984). The neuropsychology of writing and spelling: Semantic, phonological, motor, and perceptual processes. *Quarterly Journal of Experimental Psychology*, *36A*, 459–89.

Markowitsch, H. J., Calabrese, P. and Liess, J. et al. (1992). Retrograde amnesia after traumatic injury of the fronto-temporal cortex. *Journal of Neurology, Neurosurgery and Psychiatry*, *56*, 988–92.

Marr, D. (1976). *Vision*. San Francisco: W. H. Freeman.

Marr, D. and Nishihara, H. K. (1978). Representation and recognition of the spatial organisation of three-dimensional shapes. *Proceedings of the Royal Society of London*, *B200*, 269–94.

Marshall, J. C. (1988). Sensation and semantics. *Nature*, *334*, 378.

Marshall, J. C. and Halligan, P. W. (1988). Blindsight and insight in visuospatial neglect. *Nature*, *336*, 766–7.

Marshall, J. C. and Halligan, P. W. (1989). Does the midsagittal plane play any privileged role in 'left' neglect? *Cognitive Neuropsychology*, *6*, 403–22.

Marshall, J. C. and Halligan, P. W. (1990). The psychophysics of visuo-spatial neglect: a new orientation. *Medical Science Research*, *18*, 429–30.

Marshall, J. C. and Halligan, P. W. (1993). Visuo-spatial neglect: a new copying test to assess perceptual parsing. *Journal of Neurology*, *240*, 37–40.

Marshall, J. C., Halligan, P. W. and Robertson, I. H. (1993). Contemporary theories of unilateral neglect: A critical review. In I. H. Robertson and J. C. Marshall (eds), *Unilateral Neglect: Clinical and Experimental Studies*. Hove: Erlbaum.

Marshall, J. C. and Newcombe, F. (1973). Patterns of paralexia: A psycholinguistic approach. *Journal of Psycholinguistic Research*, 2, 175–99.

Martin, N. and Saffran, E. M. (1992). A computational account of deep dysphasia: Evidence from a single case study. *Brain and Language*, 43, 240–74.

Marzi, C.A., Tassinaari, G., Aglioti, S. and Lutzemberger, L. (1986). Spatial summation across the vertical meridian in hemianopics: A test of blindsight. *Neuropsychologia*, 24, 749–58.

Mauner, G., Fromkin, V. A. and Cornell, T. L. (1993). Comprehension and acceptability judgments in agrammatism: Disruptions in the syntax of referential dependency. *Brain and Language*, 45, 340–70.

Mayes, A. R. (1988). *Human Organic Memory Disorders*. Cambridge: Cambridge University Press.

Meeres, S. L. and Graves, R. E. (1990). Localization of unseen visual stimuli by humans with normal vision. *Neuropsychologia*, 28, 1231–7.

Mennemeier, M., Wertman, E. and Heilman, K. M. (1992). Neglect of near peripersonal space. *Brain*, 115, 37–50.

Mesulam, M. M. (1985). Attention, confusion states and neglect. In M. M. Mesulam (ed.), *Principles of Behavioural Neurology*. Philadelphia: F. A. Davis.

Meudell, P. R., Mayes, A. R., Ostergaard, A. and Pickering, A. (1985). Recency and frequency judgments in alcoholic amnesias and normal people with poor memory. *Cortex*, 21, 487–511.

Miceli, G., Silveri, C. and Caramazza, A. (1985). Cognitive analysis of a case of pure dysgraphia. *Brain and Language*, 25, 187–212.

Miceli, G., Silveri, M. C., Romani, C. and Caramazza, A. (1989). Variation in the pattern of omissions and substitutions of grammatical morphemes in the spontaneous speech and so-called agrammatic patients. *Brain and Language*, 36, 447–92.

Milner, B. (1963). Effects of brain lesions on card sorting. *Archives of Neurology*, 9, 90–100.

Milner, B. (1964). Some effects of frontal lobectomy in man. In J. Warren and K. Akert (eds), *The Frontal Granular Cortex and Behavior* (pp. 313–34). New York: McGraw-Hill.

Milner, B. (1966). Amnesia following operation on the temporal lobes. In C. W. M. Whitty and O. L. Zangwill (eds), *Amnesia*. London: Butterworths.

Milner, B. (1971). Interhemispheric differences in the localization of psychological processes in man. *British Medical Bulletin*, 27, 272–7.

Milner, B., Corsi, P. and Leonard, G. (1991). Frontal-lobe contribution to recency judgements. *Neuropsychologia*, 29, 601–18.

Monsell, S. (1991). The nature and locus of word frequency effects in reading. In D. Besner and G. W. Humphreys (eds), *Basic Processes in Reading: Visual Word Recognition*. Hillsdale, NJ: Lawrence Erlbaum.

Moonen, C. T. W. (1995). Imaging of human brain activation with functional MRI. *Biological Psychiatry*, 37, 141–3.

Morris, R. G., Ahmed, S., Syed, G. M. and Toone, B. K. (1993). Neural correlates of planning ability: Frontal lobe activation during the Tower of London test. *Neuropsychologia*, 31, 1367–78.

Morton, J. and Patterson, K. E. (1987). A new attempt at an interpretation, or, an attempt at a new interpretation. In M. Coltheart, K. E. Patterson and J. C. Marshall (eds), *Deep Dyslexia* (2nd edn). London: Lawrence Erlbaum.

Moscovitch, M. and Berhmann, M. *Personal Communication.*

Moscovitch, M. (1989). Confabulation and the frontal system: Strategic versus associative retrieval in neuropsychological theories of memory. In H. L. Roediger and F. I. M. Craik (eds), *Varieties of Memory and Consciousness: Essays in honour of Endel Tulving*, (pp. 133–60). Hillsdale, New Jersey: Lawrence Erlbaum Associates.

Musen, G. and Squire, L. R. (1991). Normal acquisition of novel verbal information in amnesia. *Journal of Experimental Psychology: Learning Memory and Cognition*, *17*, 1095–104.

Musen, G. and Squire, L. R. (1993). On the implicit learning of novel associations by amnesic patients and normal subjects. *Neuropsychology*, *7*, 119–35.

Mutter, S. A., Howard, D. V., Howard, J. H. and Wiggs, C. L. (1990). Performance on direct and indirect tests of memory after mild closed head injury. *Cognitive Neuropsychology*, *7*, 329–46.

Myers, J. J. and Sperry, R. W. (1985). Interhemispheric communication after section of the forebrain commissures. *Cortex*, *21*, 249–60.

Nelson, H. E. (1976). A modified card sorting test sensitive to frontal lobe defects. *Cortex*, *12*, 313–24.

Nichelli, P., Rinaldi, M. and Cubelli, R. (1989). Selective spatial attention and length representation in normal subjects and in patients with unilateral spatial neglect. *Cognition*, *9*, 57–70.

Nolan, K. A. and Caramazza, A. (1982). Modality-independent impairments in word processing in a deep dyslexic patient. *Brain and Language*, *16*, 237–64.

Norman, D. A. and Bobrow, D. G. (1979). Descriptions: An intermediate stage in memory retrieval. *Cognitive Psychology*, *11*, 107–23.

Norman, D. A. and Shallice, T. (1986). Attention to action: Willed and automatic control of behaviour. In R. J. Davidson, G. E. Schwartz and D. E. Shapiro (eds), *Consciousness and Self-Regulation* (vol. 4). New York: Plenum Press.

O'Connor, M., Butters, N., Miliotis, P., Eslinger, P. and Cermak, L. S. (1992). The dissociation of anterograde and retrograde amnesia in a patient with Herpes encephalitis. *Journal of Clinical and Experimental Neuropsychology*, *14*, 159–78.

O'Keefe, J. and Nadel, L. (1978). *The Hippocampus as a Cognitive Map.* London: Oxford University Press.

Ogden, J. (1985). Contralesional neglect of constructed visual images in right and left brain-damaged patients. *Neuropsychologia*, *23*, 273–7.

Ogden, J. (1993). Visual object agnosia, prosopagnosia, achromatopsia, loss of visual imagery, and autobiographical amnesia following recovery from cortical blindness. Case M. H. *Neuropsychologia*, *31*, 571–89.

Okada, S., Hannada, M., Hattori, H. and Shoyama, T. (1963). A case of pure word-deafness (about the relation between auditory perception and recognition of speech-sound). *Studia Phonologica*, *14*, 58–65.

Owen, A. M., Downes, J. J., Sahakian, B. J., Polkey, C. E. and Robbins, T. W. (1990). Planning and spatial working memory following frontal lobe lesions in man. *Neuropsychologia, 28,* 1021–34.

Paller, K. A. and Mayes, A. R. (1994). New association priming of word identity in normal and amnesic subjects. *Cortex, 30,* 53–73.

Papagno, C. (1992). A case of peripheral dysgraphia. *Cognitive Neuropsychology, 9,* 259–70.

Parkin, A. J. (1982). Phonological recoding in lexical decision: Effects of spelling-to-sound irregularity depend on how regularity is definded. *Memory and Cognition, 10,* 43–53.

Parkin, A. J. (1982). Residual learning capability in organic amnesia. *Cortex, 18,* 417–40.

Parkin, A. J. (1991). The relation between anterograde and retrograde amnesia in alcoholic Korsakoff Syndrome. *Psychological Medicine, 21,* 11–14.

Parkin, A. J. (1992). Functional significance of etiological factors in human amnesia. In L. R. Squire and N. Butters (eds), *Neuropsychology of Memory,* (2nd edn). New York: Guildford Press.

Parkin, A. J. (1993a). *Memory: Phenomena, Experiment and Theory.* Oxford: Blackwells.

Parkin, A. J. (1993b). Progressive aphasia without dementia: A clinical and cognitive neuropsychological analysis. *Brain and Language, 44,* 201–20.

Parkin, A. J. (1996a). The Alien Hand. In P. Halligan and J. C. Marshall (eds), *Cognitive Neuropsychiatry.* Hove: Earlbaum.

Parkin, A. J. (1996b). *Memory and Amnesia: An Introduction,* 2nd edn. Oxford: Basil Blackwell.

Parkin, A. J. (1996c). HM – The Medial Temporal Lobes and Memory. In Code, C., Wallesch, C., Lecours, A-R. and Joanette, Y. (eds), *Classic Cases in Neuropsychology.* Hove: Erlbaum

Parkin, A. J. (1996d) Focal retrograde amnesia: A multi-faceted deficit? *Acta Neuropathologica Belgica.*

Parkin, A. J. and Barry, C. (1991). Alien hand sign and other cognitive deficits following ruptured aneurysm of the anterior communicating artery. *Behavioural Neurology, 4,* 167–79.

Parkin, A. J., Bindschaedler, C., Harsent, L. and Metzler, C. (1996). Pathological false alarm rates following frontal lobe pathology. *Brain and Cognition.*

Parkin, A. J., Bindschaedler, C. and Poz, R. (in preparation). Explaining pathological false alarms in recognition memory.

Parkin, A. J., Blunden, J., Rees, J. E. and Hunkin, N. M. (1991). Wernicke-Korsakoff Syndrome of non-alcoholic origin. *Brain and Cognition, 15,* 69–82.

Parkin, A. J. and Hunkin, N. M. (1993). Impaired temporal context memory on anterograde but not retrograde tests in the absence of frontal pathology. *Cortex, 29,* 267–80.

Parkin, A. J. and Lawrence, A. (1994). A dissociation in the relation between memory tasks and frontal lobe tests in the normal elderly. *Neuropsychologia, 32,* 1523–32.

Parkin, A. J. and Leng, N. R. C. (1993). *Neuropsychology of the Amnesic Syndrome.* Hove: Lawrence Erlbaum.

Parkin, A. J., Leng, N. R. C. and Hunkin, N. M. (1990). Differential sensitivity to contextual information in diencephalic and temporal lobe amnesia. *Cortex,* 26, 373–80.

Parkin, A. J., Montaldi, D., Leng, N. R. C. and Hunkin, N. M. (1990b). Contextual cueing effects in the remote memory of alcoholic Korsakoff patients. *Quarterly Journal of Experimental Psychology,* 42A, 585–96.

Parkin, A. J., Rees, J. E., Hunkin, N. M. and Rose, P. E. (1994). Impairment of memory following discrete thalamic infarction. *Neuropsychologia,* 32, 39–51.

Parkin, A. J. and Stewart, F. (1993). Category-specific impairment? No. A critique of Sartori et al. *Quarterly Journal of Experimental Psychology,* 46A, 505–9.

Parkin, A. J. and Walter, B. M. (1992). Recollective experience, normal aging, and frontal dysfunction. *Psychology and Aging,* 7, 290–8.

Parkin, A. J., Walter, B. M. and Hunkin, N. M. (1995). Normal aging, frontal lobe dysfunction, and memory for temporal and spatial information. *Neuropsychology,* 2, 304–12.

Parkin, A. J. and Williamson, P. (1986). Cerebral lateralisation at different stages of facial processing. *Cortex,* 23, 99–110.

Parkin, A. J., Yeomans, J. and Binschaedler, C. (1994). Further characterization of the executive memory impairment following frontal lobe lesions. *Brain and Cognition,* 26, 23–42.

Patterson, K. E., Marshall J. C. and Coltheart M. (eds). (1985). *Surface Dyslexia: Neuropsychological and Cognitive Studies of Phonological Reading.* London: Lawrence Erlbaum.

Patterson, K. E. (1986). Lexical but nonsemantic spelling? *Cognitive Neuropsychology,* 3, 341–67.

Patterson, K. E. (1990). Alexia and neural nets. *Japanese Journal of Neuropsychology,* 6, 90–9.

Patterson, K. E., Graham, N. and Hodges, J. R. (1994). The impact of semantic memory loss on phonological representations. *Journal of Cognitive Neuroscience,* 6, 57–69.

Patterson, K. E. and Hodges, J. R. (1992). Deterioration of word meaning: Implications for reading. *Neuropsychologia,* 30, 1025–40.

Patterson, K. E., Seidenberg, M. S. and McClelland, J. L. (1989). Connections and disconnections: Acquired dyslexia in a computational model of reading processes. In R. G. M. Morris (ed.), *Parallel Distributed processing: Implications for Psychology and Neurobiology* (pp. 131–81). London: Oxford University Press.

Patterson, K. E. and Besner, D. (1984). Is the right hemisphere literate? *Cognitive Neuropsychology,* 1, 315–41.

Patterson, K. E. and Shewell, C. (1987). Speak and spell: Dissociations and word-class effects. In M. Coltheart, G. Sartoir and R. Job (eds), *The Cognitive Neuropsychology of Language* (pp. 273–94). Hillsdale, NJ: Erlbaum.

Patterson, K. E., Seidenberg, M. S., & McClelland, J. L. (1989). Connections and disconnections: Acquired dyslexia in a computational model of reading processes. In R. G. M. Morris (Ed.) *Parallel Distributed Processing: Implications for Psychology and Neurobiology.* London: Oxford University Press.

Patterson, K. E., Vargha-Khadem, F. and Polkey, C. E. (1989). Reading with one hemisphere. *Brain*, *112*, 39–63.

Patterson, K. E. and Wing, A. M. (1989). Processes in Handwriting: A case for a case. Hove: LEA.

Perani, D., Bressi, S. and Cappa, S. F. (1993). Evidence of multiple memory systems in the human brain: A [18F] FDG PET metabolic study. *Brain*, *116*, 903–19.

Petrides, M., Alivisatos, B., Evans, A. C. and Meyer, E. (1993a). Dissociation of human mid-dorsolateral from posterior dorsolateral frontal cortex in memory processing. *Proceedings of the National Academy of Sciences USA*, *90*, 873–7.

Petrides, M., Alivisatos, B., Meyer, E. and Evans, A. C. (1993b). Functional activation of the human frontal cortex during the performance of verbal working memory tasks. *Proceedings of the National Academy of Sciences USA*, *90*, 878–82.

Petrides, M. and Milner, B. (1982). Deficits on subject-ordered tasks after frontal-and temporal-lobe lesions in man. *Neuropsychologia*, *20*, 249–62.

Phillips, W. G. and Goodall, W. C. (1995). Lexical writing can be non-semantic and it can be fluent without practice. *Cognitive Neuropsychology*, *12*, 149–74.

Pick, A. (1903). Clinical studies 111. On reduplicative paramnesia. *Brain*, *26*, 260–7.

Pietrini, V., Nertempi, P., Vaglia, A., Revello, M. G., Pinna, V. and Ferro-Milone, F. (1988). Recovery from herpes simplex encephalitis: Selective impairment of specific semantic categories with neuroradiological correlation. *Journal of Neurology, Neurosurgery and Psychiatry*, *51*, 1284–93.

Plaut, D. C., McClelland, J. L., Seidenberg, M. S. and Patterson, K. E. (in press). Understanding normal and impaired reading: Computational principles in quasi regular domains. *Psychological Review*.

Plaut, D. C. and Shallice, T. (1993). Deep Dyslexia: A case study of connectionist neuropsychology. *Cognitive Neuropsychology*, *10*, 377–500.

Poppel, E., Held, R. and Frost, D. (1973). Residual visual function after brain wounds involving the central visual pathways in man. *Nature*, *243*, 295–6.

Posner, M. I., Cohen, Y. and Rafal, R. D. (1982). Neural system control of spatial orienting. *Philosophical Transactions of the Royal Society of London*, *298*, 187–98.

Posner, M. I., Rafal, R. D., Choate, L., & Vaughan, J. (1985) Inhibition of return: Neural basis and function. *Cognitive Neuropsychology*, *2*, 211–28.

Posner, M. I. and Raichle, M. E. (1994). *Images of Mind*. New York: Freeman.

Price, C. J. and Humphreys, G. W. (1993). Attentional dyslexia: The effect of co-occurring deficits. *Cognitive Neuropsychology*, *10*, 569–92.

Prisko, L. H. (1963). *Short Term Memory in Focal Cerebral Damage*. Unpublished PhD, McGill University.

Rafal, R. Smith, J., Krantz, J., Cohen, A. and Brennan, C. (1990). Extrageniculate vision in hemianopic humans: inhibition by signals in the blind field. *Science*, *250*, 118–21.

Ramachandran, V. S., Cronin-Golomb, A. and Myers, J. J. (1986). Perception of apparent motion by commissurotomy patients. *Nature, 320*, 358–9.

Rapcsak, S. Z., Beeson, P. M. and Rubens, A. B. (1991). Writing with the right hemisphere. *Brain and Language, 41*, 510–30.

Rapcsak, S. Z., Cimino, C. R. and Heilman, K. M. (1988). Altitudinal neglect. *Neurology, Cleveland, 38*, 277–81.

Rapcsak, S. Z., Comer, J. F. and Rubens, A. B. (1993). Anomia for Facial Expressions: Neuropsychological Mechanisms and Anatomical Correlates. *Brain and Language, 45*, 233–52.

Rapp, B. C. and Caramazza, A. (1991). Spatially determined deficits in letter and word processing. *Cognitive Neuropsychology, 8*, 275–311.

Rapp, B. C., Hillis, A. E. and Caramazza, A. (1993). The role of representations in cognitive theory: More on multiple semantics and the agnosias. *Cognitive Neuropsychology, 10*, 235–49.

Reber, A. S. (1967). Implicit learning of artificial grammars. *Journal of Verbal Learning and Verbal Behavior, 6*, 855–63.

Reuter-Lorenz, P. A. and Baynes, K. (1992). Modes of lexical access in the callosotomized brain. *Journal of Cognitive Neuroscience, 4*, 155–64.

Reuter-Lorenz P. A. and Brunn, J. L. (1990). A prelexical basis for letter-by-letter reading: A case study. *Cognitive Neuropsychology, 7*, 1–20.

Ribot, T. (1882). *Disease of Memory*. New York: Appleton.

Riddoch, M. J. (1990). Loss of visual imagery: A general deficit. *Cognitive Neuropsychology, 7*, 249–73.

Riddoch, M. J. and Humphreys, G. W. (1987a). A case of integrative visual agnosia. *Brain, 110*, 1431–62.

Riddoch, M. J. and Humphreys, G. W. (1987b). Visual object processing in optic aphasia: A case of semantic access agnosia. *Cognitive Neuropsychology, 4*, 131–85.

Riddoch, M. J. and Humphreys, G. W. (1995). *Birmingham Object Recognition Battery*, Hove: Lawrence Erlbaum.

Robertson, L. C., Knight, R. T., Rafal, R., and Shimamura, A. P. (1993). Cognitive Neuropsychology is more than single case studies. *Journal of Experimental Psychology: Learning, Memory, and Cognition, 19*, 710–17.

Robertson, L. C., and Lamb, M. R. (1991). Neuropsychological contributions to theories of part/whole organization. *Cognitive Psychology, 23*, 299–330.

Rocchetta, della, A. I. (1986). Classification and recall of pictures after unilateral frontal or temporal lobectomy. *Cortex, 22*, 189–211.

Rocchetta, della, A. I., and Milner, B. (1993). Strategic search and retrieval inhibition: the role of the frontal lobes. *Neuropsychologia, 31*, 503–24.

Roediger, H. L. (1990). Implicit memory: A commentary. *Bulletin of the Psychonomic Society, 28*, 373–80.

Roediger, H. L., and McDermott, K. B. (1994). The problem of differing false alarm rates for the process dissociation procedure: Comment on Verfaellie and Treadwell (1993). *Neuropsychology, 8*, 284–8.

Roeltgen, D. P., Rothi, L. G., and Heilman, K. M. (1986). Linguistic semantic agraphia. *Brain and Language, 27*, 257–80.

Ross, E. (1981). The aprosodias: Functional-anatomic organization of the affective components of language in the right hemisphere. *Archives of Neurology, 38*, 561–9.

Sacchett, C., and Humphreys, G. W. (1992). Calling a squirrel a squirrel but a canoe a wigwam: A category-specific deficit for artefactual objects and body parts. *Cognitive Neuropsychology, 9*, 73–86.

Sacks, O. (1985). *The Man who Mistook His Wife for a Hat*. London: Duckworth.

Saffran, E. M., Bogyo, L. C., Schwartz, M. F., and Marin, O. S. M. (1987). Does deep dyslexia reflect right hemisphere reading? In M. Coltheart, K. E. Patterson, and J. C. Marshall (eds), *Deep Dyslexia* (2nd edn). London: Routledge and Kegan Paul.

Saffran, E. M., Schwartz, M. F., and Marin, O. S. M. (1980). Evidence from aphasia: Isolating the components of a production model. In B. Butterworth (ed.), *Language Production: Speech and Talk* (vol. 1). New York: Academic Press.

Sandson, J., and Albert, M. (1984). Varieties of perseveration. *Neuropsychologia, 22*, 715–32.

Sartori, G., and Job, R. (1988). The oyster with four legs: A neuropsychological study on the interaction of visual and semantic information. *Cognitive Neuropsychology, 5*, 105–32.

Sartori, G., Miozzo, M. and Job R. (1993). Category-specific naming impairments? Yes. *Quarterly Journal of Experimental Psychology, 46A*, 489–504.

Saver, J. L., and Damasio, A. R. (1991). Preserved access and processing of social knowledge in a patient with acquired sociopathy due to ventromedial frontal damage. *Neuropsychologia, 29*, 1241–9.

Schacter, D. L. (1987). Implicit memory: History and Current Status. *Journal of Experimental Psychology: Learning, Memory and Cognition, 13*, 501–18.

Schacter, D. L. (1990). Perceptual representation systems and implicit memory: Toward a resolution of the multiple memory systems debate. In A. Diamond (ed.), *The Development and Neural Bases of Higher Cognitive Functions*. New York: New York Academy of Sciences.

Schacter, D. L. (1992). Priming and multiple memory systems: Perceptual mechanisms of implicit memory. *Journal of Cognitive Neuroscience, 4*, 244–56.

Schacter, D. L., Cooper, L. A., and Delaney, S. M. (1990). Implicit memory for unfamiliar objects depends on access to structural descriptions. *Journal of Experimental Psychology: General, 119*, 5–24.

Schacter, D. L., Curran, T., and Galluccio, L. (in press). False recognition and the right frontal lobe. *Neuropsychologia*.

Schacter, D. L., Harbluk, J. L., and McLachlan, D. R. (1984). Retrieval without recollection: An experimental analysis of source amnesia. *Journal of Verbal Learning and Verbal Behavior, 23*, 593–611.

Schacter, D. L., McGlynn, S. M., Milberg, W. P., and Church, B. A. (1993). Spared priming despite impaired comprehension: Implicit memory in a case of word-meaning deafness. *Neuropsychology, 7*, 107–18.

Schacter, D. L., Osowiecki, D., Kaszniak, A. W., Kihlstrom, J. F., and Valdiserri,

M. (1991). Source memory: Extending the boundaries of age-related deficits. *Psychology and Aging*, *9*, 81–9.

Schacter, D. L., and Tulving, E. (1994). What are the memory systems of 1994. In D. L. Schacter and E. Tulving (eds), *Memory Systems 1994*. Cambridge, MIT Press.

Schinder, A., Benson, D. F., and Schaure, D. W. (1994). Visual agnosia and optic aphasia: Are they anatomically distinct? *Cortex*, *30*, 445–58.

Schneider, G. E. (1967). Contrast in visuomotor functions of tectum and cortex in the golden hamster. *Psychol. Forsch.*, *31*, 52–62.

Schneiderman, E. I., Murasugi, K. G., and Saddy, J. D. (1992). Story arrangement ability in right brain-damaged patients. *Brain and Language*, *43*, 107–20.

Seidenberg, M., and McClelland, J. L. (1989). A distributed, developmental model of word recognition and naming. *Psychological Review*, *96*, 523–68.

Semenza, C., and Sgarmella, T. (1993). Proper names production: A clinical case study of the effects of phonemic cueing. *Memory*, *1*, 265–80.

Semenza, C., and Zettin, M. (1989). Evidence from aphasia for the role of proper names as pure referring expressions. *Nature*, *342*, 678–9.

Sergent, J. (1986). Subcortical coordination of hemisphere activity in commissurotomized patients. *Brain*, *109*, 357–69.

Sergent, J. (1987). A new look at the human split brain. *Brain*, *110*, 1375–92.

Sergent, J. (1990). Furtive incursions into bicameral minds. *Brain*, *113*, 537–68.

Sergent, J., and Signoret, J.-L. (1992). Varieties of functional deficits in prosopagnosia. *Cerebral Cortex*, *2*, 375–88.

Seymour, S. E., Reuter-Lorenz, P. A., and Gazzaniga, M. S. (1994). The disconnection syndrome. *Brain*, *117*, 105–15.

Shallice, T. (1981). Neurological impairment of cognitive processes. *British Medical Bulletin*, *37*, 187–92.

Shallice, T. (1988a). *From Neuropsychology to Mental Structure*. Cambridge: Cambridge University Press.

Shallice, T. (1993). Multiple semantics: Whose confusions? *Cognitive Neuropsychology*, *10*, 251–61.

Shallice, T., and Burgess, P. W. (1991). Deficits in strategy application following frontal lobe damage in man. *Brain*, *114*, 727–41.

Shallice, T., Burgess, P. W., Schon, F., and Baxter, D. M. (1989). The origins of utilisation behavior. *Brain*, *112*, 1587–98.

Shallice, T., Fletcher, P., Grasby, P., Frackowiak, R. S., and Dolan, R. J. (1994). Brain regions associated with acquisition and retrieval of verbal episodic memory. *Nature*, *368*, 633–5.

Shallice, T., and Warrington, E. K. (1977). The possible role of selective attention in acquired dyslexia. *Neuropsychologia*, *15*, 31–41.

Shankweiler, D., and Studdert-Kennedy, M. (1967). Identification of consonants and vowels presented to the left and right ears. *Quarterly Journal of Experimental Psychology*, *19*, 59–63.

Shelton, P. A., Bowers, D., and Heilman, K. M. (1990). Peripersonal and vertical neglect. *Brain*, *113*, 191–205.

Sheridan, J., and Humphreys, G. W. (1993). A verbal-semantic category-specific recognition impairment. *Cognitive Neuropsychology*, *10*, 143–84.

Shimamura, A., and Squire, L. R. (1987). A neuropsychological study of fact memory and source amnesia. *Journal of Experimental Psychology: Learning Memory and Cognition, 13*, 464–73.

Shimamura, A., and Squire, L. R. (1989). Impaired priming of new associations in amnesia. *Journal of Experimental Psychology: Learning, Memory and Cognition, 15*, 721–8.

Shuttleworth, E. C., Syring, V., and Allen, N. (1982). Further observations on the nature of Prosopagnosia. *Brain and Cognition, 1*, 307–22.

Silveri, M. C., and Gainotti, G. (1988). Interaction between vision and language in category specific impairment. *Cognitive Neuropsychology, 5*, 677–709.

Small, S. L., Hart, J., Nguyen, T., and Gordon B. (1995). Distributed representations of semantic knowledge in the brain. *Brain, 118*, 441–53.

Smith, M. L., and Milner, (1984). Differential effects of frontal-lobe lesions on cognitive estimation and spatial memory. *Neuropsychologia, 22*, 697–705.

Smith, M. L., and Milner, B. (1988). Estimation of frequency of occurrence of abstract designs after frontal or temporal lobectomy. *Neuropsychologia, 26*, 297–306.

Snodgrass, J. G., and Vanderwart, M. (1980). A standardised set of 260 pictures: Norms for name agreement, image agreement, familiarity and visual complexity. *Journal of Experimental Psychology: Human Learning and Memory, 6*, 174–215.

Sokol, S. M., McCloskey, M., Cohen, N. J., and Alimnosa, D. (1991). Cognitive representations and processes in arithmetic: Inferences from the performance of brain-damaged patients. *Journal of Experimental Psychology: Learning, Memory, and Cognition, 17*, 355–76.

Spencer, W. D. & Raz, N. (1994) Memory for facts, source and context. Confrontal lobe function explainage-related differences? *Psychology & Aging, 9*, 149–59.

Sperry, R. W., and Gazzaniga, M. S. (1967). *Language Following Surgical Disconnection of the Hemispheres.* New York: Grune, Stratton.

Sperry, R. W., Zaidel, E., and Zaidel, D. (1979). Self-recognition and social awareness in the deconnected hemisphere. *Neuropsychologia, 17*, 153–66.

Spier, S. A. (1992). Capgras' Syndrome and the delusions of misidentification. *Psychiatric Annals, 22*, 270–85.

Squire, L. R. (1982). Comparisons between forms of amnesia: Some deficits are unique to Korsakoff's syndrome. *Journal of Experimental Psychology: Learning, Memory and Cognition, 8*, 560–71.

Squire, L. R. (1987). *Memory and Brain.* New York: Oxford University Press.

Squire, L. R., Amaral, D. G., Zola-Morgan, S., Kritchevsky, M., and Press, G. (1989). Description of brain injury in the amnesic patient NA based on magnetic resonance imaging. *Experimental Neurology, 105*, 23–35.

Squire, L. R., Cohen, N. J., and Nadel, L. (1984). The medial temporal region and memory consolidation: A new hypothesis. In H. Weingartner and E. Parker (eds), *Memory Consolidation* (pp. 635–40). Hillsdale, New Jersey: Erlbaum.

Squire, L. R., and Frambach, M. (1990). Cognitive skill learning in amnesia. *Psychobiology, 18*, 109–117.

Squire, L. R. and Moore, R. Y. (1979). Dorsal thalamic lesions in a noted case of human amnesia. *Annals of Neurology, 6,* 603–6.

Stagno, S. J., and Gates, T. J. (1991). Palinopsia: a review of the literature. *Behavioural Neurology, 4,* 67–74.

Stemmer, B., Giroux, F., and Joanette, Y. (1994). Production and evaluation of requests by right hemisphere brain damaged individuals. *Brain and Cognition, 47,* 1–31.

Stewart, F., Parkin, A. J., and Hunkin, N. M. (1992). Naming impairments following recovery from Herpes Simplex Encephalitis: Category-specific? *The Quarterly Journal of Experimental Psychology, 44A,* 261–84.

Stoerig, P. (1993). Spatial summation in blindsight. *Visual Neuroscience, 10,* 1141–9.

Stoerig, P., and Cowey, A. (1992). Wavelength discrimination in blindsight. *1992, 115,* 425–44.

Stuss, D. T., and Benson, D. F. (1987). The Frontal Lobes and Control of Cognition and Memory, *The Frontal Lobes Revisited* (pp. 141–58): IRBN Press.

Sutherland, N. S. (1973). Object recognition. In E. C. Carterette and M. P. Friedman (eds), *Handbook of Perception* (vol. 3, pp. 157–85). New York: Academic Press.

Sutherland, N. S. (1989). *A Dictionary of Psychology.* London: MacMillan.

Takahashi, N., Kawamura, M., Shinotou, H., Hirayama, K., Kaga, K., and Shindo, M. (1992). Pure word deafness due to left hemisphere damage. *Cortex, 28,* 295–303.

Tanji, J., and Kurata, K. (1982). Comparison of movement-related activity in two cortical motor areas of primates. *Journal of Neurophysiology, 48,* 633–53.

Tegner, R., and Levander, M. (1991). The influence of stimulus properties on visual neglect. *Journal of Neurology, Neurosurgery, and Psychiatry, 54,* 882–7.

Teuber, H.-L. (1965). Somato-sensory disorders due to cortical lesions. *Neuropsychologia, 3,* 287–94.

Thaiss, L., and DeBleser, R. (1992). Visual agnosia: A case of reduced attentional 'spotlight'? *Cortex, 28,* 601–21.

Tomasch, J. (1957). A quantitative analysis of the human anterior commissure. *Acta Anatomica, 30,* 902–6.

Tranel, D., and Damasio, A. R. (1988). Nonconscious face recognition in patients with face agnosia. *Behavioral Brain Research, 30,* 235–49.

Tranel, D., Damasio, A. R., and Damasio, H. (1988). Intact recognition of facial expression, gender, and age in patients with impaired recognition of face identity. *Neurology, 38,* 690–6.

Trojana, L., Crisci, C., Lanzillo, B., Elefante, R., and Caruso, G. (1993). How many alien hand syndromes? Follow up of a case. *Neurology, 43,* 2710–12.

Tucker, D. M., Watson, R. T., and Heilman, K. M. (1977). Affective discrimination and evocation in patients with right parietal disease. *Neurology, 17,* 947–50.

Tulving, E. (1989). Memory, performance, knowledge and experience. *European Journal of Cognitive Psychology, 1,* 3–26.

Tulving, E., Hayman, C. G., and MacDonald, A. (1991). Long-lasting perceptual priming and semantic learning in amnesia: A case experiment. *Journal of Experimental Psychology: Learning, Memory and Cognition, 17,* 595–617.

Tulving, E., Kapur, S., Craik, F. I. M., Moscovitch, M., and Houle, S. (1994). Hemispheric encoding/retrieval asymmetry in episodic memory: Positron emission tomography findings. *Proceedings of the National Academy of Sciences. USA, 91,* 2016–20.

Tulving, E., and Schacter, D. L. (1990). Priming and human memory systems. *Science, 247,* 301–6.

Vallar, G., and Baddeley, A. D. (1984). Fractionation of working memory: Neuropsychological evidence for a phonological short-term store. *Journal of Verbal Learning and Verbal Behavior, 23,* 151–61.

Vallar, G., and Baddeley, A. D. (1987). Phonological short-term store and sentence processing. *Cognitive Neuropsychology, 4,* 417–38.

Vallar, G., and Baddeley, A. D. (1989). Development disorders of verbal short-term memory and their relation to sentence comprehension: A reply to Howard and Butterworth. *Cognitive Neuropsychology, 6,* 465–73.

Vallar, G., and Papagno, C. (1995). Neuropsychological impairments of short-term memory. In A. D. Baddeley, B. A. Wilson and F. N. Watts (eds), *Handbook of Memory Disorders,* Chichester: Wiley.

Velmans, M. (1991). Is human information processing conscious? *Behavioural and Brain Sciences, 14,* 651–726.

Verfaellie, M. (1994). A re-examination of recognition memory in amnesia: A reply to Roediger and McDermott. *Neuropsychology, 8,* 289–92.

Verfaellie, M., and Treadwell, J. R. (1993). Status of recognition memory in amnesia. *Neuropsychology, 7,* 5–13.

Verfaellie, M. & Roth, H. L. (in press) Knowledge of English vocabulary in amnesia: An examination of premorbidly acquired semantic memory. *Journal of the International Neuropsychology Society.*

Walker, R., Findlay, J. M., Young, A. W., and Welch, J. (1991). Disentangling neglect and hemianopia. *Neuropsychologia, 29,* 1019–27.

Warrington, E. K. (1981). Concrete word Dyslexia. *British Journal of Psychology, 72,* 175–96.

Warrington, E. K. (1982). Neuropsychological studies of object recognition. *Philosophical Transactions of the Royal Society of London, Series B: Biological Sciences, 298,* 15–33.

Warrington, E. K. (1985). Agnosia: the impairment of object recognition. In P. J. Vinken, G. W. Bruyn, and H. L. Klawans (eds), *Handbook of Clinical Neurology* (vol. 45, pp. 333–49). Amsterdam: Elsevier Science Publishers.

Warrington, E. K., Cipolotti, L., and McNeil, J. (1993). Attention dyslexia: A single case study. *Neuropsychologia, 31,* 871–86.

Warrington, E. K., and James, M. (1986). Visual object recognition in patients with right hemisphere lesions: Axes or features? *Perception, 15,* 355–6.

Warrington, E. K., and James, M. (1988). Visual apperceptive agnosia: A clinico-anatomical study of three cases. *Cortex, 24,* 13–32.

Warrington, E. K., and McCarthy, R. A. (1988). The fractionation of retrograde amnesia. *Brain and Cognition, 7,* 184–200.

Warrington, E. K., and McCarthy, R. A. (1994). Multiple meaning systems in the brain: A case for visual semantics. *Neuropsychologia, 32*, 1465–73.

Warrington, E. K., and Shallice, T. (1969). The selective impairment of auditory-verbal short-term memory. *Brain, 92*, 885–96.

Warrington, E. K., and Shallice, T. (1980). Word form dyslexia. *Brain, 103*, 99–112.

Warrington, E. K., and Shallice, T. (1984). Category-specific semantic impairments. *Brain, 107*, 829–54.

Warrington, E. K., and Taylor, A. M. (1973). The contribution of the right parietal lobe to object recognition. *Cortex, 9*, 152–64.

Warrington, E. K., and Taylor, A. M. (1978). Two categorical stages of object recognition. *Perception, 7*, 695–705.

Warrington, E. K., and Weiskrantz, L. (1970). Amnesic syndrome: Consolidation or retrieval? *Nature, 228*, 628–30.

Warrington, E. K., and Weiskrantz, L. (1982). Amnesia: A disconnection syndrome? *Neuropsychologia, 20*, 233–48.

Waters, G., Caplan, D., and Hildebrandt, N. (1991). On the structure of verbal short-term memory and its functional role in sentence comprehension: Evidence from neuropsychology. *Cognitive Neuropsychology, 9*, 81–126.

Weintraub, S., Mesulam, M. M., and Kramer, L. (1981). Disturbances in prosody. *Archives of Neurology, 38*, 742–4.

Weiskrantz, L. (1985). Issues and theories in the study of the amnesic syndrome. In N. M. Weinberger et al (eds), *Memory Systems of the Brain*. New York: Guilford.

Weiskrantz, L. (1986). *Blindsight: A Case Study and Implications*. Oxford: Clarendon Press.

Weiskrantz, L. (1989). Blindsight. In F. Boller and J. Grafman (eds), *Handbook of Neuropsychology* (vol. 2, pp. 375–85). Amsterdam, New York and Oxford: Elsevier Publishers.

Weizkrantz, L. (1990). Outlooks for blindsight: Explicit methodologies for implicit processes. The Ferrier Lecture 1989. *Proceedings of the Royal Society of London, B239*, 247–78.

Weiskrantz, L., Harlow, A., and Barbur, J. L. (1991). Factors affecting visual sensitivity in a hemianopic subject. *Brain, 114*, 2269–82.

Wilson, B. A., and Davidoff, J. (1993). Partial recovery from visual object agnosia: A 10-year follow-up study. *Cortex, 29*, 529–42.

Wilson, B. A., and Wearing, D. (1995). Amnesia in a musician. In R. Campbell and M. Conway (eds), *Broken Memories*. Oxford: Blackwell.

Wilson, D. H., Reeves, A., Gazzaniga, M. S., and Culver, C. (1977). Cerebral commissurotomy for the control of intractable seizures. *Neurology, 27*, 708–15.

Winocur, G., and Kinsbourne, M. (1978). Contextual cueing as an aid to Korsakoff amnesics. *Neuropsychologia, 16*, 6741–82.

Wolpert, I. (1924). Die simultanagnosie: Storung der gasamtauffassung. *Z Ges Neurol Psychiat, 93*, 397–415.

Yaqub, B. A., Gascon, G. G., Alnosha, M., and Whitaker, H. (1988). Pure word deafness (acquired verbal auditory agnosia) in an Arabic speaking patient. *Brain, 111*, 457–66.

Young, A. W., Aggleton, J. P., Hellawell, D. J., Johnson, M., Broks, P., and Hanley, J. R. (1995). Face processing impairments after amygdalotomy. *Brain*, *118*, 15–24.

Young, A. W., deHaan, E. H. F., Newcombe, F., and Hay, D. C. (1990). Facial neglect. *Neuropsychologia*, *28*, 391–415.

Young, A. W., Ellis, H. D., Szulecka, T. K., and dePauw, K. W. (1990). Face processing impairments and delusional misidentification. *Behavioural Neurology*, *3*, 153–68.

Young, A. W., Hay, D. C., and Ellis, A. W. (1985). The faces that launched a thousand slips: everyday difficulties and errors in recognising people. *British Journal of Psychology*, *76*, 495–523.

Young, A. W., Hellawell, D. J., and Welch, J. (1992). Neglect and visual recognition. *Brain*, *115*, 51–71.

Young, A. W., Humphreys, G. W., Riddoch, M. J., Hellawell, D. J., and de Haan, E. H. F. (1994). Recognition impairments and face imagery. *Neuropsychologia*, *32*, 693–702.

Young, A. W., Newcombe, F., De Haan, E. H. F., Small, M., and Hay, D. C. (1993). Face perception after brain injury. *Brain*, *116*, 941–59.

Young, A. W., Reid, I., Wright, S., and Hellawell, D. J. (1993). Face-processing impairments and the Capgras delusion. *British Journal of Psychiatry*, *162*, 695–8.

Zaidel, E. (1983a). Disconnection syndrome as a model for laterality effects in the normal brain. In J. B. Hellige (ed), *Cerebral Hemisphere Asymmetry: Method theory and application* (pp. 95–151). New York: Praeger Publishers.

Zaidel, E. (1983b). Language in the right hemisphere, convergent perspectives. *American Psychologist* (May), 542–46.

Zaidel, E. (1990). Language functions in the two hemispheres following complete cerebral commissurotomy and hemispherectomy. In Boller and J. Grafman (eds), *Handbook of Neuropsychology* (pp. 115–50). B. V.: Elsevier Sciences Publishers.

Zaidel, E., and Schweiger, A. (1984). On wrong hypotheses about the right hemisphere: Commentary on K. Patterson and D. Besner, 'Is the right hemisphere literate?' *Cognitive Neuropsychology*, *1*, 351–64.

Zaidel, E., Zaidel, D. W., and Sperry, R. W. (1981). Left and right intelligence: Case studies of Raven's Progresive Matrices following brain bisection and hemi-decortication. *Cortex*, *17*, 167–86.

Zihl, J., and Werth, R. (1984). Contributions to the study of 'blindsight' – II. The role of specific practice for saccadic localization in patients with postgeniculate visual field defects. *Neuropsychologia*, *22*, 13–22.

Zola-Morgan, S., Squire, L. R., and Amaral, D. G. (1986). Human amnesia and the medial temporal region: Enduring memory impairment following a bilateral lesion limited to field CA1 of the hippocampus. *Journal of Neuroscience*, *6*, 2950–67.

Zurif, E., Swinney, D., and Fodor, J. A. (1991). An evaluation of assumptions underlying the single-patient-only position in neuropsychological research: A reply. *Brain and Cognition*, *16*, 198–210.

Zurif, E. B., Gardner, H., and Brownell, H. H. (1989). The case against the case against group studies. *Brain and Cognition*, *10*, 237–55.

Subject Index

Author Index